suffragettes to She-Devils

Women's Liberation and Beyond

Liz McQuiston

Foreword by Germaine Greer

Φ

For all of us:
Petronela, Nellie, Liz, June, Lee and Nela

Phaidon Press Ltd
Regent's Wharf
All Saints Street
London N1 9PA

© 1997 Phaidon Press Ltd

ISBN 0 7148 3619 2

A CIP catalogue record for this book is
available from the British Library.

Printed in Hong Kong

Acknowledgements

The author wishes to give special thanks
to the following for consultation and generous assistance
in the making of this book.

Zurayah Abass, Molo Songololo, Cape Town
Ghalia and Widad Abbas, Dubai
Fatma Alloo, Tanzania Media Women's Association (TAMWA),
Dar es Salaam
Jeremy Barr, London
Astra Blaug, Older Feminists Network, London
Tania Chalfoun, Lebanon
Cynthia Chris, Printed Matter Bookstore at Dia, New York City
Julia Church, Melbourne
Vivian Constantinopoulos, Phaidon Press, London
John Davis, Newham College of Further Education, London
David Doughan and Veronica Perkins, Fawcett Library,
London Guildhall University
Noemi Escudero and Richard Oliver, London
The Feminist Library, London
Roz Foley, Association of London Authorities
Joan Hammond and the Feminist Archive, Bristol
Muneera Hashwani, Karachi
Chris, Leslie and Kate Mees, Design Documentation, UK
Melanie Keen, London
John McKay, Ravensbourne College of Design and Communication, UK
Caroline Nursey, World University Services, UK
Sarah Robinson and Georgina Ashworth, Change, London
Sue Roscow, London
Paula Scher, Lisa Mazur, Esther Bridavsky and Anke Stohlmann
Pentagram, New York, who designed the book and jacket
Jane Zeuner, Museum of London

Contents

One of the Striking Features of Kew Gardens

Foreword
Germaine Greer

On formal occasions, in the main dining hall of Newnham College, a handworked silk banner is hung from the rafters. In the corners are bursts of daisies; in the centre is an appliquéd escutcheon featuring an open book, a castellated bridge and three sailing ships; the legend reads, 'Better is wisdom than weapons of war'. The banner was designed and worked in 1908 by the women students of Cambridge University, as part of the extraordinarily sophisticated propaganda campaign waged by the Women's Social and Political Union (see page 138 fig 2 for banner).

As a student at Newnham from 1964 to 1967 I was unaware of the existence of the banner, for it was lying forgotten in one of the college's many repositories of valuable possessions. For Newnham's suffragette past I had scant respect, thinking it of a piece with quaint behaviours like hockey and guiding. Women had got the vote, I thought, and what good had it done them? Before many more months elapsed I had come to understand that the work of feminism was far from complete and that the woman question remained unanswered. As feminist consciousness was raised over the ensuing years, a younger generation of Newnham women discovered the banner and restored it. It is now the college's most treasured and most famous possession. Today's students are more aware of the struggles of an earlier generation and far more thoughtful in their approach to women's issues than I was.

In the summer of 1970, after years as an unpaid and disenfranchised writer for the underground press, with no say in editorial policy or procedure, I was asked to guest-edit Oz, issue number 29 – 'Female Energy' Oz, according to the cover, within, 'Cuntpower' Oz. The men who ran Oz were aware only that feminism was flavour of the month, but I saw my chance of getting beyond defining the problem to something more creative, a new positive way of seeing women as they really are, hairy, smelly, energetic and strong. Up till then women had been represented in Oz principally by wispy bare-breasted flower children and the pneumatic creations of Robert Crum. The sixties was the hey-day of male display; the most successful sixties women were scented, decorative and slender, voluptuously dressed in diaphanous chiffons, old embroideries, baubles, bangles, beads and boots, and spoke in blurred voices – if they spoke at all. The women of the English underground did as they did in youth underground groups the world over, that is, they handled the secretarial work, made coffee and love and rolled joints, as required. They also got pelvic infections, got pregnant, had abortions, used IUDs, took pills and anything else that was necessary to make the lives of the men as easy as possible. In fealty to the spurious dogma of sexual liberation they made few demands. A few women got loudly sick of this and the rest is history, or herstory if you prefer.

If I had been able to cover Oz with strong-scented pubic hair I would have done it but I had to settle for graphic media that were within our resources, which were more than usually straitened because, during the preparation of the issue, Scotland Yard's Obscenity Squad twice raided us and took away anything it felt like lifting, including artwork. I would have liked to avoid using the over-worked imagery of the female body altogether but, as there was no time to develop a visual language of female energy, we had to agree on transforming the imagery of the female, who became a creature of springing hairs and thundering thighs rather than dewy eyes and perky tits. The female sex is sweet and powerful and we were going to rub every reader's face in it. 'In your face' being the method of choice, I decided on an anti-fashion spread, and crocheted stick-out nipples and an enormous bush on to a modest bikini which, as it turned out, was modelled for the photographs by a girl-child – not my idea at all.

The principal difficulty facing the feminist creator of propaganda images in 1970 was that so little of the process of producing, publishing and placing the images was controlled by women. Virtually all the artwork for Oz 29 was done by men who let me bully them to a point, but not even I was involved in the final lay-out and the selection of colour. Production values are not absolute, but time and again the women who were struggling to utter their own vision were intimidated by the men who controlled production into smoothing their rough graphics and turning out something slick and 'professional'. The art of the counter-culture was conservative, to say the least, the approach to lettering and typography naive in the extreme. Time and again we found our ideas tidied up, or printed in lavender what we had thought in blood-red and ink-black. It is not surprising then that some of the most powerful feminist graphics appeared dashed onto walls by actual brushes loaded with real paint. Eventually it was understood that women's propaganda had to be produced in a different, non-hierarchical way, and so began the series of work-place experiments with roles in production moving from member to member of a co-operative, within a network structure that reflected women's traditional methods of making and distributing.

The idea of women's equality threatened nobody, for it took the status of men as the ultimate that women could aspire to; the question of liberation was far more disturbing in its implications. An unfettered woman would be incessantly redrawing the limits, redefining her own nature and the relations she might have with others. The essential characteristic of a genuinely unfettered woman would be access to her own creativity. The strategy I adopted at *Oz* remained one of the principal methods of feminist exploration in the decades that followed. It seemed important to us then and it remained important to bring the female sex out of its veil of modesty and show it in all its manifestations, bloody, engorged, toothed, split. Women's bodies had always been the subject of art; individual women would come to treat their bodies as media, carving new statements about oppression and rebellion into their very flesh, immolating themselves in the search for a new truth.

Historically, in the male-dominated domain of fine art, women's creativity had been recognized as long as it was derivative and offered men's work the supreme flattery of imitation. A woman reacting against male expertise and rejecting the right of male authorities to evaluate her work was flying in the face of the whole art establishment. No galleries existed to hang the work of feminist artists, who in any case had small appetite for the lucrative art game. The arena in which radical women's graphic art developed had to be the same one in which Käthe Kollwitz chose to work, the world of cheap publishing and mass propaganda. The development of personal computers and affordable page-making software enabled hard-line feminist co-operatives to control every stage of production. The countless small magazines that appeared on the streets for a few months and then disappeared are now a priceless resource, though the cheap pages have yellowed and become brittle. This book is a valuable record of the scale and extent of ephemeral feminist publishing.

There are few successful female practitioners of the fine arts who have not taken on board the message of liberation and profited by it, though they may be loath to admit the fact. All successful artists reap energy from the assiduous activity of the many, who generate the pressure that forces a great talent upwards into the kind of single-minded career that most of us would not envy. In England in the last months of 1996 women's guerrilla art received a shot in the arm from the failure of the Turner Art Prize Committee to short-list a single woman. An underground group calling itself Cunst began an extended campaign of disruption of the event which had all the hallmarks of an old-fashioned happening.

These have been difficult years for women, but they have also been good years, when the scent of battle was in our nostrils. We have suffered casualties but, from Orlan to Madonna to the glorious Guerrilla Girls and back again, the subversive power of women's art is now undeniable. It remains outside the art establishment partly by choice, because it insists upon communication, accessibility and immediate, tangible relevance to the everyday lives of women. In women's aesthetic, life is greater than art and art is an essential part of life. In the growth and development of women's 'alternative site' the graphic art of ephemeral feminist propaganda was and is the flash point from which female energy explodes again and again, wherever there are women daring to think that they have something to say and the right to say it and to make themselves heard.

1

2

1, 2 *Cover and inside page of Oz, 'Cuntpower' issue number 29, guest-edited by Germaine Greer, Britain, July 1970.*

Introduction

The fight for women's rights has been one of the great power struggles of our century, and promises to have a profound influence on the next. A long tradition of women's rights activism leads up to the modern women's movement; but it took the organized strength of twentieth-century feminism to strike at the heart of the problem and challenge existing power relationships between men and women. Modern feminists have analysed and interrogated patriarchy in all its forms – religion, education, language, history, the arts and culture – resulting in a shift in our definition of politics, and indeed in our expectations of society itself.

1

Although it can have other connotations and far more complex meanings, the word 'feminism' has been used broadly thoughout this book to mean 'the struggle for women's rights'. All of the visual material included here can be said to be relevant to feminism's wide-ranging concerns and principles. That does not, however, mean that all of the creators of that material would call themselves feminists, nor are they all women. As an evolving movement, the struggle for women's rights has involved not one philosophy, but many. Over the years it has comprised diverse fields of activity, each with its own intent and point of focus: the militant suffragettes of the first wave of feminism; the collectives of the Women's Liberation Movement, the activist groups of America's 'third wave', and many others. Their methods have also varied tremendously, ranging from violent militancy to satire or even masquerade. Yet all could be drawn together by a common bond: the will to change and improve the lives of women, and in doing so, to transform the lives of all.

WOMEN never, never, never shall be slaves

3

2

4

Graphic expression, in its many forms, has been crucial to this effort. It has, most significantly, provided the agents and carriers of the ongoing call for change. Every battle needs identifiable heralds and uniforms; every propaganda campaign needs its visual aids and modes of dissemination; every communications network needs graphic or electronic formats through which to talk and exchange information. The imagery of feminism may also have a tangential relation to its cause. It may exist in the creation of a tough, comic-book heroine or a new abrasive kind of street fashion or style. It may operate as education, or as therapy in a community art memorial dedicated to suffering or death resulting from violence against women.

This book's broad concern, then, is with the developing role of graphics and related media in the struggle this century for women's liberation and women's rights. It focuses more specifically on how women themselves have used graphics as a means of empowerment, and on the notion of women 'finding a voice' through graphic or visual means. It is to do with how they have used that graphic voice to articulate their own concerns and beliefs, to create propaganda, to conduct tough social critique, or to wage war against their misrepresentation by the media. It also examines how that voice has changed over the decades,

Graphics has played a crucial role in the call to action for women's rights this century:
1 'The Bugler Girl', poster designed by Caroline Watts, published by the Artists' Suffrage League, Britain 1908. Originally intended to announce the NUWSS procession of 13 June 1908.
2 Photo of Japanese suffragist Kimura Komako joining a suffrage demonstration on a visit to New York in 1917. The lettering reads: 'Women Join in the Vote'.

3 Poster published by Manchester Women's Co-operative Printers, Britain, 1970s.
4 Poster advertising Issue 33 (1991) of Speak, a South African women's rights magazine.
5 Trans, moving downwards: 'Democratic Movement of the Women of Valencia', (the woman shouts 'Liberty'), 'Women of Valencia, Join the Struggle for your Liberation'. Spain, late 1970s.

5

particularly in the light of recent developments in the new technologies. At the beginning of this century, women 'found their voice' through print media; now, at the end of the century, they are determined to exercise it to the full in digital media. The internet, e-mail and other contingents of cyberspace have become our conceptual 'print room'.

The word 'graphics', therefore, is not used here in its strict, traditional design sense – two-dimensional design for print. Instead it refers to the various designed elements of the 'graphic environment': an active, evolving mix of visual codes, symbols, ephemera and papers, flashing signs, information bytes and messages, personal marks and tattoos, all working to inform and influence our thinking. The visual material collected here aims to reflect this variety (while hinting at its future state) and consequently includes everything from billboards, banners, books, posters and magazines, to t-shirts, comics, computer graphics and virtual reality experiments, and includes both professional and influential amateur contributions.

It is also important to recognize that this book is, first and foremost, a design source book. It does not attempt to be a history book, and hence it does not provide a complete historical survey of women's liberation. Nor does it provide in-depth coverage of any particular event, personality or campaign. Its interests are design-led, and although visual material is culled from a great variety of sources – including fine art, fashion, advertising and other associated professions – it is all discussed within a design-related context.

Humour has often, but not always, softened the anger raging between the sexes.
1 Photomontage poster by the SisterSerpents art collective, USA, 1990.
2 'Renew his Interest in Carpentry', an example of guerrilla graffiti in London photographed by Jill Posener, and produced as a postcard by The Women's Press, Britain, 1981.
3 Badges, Britain, 1970s.
4 Badges, Britain late 1970s/early 1980s.
5 Back cover of the US feminist magazine Heresies, issue 20, 1985, showing a counter-demonstrator's comment on a women's peace rally held at Sampson State Park near Seneca Army Depot in Seneca, New York on 22 October 1983. Photo by Ruth Putter.
6 'Stray Dags', poster by Leonie Lane of Lucifoil Poster Collective, Australia, 1980, announcing a performance by the women's band Stray Dags at the Wimmin's Warehouse, a women-only centre and dance venue.

4

5

WEDDING ?
WEDDING ?

WEDDING ?
WHAT
WEDDING ?

The chapters describe broad 'eras' of social and design activity and are roughly chronological, although there are various overlaps of detail, particularly in recent decades. The first chapter deals largely with the graphics surrounding the British militant suffragettes and their campaign for the vote at the beginning of the century – for this marks the start of the organized and demonstrative use of graphics to broadcast women's struggle for their rights. The visual propaganda campaign of the Women's Social and Political Union (the WSPU) is described in detail, and then set within a broader context that includes the other suffrage societies of that time. The chapter then moves on through two World Wars to show how women were presented with notions of so-called 'liberation' by governments and advertisers in pursuit of their labour or commercial power. It finally arrives in the post-war consumerism of 1950s USA and the hard-sell of the 'happy housewife', which brought about rebellion against what Betty Friedan was to call the 'feminine mystique'. Chapter Two then

6

deals with the revolution of the Women's Liberation Movement: its consciousness-raising, poster collectives, communications networks and attempts to help women 'find a voice' throughout the 1960s and 1970s.

The following decade, outlined in Chapter Three, brought years of conservatism that drove feminism underground; and then saw it surface again through extraordinary new forms of social critique (ranging from Punk to the Guerrilla Girls) and radical activism

over the defence of abortion rights in the USA. Chapter Four then looks at the 1990s and beyond, with a new 'culture of resistance' committed to targeting and counter-attacking all manner of stereotyping, sexism and media misogyny. It also explores the possibilities opening up for women's expression through use of the new digital technologies. The final chapter places these developments within the wider context of the international women's movement, illustrating how graphics have built up a visual profile of women's lives around the world, the role they have played in various political struggles, and their present use in global communications media.

The development of women's graphic expression remains the central underlying theme throughout this book. The early suffrage movement broke the ground and set a precedent for women's

expression; the analysis of the Women's Liberation Movement (1960s/1970s) then defined that expression and gave it momentum. But from the very start, a developing visual language based on women's experience began to emerge and – as a scan through this book will show – has continued to expand ever since. It has none of the soothing or graceful qualities that characterize traditional representations of femininity. The visual commentary and expression surrounding women is much stronger and more brutal, as is women's experience itself.

Evidence of a global women's movement:
1 Poster announcing an event for all women organized by the Women's Action Forum of Lahore, Pakistan, 1987. Trans, moving downwards: '12th February', 'Pakistani Women's Liberation Day', 'Special meeting of the Women's Movement'. It continues to state time, venue, programme (speeches, drama and ballads), and guest speakers.
2 Poster for the First Meeting of Latin American Women, held in Paris on 8 March 1986 (International Women's Day). Designed by the Studio of Latin American Women in Paris. Cartoon trans: 'What is the difference between the wolf on the left and the wolf on the right?', 'NONE: They'll both always be wolves'. The poster is referring to similarities between Left and Right politics, and particularly the notion that Latin American men of the Left (Revolutionaries) were often just as sexist as men of the Right. There is also an insinuation that all men are wolves, ie cunning, vicious predators.

V ENCUENTRO FEMINISTA LATINOAMERICANO Y DEL CARIBE

San Bernardo, Argentina
18 al 24 de noviembre de 1990

MUJER

REVOLUCION

O ne of the central tenets of women's experience is the polarity of the public versus the private, the outer and the inner worlds. Consequently, this maintains a ghost-like presence, both conceptually and stylistically, throughout these pages. The image of a split-woman or a multi-armed woman, seen in posters and other graphics throughout the decades, has become a symbolic recognition of women's existence between (and control by) those two worlds. It represents the 'double shift' of work at home, coupled with employment outside the home; also, the way in which women have been devalued by being defined within the domestic world or private sphere, rather than the professional world or public sphere. Barbara Kruger's famous Pro-Choice poster 'Your Body is a Battleground', showing a woman's face split into a positive and negative (x-ray style) image, becomes a questioning of outer and inner. Should outer forces be allowed to control the inner choice? Suddenly the division can be seen for what it is: a means of creating a prison for purposes of control.

W hen the private world is transcended and the barriers between the two spheres are broken down, the effect is both shocking and liberating. It can be found in the act of stylizing the intimate image of female genitalia and then promoting it to the level of a public icon, a strategy which grew popular in feminist art and posterwork in the 1970s and continues today. Transgression between the two worlds also points to new territory for artistic exploration in the medium of modern technology. In Diane Gromala's virtual reality experiments, a journey though her virtual 'body' merges the private and the public realms.

3 Young woman wearing a banned t-shirt (from the End Conscription campaign) at a funeral in the Eastern Cape, South Africa, late 1980s.
4 Poster announcing the fifth meeting of feminists of Latin America and the Caribbean, held in Argentina in 1990. Design by Patricia Jastrzebski.

5 A broadsheet published by AMNLAE, July 1981. (AMNLAE is the Luisa Amanda Espinoza Nicaraguan Women's Association.) Women played an important fighting role in Nicaragua's protracted struggle for independence. Trans: 'Women', 'Revolution'.

Shock becomes another highly important tactic of women's graphic expression. Some people may find certain examples of language or imagery in this book to be offensive or overly crude: that is exactly the point, and is the very crux of the matter. From the suffragettes early this century to the modern-day SisterSerpents, women activists have had to combat the continuous force of control, oppression and violence launched against them with equal aggression. It should not be surprising to find anger, threats, provocation, bad language and emotional outbursts rushing through these pages: they indicate the tone of the battle, and a vicious battle it can be at times, too.

One of women's greatest instruments for visual shock has been the female body itself, assigned political status for the first time by the Women's Liberation Movement in the 1960s. As the female body had so often been stigmatized, exploited in the rhetoric of misogyny, women suddenly took a firm stand and began to use their bodies to make political statements. In work such as 'cunt art', they derived symbolism from the body for the visual language of their new culture. The newly accurate and unprurient depiction of the female body was important in health education and family planning, which diagrammed self-examination, reproductive processes and other issues that became part of the movement to reclaim control over women's own bodies. They used the body for shock value and as a symbol of new freedom and determination, and the new value attached to women's personal experience. And the body has continued ever since to work as a canvas on which defiance can be expressed: Punks wrote 'sex' on their bottoms, Riot Grrrls scrawled

Examples of woman-power confronting, criticising and using the media:
1   'Thank You America', illustration by Sue Coe showing Anita Hill being burned as a witch, USA, 1991. (See page 150.)
2   Sign at entrance to Yellow Gate at Greenham Common (Women's Peace Camp), photographed by Astra Blaug, Britain, c1985.
3   Trans: 'Your testimony has power!', poster by Yossi Lemel, Israel, 1991. Part of an influential telephone campaign in which victims of rape, abuse, harassment at work, etc, were asked to call and give their story, with the result that laws concerning women's rights in Israel were changed.
4   Cover of Ms. magazine, November 1973, USA.

'slut' on their stomachs, and there are many other forms of body graphics and personal branding in t-shirts, tattoos and piercings.

Body politics also cuts across the issue of violence against women in all its forms: rape, battering, domestic abuse, sexual harassment at work, and so on. It is an issue which runs under a great deal of the material in this book, and accounts for the brutal nature of some of the imagery. But that's as it should be. After all, why should the protest be more delicate than the oppression? Violence makes a necessary appearance throughout the book, and the last chapter presents a number of campaigns from different countries, to dispel any idea that violence against women is purely a problem of poorer countries or 'other' cultures. It is, unfortunately and unbelievably, endemic to all cultures.

The last and perhaps most extraordinary aspect of women's graphic expression is its universality: its symbolic reference to a global community. Over the entire span of a century, the women's movement has claimed an international reach, and the principles of connecting have served to provide women's visual language with the power of unity.

1

2

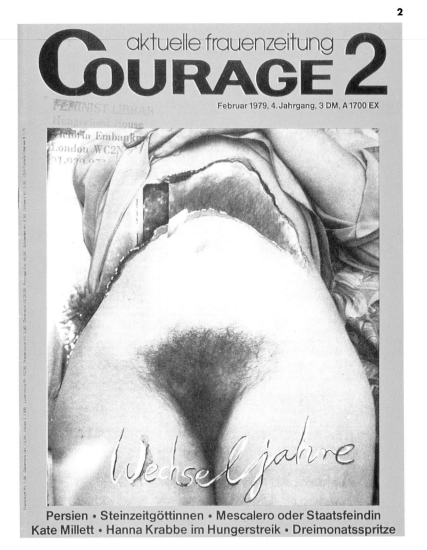

aktuelle frauenzeitung
COURAGE 2
Februar 1979, 4. Jahrgang, 3 DM, A 1700 EX

Persien · Steinzeitgöttinnen · Mescalero oder Staatsfeindin
Kate Millett · Hanna Krabbe im Hungerstreik · Dreimonatsspritze

3

Whether experienced as the cyber-explorations of digital technology or the chalk writing of graffiti on a city wall, each message, each image has within it a part of us all. Throughout this century and into the next, the power of the network maintains a constant watchful presence: the struggle of one is the struggle of all, the strength of one is the strength of all.

5

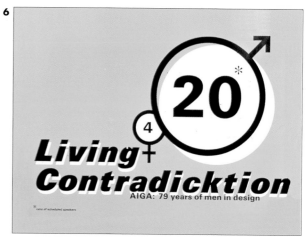

6

4

Body politics, plus jokes and jibes:

1   'Boobs Bite Back', t-shirt by designer Karen Savage, in the 'Stereotypes with Attitude' collection, Britain, Spring/Summer 1993.

2   Cover of Courage magazine, issue 2, February 1979, (West) Germany. The lettering on the image reads 'Menopause'.

3   Punk personality Jordan wears a t-shirt bearing a printed definition of 'masculine' pulled over a lace dress, London c1976.

4   Day-glo stickers by the Chicago-based SisterSerpents art collective, the self-proclaimed 'guerrillas in the war against sexism', USA, 1990–95.

5   Postcard with cartoon by Marc, published by Spellbound Cards in Dublin, Ireland c1995.

6   'Living Contradicktion', an alternative poster for a conference in Miami entitled 'Living Contradictions', held by the AIGA (the USA's largest organization of professional graphic designers). The poster protested against the five to one ratio of male to female speakers at the conference. Produced by Class Action (project team: Lisa Ashworth, David Comberg, Tom Starr), USA, 1993.

Promises of Emancipation

From First Wave Feminism (1850–1914) to the 1960s

Feminism, or the fight for women's rights, emerged throughout the mid-nineteenth and early twentieth century as an organized mass movement devoted to ending women's subordination; this has become known in recent times as the 'first wave' of feminism. It is little wonder that the modern feminist movement, or 'second wave', placed such emphasis on studying this rich early heritage – not only as a source of inspiration, but often as a model for methods and strategies. For the first time, the struggle for women's rights could be understood as part of a continuum, so that women began to see themselves in league with a long line of freedom fighters. A blow for one was a blow for all; not just in relation to the present, but also in communion with the ghosts of the past. This notion of 'connectivity' – of women connecting across countries, cultures, even generations – became one of the great themes of the twentieth-century feminist revolution (and its graphics) through all of its various stages of development up to the present day.

One of the richest historical sources, and of greatest interest graphically, was the battle for women's suffrage waged by the militants of England, otherwise known as the suffragettes. Their visual propaganda was characterized by the highly inventive use of the communication media of the time, as well as extraordinary innovations in marketing and fashion. The Women's Social and Political Union, founded in 1903 and led by the dynamic Pankhursts, particularly stands out for its visual contribution, including an imaginative, co-ordinated approach to visual identity and corporate image-building. This was expressed through their use of colours; a uniform; paraphernalia, such as certificates and badges, designed as part of an elaborate support system for imprisoned members; and the promotion of their political message through traditional formats such as posters, postcards and magazines, as well as through an innovative use of merchandising. Both

their propaganda techniques and their use of direct action drew attention and were copied around the world by other political movements. Although their achievements fell short of their aim (the vote for women over the age of thirty didn't arrive until 1918), the century's first major attack on male-dominated culture and its power systems had been mounted; and one of its most successful instruments had been a highly organized visual campaign.

The onset of the First World War shifted attention away from the campaign for the vote. Women no longer called for their liberation through their own media and imagery. The decades that followed produced instead a number of graphic trends or campaigns whereby women were presented with images and the rhetoric of their so-called 'liberation', particularly by governments or advertisers, solely for the purpose of acquiring their labour or commercial power.

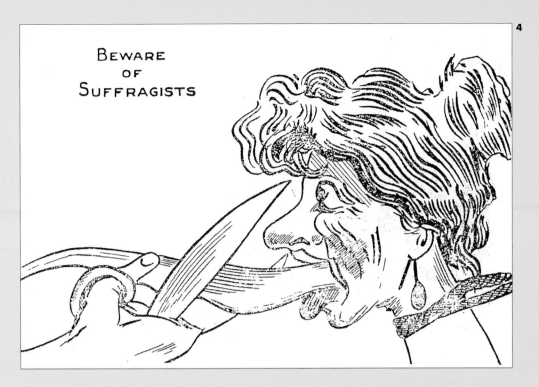

BEWARE
OF
SUFFRAGISTS

The graphic culture of the Edwardian period reinforced Victorian attitudes towards women, depicting them as decorative, empty-headed beauties – and above all, as passive possessions of their husbands (hence prisoners in their own homes).

1   Illustration taken from Queen magazine, showing the corsetted fashions of the time, Britain, 1905.
2   Packaging for liver salts, lozenges and other products, Britain, 1905.
3   'Ivens & Co Foto-Artikelen', poster by C van Caspel, Holland, 1900.
4   'Beware of Suffragists', card, copyright of E Dusédau, Jersey, 1909.
5   'A Woman's Mind Magnified', poster, Britain, 1900–14.

The liberated spirit of women working to build a new Soviet future after the Russian Revolution was short-lived, and soon gave way to the lifeless years of Stalinism. In both World Wars, governments offered women the chance to be liberated, take on men's jobs and join in war work – and then promptly bustled them back into the kitchen the minute their services were no longer needed. After the Second World War, the commercialism of the 1950s and 1960s promised liberation in the form of labour-saving domestic technology and products, while delivering rigid roles and limited ambitions which only trapped women further in their 'natural sphere' – a domestic prison. It wasn't until the social revolution of the 1960s occurred, and with it the 'second wave' of feminism, that women themselves once again used communication media and other innovative formats to produce their own visual and verbal messages for 'women's liberation'.

Approaching the twentieth century: background to the British suffrage campaign

By the start of the twentieth century, the organized campaign for women's rights was already over half-a-century old on both sides of the Atlantic. In the USA, the first wave of feminism had grown out of the movement against slavery. Inspired by the heroism and courage of the black slave freedom-fighters, the early feminist pioneers defied social convention, upbringing and at times even religion, and spoke out for the emancipation of slaves as well as women. In 1848, abolitionists Elizabeth Cady Stanton and Lucretia Mott organized The First Women's Rights Convention in Seneca Falls, New York. As a result of that meeting, Elizabeth Cady Stanton was joined by Susan B Anthony and together they launched the US women's rights movement. For many years thereafter they were its main organizers and driving force, maintaining a central focus on campaigning for women's suffrage.

In Europe, the seeds were sown as early as the eighteenth century when the French Revolution (1789) and its call for freedom from tyranny provided the climate for women's groups such as the *Citoyennes Républicaines Révolutionnaires* (Revolutionary Republican Women-Citizens) to fight for political rights, including the vote, in the emerging new Republic. At the same time, calls for freedom from tyranny could also be heard from Britain in Tom Paine's book *The Rights of Man* (1791–2), closely followed by Mary Wollstonecraft's *A Vindication of the Rights of Woman* (1792) which challenged domestic tyranny and called for political status for women. Perhaps even more shockingly, it introduced the notion that women were taught or programmed into subordination, while expectations of equality were repressed in them – ideas so radical that this document has remained the foundation text of modern feminism, and

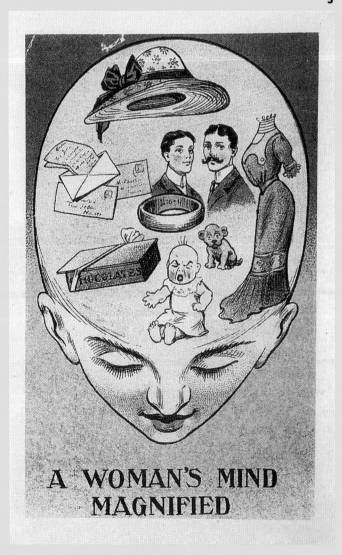

A WOMAN'S MIND MAGNIFIED

continues to be widely read two centuries on.

However, an organized movement did not emerge until the 1850s when early British feminists struggled against Victorian attitudes and laws which denied many of the most basic civil rights to women. They were, for example, excluded from education and the professions. Hence Barbara Leigh-Smith (later Bodichon), Bessie Rayner Parkes and other feminists came together in 1855 as the London-based Langham Place Group, working to promote women's rights in work, education and property matters. (They produced many notable collaborations, among them the Society for Promoting the Employment of Women which set up a women's printshop called the Victoria Press, run by Emily Faithfull and her compositors.) In 1865 they took on the issue of the vote, and the following year drew up Parliament's first women's suffrage petition. This was the start of a growing suffrage movement. But for the following twenty years, despite the extraordinary activity and public-speaking of such feminists as Lydia Becker in Manchester, and Millicent Fawcett in London, bills for women's suffrage were voted down.

The turn of the century brought a fresh spirit of change. Throughout Europe, industrialization and rejection of the old traditions and old social order brought new expectations for the future – and a rising wave of social and labour reform. In Britain, it also brought a new generation of women, determined to fight for their rights. As the forces mustered, the broader issues of women's civil rights began to merge into one objective – the franchise (or the vote) was viewed as the pathway to other freedoms. But as the Victorian age passed into the Edwardian era, opposition to reform remained firm. The popular Edwardian attitude was that women should remain passive possessions of their husbands, prisoners in his 'castle', seen but not heard, and subject to beatings or mistreatment by his hand. Not only that, but there was no question that women could be anything else, for they were believed to be empty-headed and unworthy of education. The popular graphic culture of the time reinforced this – in books, newspapers, magazines, advertising – and as the only existing mass media, they carried a great deal of weight. So the scene was set; and although women's suffrage was a burning issue on the international political agenda, Britain and its climate of resistance became the acknowledged focal point of the battle for the vote.

Early days of an escalating struggle:
1 'A Garland for May Day 1895', by British artist Walter Crane whose socialist cartoons and illustrations influenced the work of Sylvia Pankhurst, creator of many suffrage designs.

2 'The Haunted House', poster showing the ghost of a suffragette hovering over the Houses of Parliament, drawing by David Wilson of the Daily Chronicle, Britain, 1907.

A·GARLAND·FOR·MAY·DAY·1895·
DEDICATED·TO·THE·WORKERS·BY·WALTER·CRANE·

MRS PANKHURST.

THE IMPRISONED SUFFRAGIST LEADERS.

MAY 22nd 1912.

MrPETHICK·LAWRENCE.   MrPETHICK·LAWRENCE.

4

Creative influences and communications media

The artistic and graphic scenes developing at this time were equally interesting, and are certainly worth a quick review. The new century found the 'artistic poster' past its golden age, but still highly influential both in Europe and the USA, and beginning its slow development into a formidable advertising medium, particularly in Germany. Berlin poster artists achieved world renown in the period up to the outbreak of the First World War. It was also the timely meeting point for a mixture of styles and influences, as artists allowed themselves to be swayed by the spirit of the 'new'. Art Nouveau, with its organic shapes and fluid lines, was the overriding style in both the fine and the applied arts, and was influential on an international scale: Will Bradley in the USA, Aubrey Beardsley in England and Alphonse Mucha working in Paris were a few of the leading practitioners.

British stylistic sources also included the Pre-Raphaelites and, in particular, William Morris and the Arts and Crafts Movement. Out of this tradition grew the Beggarstaff Brothers, whose pioneering use of flat areas of colour and simple composition created an ultimately modern poster style of its own, which in turn influenced German poster art. It also yielded the socialist cartoons and illustrations of Walter Crane, who created much of the imagery of the Labour Movement, and had a direct influence on the work of Sylvia Pankhurst, creator of many suffrage designs. In short, the tone of the period was one of rich, creative exchange and communication, by means of journals, exhibitions, institutes of study and personal travel. The artists and designers working for the suffrage movement would certainly have been party to this exchange.

The communications media of the time were equally exciting, ripe with opportunities for exploitation. Colour printing by lithography was now sophisticated and cheap enough to produce richly-coloured, pictorialized packaging and all manner of graphic ephemera, while picture posters displayed as advertisements in the urban environment were a commercial and artistic presence.

Illustrated magazines and newspapers, such as *The Times* and the *Daily Telegraph*, were now prominent. Newspapers in particular acted as important forums for political debate, and had a pronounced effect on public opinion. Most important was the rise of the cheap, national dailies such as the *Daily Mail*, *Daily Sketch*, *Daily News* and *Daily Mirror*, all with mammoth circulations. (The *Daily Mail*, founded in 1896, was a monster: it achieved a daily circulation of one million while still in its infancy.) By 1904, the *Daily Mirror* was sporting photographic reproductions; within a

5

·LIFE·

Militants

AS THEY ARE

AS THEY THINK THEY ARE

Rodney Thomson
with apologies to
Orson Lowell

AS THEY APPEAR TO THE POLICE AND SHOPKEEPERS

few years, all of the newspapers had them. From then on, the daily press provided a photographic record and running commentary on the suffrage movement, on its use of spectacle and its acts of violence. To the suffrage societies themselves, the press also represented a prime publicity vehicle to exploit.

Another medium of the moment was postcards. The Edwardian years became the golden years of the picture postcard. At their peak from 1904 to 1914, they replaced posters as the most popular collectables. Both illustrated and photographic, they were cheap, accessible and remarkably speedy, as the British postal service offered several deliveries daily in most towns.

Finally, the early Edwardian years were still, despite a fading empire, a period of public display, procession and pageantry. Also, from the middle to late 1890s, the Labour Movement had developed a growing presence of parades, ceremonies, demonstrations with banners and large-scale marches, which the suffrage movement adopted and modified for its own purposes. Banners in particular were to become an important suffragist medium. But whereas trade union banners were essentially a male medium – large, heavy, painted pictorial representations of male heroes and the value of (male) work – suffrage banners were light, smaller, appliquéd or embroidered, and emblematic. They were designed more like flags than paintings, and carried symbols representing ideas or groups of people. Most importantly, they were being marched through the streets by women: something previously unheard of.

The last phase: suffrage societies, their studios and their communication methods

The new century, therefore, brought the British campaign for women's suffrage into its final and most volatile phase. There were three main women's organizations involved in the struggle, all with the same objective of securing 'the franchise for women on the same terms as men'. However, they differed dramatically in the means to be used to achieve it. This brought out the important distinction between the 'constitutionalists' and the 'militants'.

The first and largest organization, which included the original supporters of women's suffrage, was the National Union of Women's Suffrage Societies (NUWSS) led by Mrs Millicent Garrett Fawcett. It co-ordinated the activities of a group of affiliated suffrage societies, which grew in number from sixteen in 1903 to over 300 in 1911; their published newspaper was The Common Cause. Their supporters were known as 'suffragists', and included men in their ranks. Most importantly, however, they were constitutionalists – law-abiding, well-behaved and reasonable – a stance which unfortunately had gained the movement little ground by that point. Unlady-like conduct, let alone violence, was not tolerated, and this led to sore divisions in their relations with the other societies involved in the new revitalized movement. Soon after the first few violent demonstrations, around 1907, the NUWSS began to distance itself from the militants – and the militants obviously caused them deep concern in propaganda terms as the years went on. Most of the NUWSS's propaganda material was branded with the words 'law-abiding' or 'no party' (as they also rejected political affiliation), and much energy was spent on devising colours and publicity material that would distinguish them from the militants. It also led to their refusing invitations to march in processions with the militants.

The NUWSS's favoured methods of visual propaganda involved processions and spectacle, and the widespread use of banners. They were also the largest producers of posters, although they seem to have made less use of postcards than the other societies. They knew that their heavy visual propaganda output was very important, particularly as they could not count on the publicity gained by militancy. Much of their output was handled by the Artists' Suffrage League (see page 49), and by designers also working for other suffrage societies; their poster designs were printed by commercial lithographers.

(see page 49)

HIGHLIGHTS OF THE SUFFRAGETTES' CAMPAIGN 1903–1914

NUWSS National Union of Women's Suffrage Societies
WFL Women's Freedom League
WSPU Women's Social and Political Union

1903
October
Emmeline Pankhurst founds the Women's Social and Political Union (WSPU) in Manchester.

1904
May
Emmeline Pankhurst protests outside Houses of Parliament in London at the 'talking out' of a women's suffrage bill.

1905
October
First occurrence of militancy, Free Trade Hall, Manchester. Christabel Pankhurst and Annie Kenney disrupt a meeting of Liberal speakers (including Winston Churchill); they are arrested, refuse to pay fines, and are imprisoned.

1906
January
General election. Liberals win landslide majority over Conservatives; the young Labour Party increases its hold. Liberal and Labour promise to support woman's suffrage, but this soon vanishes. The new Chancellor of the Exchequer, Henry H Asquith, is a staunch opponent of women's suffrage.

10 January
WSPU members nicknamed 'suffragettes' by the Daily Mail.

April
Disturbance caused by WSPU at House of Commons attracts a large amount of publicity. NUWSS receives complaints and starts to distance itself from the militants.

Emmeline Pankhurst heckles Asquith at Nottingham meeting (and is ejected from meeting).

June
WSPU holds protest at Asquith's London house. Teresa Billington arrested; she refuses to accept the authority of 'man-made laws' or to pay the fine, and is sent to prison.

WSPU decides to fight the Liberals 'at all by-elections until women are given the vote'.

October
Ten WSPU members arrested in disturbance outside the House of Commons. (Emmeline Pankhurst is knocked to the ground.) They refuse to pay fines, and are sentenced to two months in prison. The severity of the sentences attracts much publicity.

The Times prints a letter from Millicent Fawcett in which she appeals to the old-fashioned suffragists to 'stand by their comrades who in my opinion have done more to bring the movement within the region of practical politics in twelve months than I and my followers have been able to do in the same number of years'.

1907
9 February
The 'Mud March': first major NUWSS demonstration (3,000 march from Hyde Park to the Strand).

February
WSPU deputation sent to House of Commons; mounted police ride down the marchers. The fighting lasts for hours; Charlotte Despard and many others arrested.

Another women's suffrage bill introduced by W H Dickinson; it loses support by the second reading on 8 March.

March
Failure of W H Dickenson's new bill for woman's suffrage causes demonstration at House of Commons; prolonged fighting and sixty women arrested.

September
Charlotte Despard and Emmeline Pankhurst part; Despard forms Women's Freedom League (WFL).

October
WSPU launches Votes for Women newspaper.

1908
Two suffragettes chain themselves to railings in Downing St (Edith New and Olivia Smith); five arrested including 'General' Flora Drummond.

NUWSS has formal meeting with Asquith; he tells them no chance of legislation without approval of a general election.

Emmeline Pankhurst targets the Liberal candidates in the upcoming by-elections (hence the slogan 'Keep the Liberal Out'). Result: a number of Liberals lose their seats. In Devon, furious Liberal supporters roll Emmeline Pankhurst in the mud; further assault prevented by police.

February
Emmeline Pankhurst, still limping from Devon incident, leads deputation to Parliament riding in a cart. She is arrested; sentenced to six weeks in prison.

Suffragettes continue to harass politicians by various means (heckling at meetings, etc); cabinet ministers ambushed while playing golf.

April
Henry H Asquith succeeds Henry Campbell-Bannerman as Prime Minister. Asquith still opposes women's suffrage.

13 June
NUWSS procession, plus mass meeting at Albert Hall (13,000 march from Embankment to Albert Hall).

21 June
'Women's Sunday': WSPU's first mass demonstration; seven processions converge on Hyde Park, half a million attend.

30 June
First suffragette window-smashing: Mary Leigh and Edith New.

Autumn brings a period of industrial unrest; parades of unemployed and hunger strikes.

October
WSPU holds public meeting in Trafalgar Square and invites all to 'rush' the House of Commons. Emmeline, Christabel, 'General' Drummond and others arrested. The Leaders are jailed for approximately three months.

1909
Militancy increases: demonstrations, fighting, imprisonment, hiding in meeting rooms, chaining themselves to railings, accosting public figures.

WSPU now has seventy-five salaried staff and branches throughout the country.

27 April
NUWSS stages The Pageant of Women's Trades and Professions.

29 June
Suffragettes smash Whitehall office windows after Asquith consistently refuses to see deputations. Fourteen smashers serve one month in Holloway Gaol.

Escalating tension.

July
First suffragette hunger-strike by Marion Wallace Dunlop. Others follow; all are released early (thus terminating their sentences).

Group of suffragettes scale the wall of Lympe Castle in Kent and shout slogans at Prime Minister Asquith (dining with his family).

September
Force-feeding of hunger-striking suffragettes; Mary Leigh is the first.

'Pestering' of cabinet ministers by suffragettes continues all over the country.

1910
January
General election. Liberals and Conservatives achieve equal seats, giving the smaller parties such as Irish Nationalists and Labour more swaying power. All parties have their own agendas regarding Parliamentary reform; women's suffrage left in a weak position (not considered a political priority).

Lady Constance Lytton, suffragette and also member of the aristocracy, dons disguise, is arrested, jailed and forcibly fed. On release she exposes the torturous feeding methods.

February
Conciliation Committee formed to draft a bill including elements of women's suffrage: known as the Conciliation Bill. (From 1910 to 1912 three such bills are drafted and debated; all fail.)

Militants call a peace truce while the Committee does its work.

14 June
Conciliation Bill passes its first reading (progress is made).

To emphasize strength of purpose in the absence of militancy (due to peace truce), women hold rallies, processions and meetings.

18 June
WSPU and WFL stage 'From Prison to Citizenship' procession in support of the Conciliation Bill; NUWSS refuses to participate (10–15,000 march, two-mile long procession).

July
Conciliation Bill fails to gain ground, and is temporarily 'buried'.

November
To satisfy Irish Nationalists, Asquith calls for General Election in December to force Parliamentary reforms – but not women's suffrage. Militants infuriated.

---

18 November
'Black Friday': violence erupts outside House of Commons; 120 women arrested, many assaulted by police.

The following week bring riots in Parliament Square.

December
General election; same results. Government survival still reliant on the smaller parties.

1911
New optimism comes with the re-drawing of a second Conciliation Bill; WSPU renews its peace truce.

April
Peaceful protest: suffragettes refuse to fill in their census forms.

Second Conciliation Bill passes its second reading in May.

17 June
To exploit the spirit of optimism, the combined women's organizations present the Women's Coronation Procession, ten days before Coronation of George V (40,000 march, seven-mile long procession)

No progress on second Conciliation Bill.

5 October
Emmeline Pankhurst leaves for the USA on a lecture tour (not to return until January 1912).

November
Asquith announces new government bill for adult male suffrage (Reform Bill), giving more votes to men and invalidating the Conciliation Bill. WSPU furious.

21 November
Large-scale window-smashing of government and commercial properties. Over 200 suffragettes arrested; sentenced up to two months in Holloway.

1912
January
Emmeline Pankhurst arrives back from the USA; urges more militant action.

1 March
Violence against property begins. Mass window-smashing: women use hammers and stones to smash shop windows from Piccadilly Circus, up Regent St and along most of Oxford St – and elsewhere. Mrs Pankhurst and colleagues throw stones at Asquith's windows at No 10 Downing St.

Violent protests escalate. Break with suffragists visibly widens.

---

5 March
Police raid WSPU headquarters and arrest WSPU leadership on charges of conspiracy to incite violence. Emmeline Pankhurst and the Pethick-Lawrences sentenced to nine months in prison.

Christabel, on hearing of the warrant for her arrest, flees to France with Annie Kenney and continues to run the WSPU from Paris, taking an increasing tough line. Annie Kenney makes weekly trips across the Channel. (Christabel does not return until September 1914.)

28 March
A third Conciliation Bill comes before the House, and is defeated.

July
WSPU campaign becomes increasingly violent: window-smashing; firing of churches, houses and public amenities. Golfing greens attacked with acid, letters burnt in pillar-boxes, buildings scrawled with slogans.

October
On release from prison, the Pethick-Lawrences disagree with the new violent militancy, and are told to leave the WSPU. They continue to edit *Votes for Women*.

The new official WSPU headquarters opens in Kingsway, run by Emmeline Pankhurst, Annie Kenney and 'General' Flora Drummond. They launch *The Suffragette*, a more militant weekly newspaper.

Individual acts of violence occur: Mary Leigh throws a hatchet at PM Asquith in Dublin; then sets fire (with others) to the Theatre Royal. But WSPU policy is directed solely against property; (unoccupied) buildings are regularly burned down.

1913
January
The Government's own Franchise (Reform) Bill stopped in the House, along with its women's suffrage amendments; calls are made for total reworking of franchise reform. No clear way ahead for women's suffrage.

February
WSPU goes on rampage and conducts arson campaign. Suffragettes break windows; burn down the orchid house at Kew and refreshment pavilion in Regent's Park; vandalize public places. They even blow up Lloyd George's new country house.

---

24 February
Emmeline Pankhurst willingly takes the blame, and is arrested for incitement to violence; sentenced to three years in prison.

Hunger-strikes and force-feeding continue.

April
The new Home Secretary, Reginald McKenna, institutes his Prisoners' Temporary Discharge for Ill-Health Act ('The Cat and Mouse Act') which allows hunger-strikers to be released early for ill health, then re-arrested when recovered. Suffragettes learn to outwit the police, with disguises, false trails, etc. The more conspicuous Emmeline Pankhurst can't hide; between April 1913 and July 1914 (and weak from many hunger-strikes), she is moved in and out of prison nineteen times.

More outrages against property; buildings burned down, golf courses ruined by acid. (Again, WSPU claims only unoccupied buildings are attacked; no one is ever hurt.)

April
WSPU headquarters in Kingsway raided by police; senior staff arrested; papers removed. WSPU shops and offices all over the country attacked by angry public.

4 June
In protest Emily Wilding Davison throws herself in front of King George V's horse at the Derby races; she dies 8 June. Her funeral on 14 June is the last great WSPU procession.

Violence continues: the burning of houses, sports pavilions, seaside piers, churches; the interruption of state occasions; skirmishes with the police.

October
Force-feeding is re-introduced.

The Albert Hall refuses to hire to the WSPU.

Doctors who condone force-feeding or are involved in it, are physically attacked by suffragettes.

December
A bomb at Holloway Gaol fails to cause much damage.

1914
January
Sylvia Pankhurst disagrees with Emmeline and Christabel's policies, and is removed from the WSPU; she remains with her East London Federation of Suffragettes.

WSPU accuses government of giving drugs to suffragette prisoners to reduce their resistance to force-feeding.

---

10 March
Mary Richardson slashes The Rokeby Venus (painting of a female nude by Velázquez) in the National Gallery, in protest of the government's treatment of Emmeline Pankhurst.

21 May
Deputation to see King George V at Buckingham Palace fails; more than sixty women arrested.

Historic houses, art galleries and museums close down or admit Men Only as a result of suffragette attacks on exhibits.

Homes of suffragette sympathizers raided by police; firms who print their newspaper are threatened by the authorities. WSPU forced further underground; moves to new offices two more times.

4 August
Britain at war. The First World War begins.

Millicent Fawcett (NUWSS) and Emmeline Pankhurst (WSPU) both urge women to back the government and support the war effort.

Emmeline and Christabel call off the militant campaign and devote themselves to supporting Britain at War (Christabel returns to Britain in September 1914.)

The Suffragette newspaper is retitled *Britannia*.

Suffragette prisoners released early and start volunteering for the war effort.

1918
The Representation of the People Act gives the vote to women over thirty who are: householders or wives of householders; occupiers of property with an annual rent of £5 or more; or, graduates of British universities. (More than eight million entitled to vote.)

1928
All women over twenty-one, irrespective of property, can vote.

The second organization, the Women's Social and Political Union (WSPU), was fired by the new spirit of agitation and militancy. Founded in Manchester in 1903 and then transferred to London in 1906, it was dominated by the Pankhursts: Emmeline, founder of the organization, and her daughters Christabel and Sylvia. Emmeline was a visionary who ruled with an iron fist; Christabel was a renowned and compelling speaker who trained in law and devised the militant strategies that drove their movement; Sylvia created many of the WSPU's visual designs and also built up the presence of the women's movement in the East End of London. Other notable figures included Annie Kenney, Flora Drummond (the 'General'), and the brilliant Pethick-Lawrences, Frederick and Emmeline, who conceived and engineered the WSPU's 'corporate identity', marketing and fund-raising strategies. Its membership was composed of militants committed to bringing direct pressure on the government by any means necessary, who did not shrink from civil disobedience or violence. In 1906 the *Daily Mail* labelled them 'suffragettes', a slur which they adopted with pride. But Emmeline Pankhurst's uncompromising rule caused an early split and the formation of a second militant group, the Women's Freedom League; from then on, the suffragette label referred to members of both societies.

The WSPU operated a highly organized and military-like structure. One of the most innovative aspects of their visual propaganda campaign was a carefully designed corporate identity used for political purposes. Posters and banners were certainly a part of their display (albeit less than for other societies), and they also made extensive use of postcards. All such visual material did, however, sit within a broader framework that involved the publishing and merchandising of a very wide range of products and fashion. Their newspaper was entitled *Votes for Women*, which also became the rallying cry of the movement, and in later years they produced a more militant paper, *The Suffragette*.

The WSPU used a small number of individuals for visual art and design. Sylvia Pankhurst's designs appeared throughout the campaign, on everything from wall murals for exhibitions, to the emancipation certificates given to those who suffered imprisonment (see page 43). Perhaps most notable are her logos: the trumpeting angel, the freed prisoner walking over broken chains, the woman sowing the seeds of suffrage, and the Joan of Arc logo, all of which were placed on products and graphics. Hilda Dallas and Mary Bartels created advertising posters for the magazines; Alfred Pearse (who signed himself 'A Patriot') created many political cartoons for *Votes for Women*, as well as posters and postcards.

The Women's Freedom League (WFL) which originally broke away from the WSPU in 1907 under the leadership of Charlotte Despard, was the third women's organization. It too was militant and deserving of the label 'suffragette', but Despard insisted on a democratically-run organization that offered women a greater chance of expression. It also seemed to excel at gaining publicity through non-violent methods, such as picketing or tax resistance. The WFL set up London offices, but also had a strong provincial network (sixty-four provincial branches); it published a newspaper called *Vote*.

In addition to the use of banners and processions, the WFL, like the other societies, established its identity through posters, picture postcards, badges and other ephemera. It had a particularly strong graphic ally in the Suffrage Atelier, an artists' society which produced innovative graphic material for the WFL by economical hand-printing methods, as well as offering women artists an educational facility covering a variety of art and design areas, including modern reproduction processes (see page 50).

The suffrage movement as a whole made exemplary and inventive use of the communications media available to them. It was, however, first and foremost, a political movement, and the graphic and visual elements of the movement were a constituent part of those strategies involved. So although the graphics displayed on the following pages are meaningful in themselves, it is interesting to look at their position within an overall scheme of events, strategies and the political climate throughout the last decade of the suffrage campaign. A list of important moments in the campaign, shown on pages 22–23, pro-

1

1 Selected cards from 'Panko' or 'Votes for Women' ('The Great Card Game: Suffragists vs Anti-Suffragists'), with illustrations by E T Reed of Punch magazine, London, c1909.
2 'Saint Christabel', a postcard depiction by Charles Sykes of Christabel Pankhurst which hints at many issues: the adoration WSPU (Women's Social and Political Union) members felt for their leaders; the martyrdom of imprisonment; the crusading fervour of the militants and their commitment to their cause; and the window-smashing of churches. Britain, 1908–14.

3 Badge for the WSPU showing the suffragette colours of purple, white and green, and the symbolic use of chains, Britain, 1908–14.
4 Anti-suffragette Christmas card showing a hunger-strike medal, Britain, 1909–14. Such medals were presented by the WSPU to suffragettes who had endured hunger-strikes or force-feeding while imprisoned.

vides a picture of the suffragette activities. (It is necessarily highly simplified, and texts are listed in the Bibliography for a more in-depth reading of these fascinating events.) The list also brings to light another interesting point about this period: it is possible to see feminism operating as something close to a focused, single-issue mass movement, despite the fragility of the links between the societies themselves. The graphics can thus be viewed as part of a prolonged campaign of diverse and combined styles and methods.

Our focus, however, finally rests on the militant WSPU and its visual propaganda, as they offer the most interesting design issues for examination, as well as the most exciting political activity. As time went on, frustrations intensified, while tactics and propaganda strategies changed; and their attempts at persuasion gave way to a declaration of all-out war.

The WSPU and its propaganda campaign

The WSPU had a very clear corporate philosophy: to achieve the vote by any means necessary, including militant tactics. To this end, they operated in two spheres of activity: the first, political protest (direct action and militant activities), the second, corporate image-building, to gain both popular and financial support. Their corporate identity sustained both of these spheres of activity in the earlier years of their campaign, 1908–12, with visual propaganda as the cornerstone. The emphasis was, however, to change in the last two years.

SAINT CHRISTABEL

With regard to the organizational structure that dominated all activities, the WSPU fashioned itself after an army. Emmeline Pankhurst was an autocratic ruler and the rest of the leadership closed ranks around her, giving the impression of a well-oiled military machine. Their cause was a crusade, and the WSPU demanded complete devotion and loyalty to that cause, bordering on religious fervour at times. This was just as well, for that crusading spirit was the sacrificial mettle that would see them through the horrors of force-feeding and other brutalities. Furthermore, the army took care of its own. Imprisoned members were provided with an elaborate support system of medals of honour, certificates, ritual welcomings and breakfast ceremonies on their release. Of those who sacrificed themselves, none did so alone.

The first sphere of activity, political protest, grew more frenetic as time went on. A variety of communication methods and strategies were used to put across the Union's message, and thereby inform and persuade the public, recruit more members, and so on. Printed pamphlets and handbills carried essays by the leadership and information on how to help. The best known (and perhaps most admirable) method was public speaking – from small impromptu corner addresses to prepared formal speeches in mass demonstrations – a form of activity normally considered unseemly for women. For speed and economy, announcements of meetings or events were sometimes chalked in the street (using coloured chalk or tailor's chalk) or run off at a local press. Illustrated posters, a far more expensive communications tool, played a smaller but nevertheless important role and tended to be used around election time to target particular issues.

Postcards, on the other hand, were used extensively by the WSPU. They put across particular political messages, showed reverence to the leadership, and seemed to document every move the Union made. They recorded, among other things, demonstrations, speeches, trials and arrests, meetings, events (bazaars, processions, the

3

4

VOTES FOR WOMEN
AND LOTS OF 'EM
THIS MERRY CHRISTMASTIME

What you'll deserve if   You can do Without 'em

We must have 'em in the 'House'
There is no doubt about 'em
We'd all be hunger strikers
If we had to do without 'em—
What's the use of Mistletoe?
What's the good of Holly?
Only Women's love and smiles
Can make Old Christmas jolly—
Votes for Women! Heaven bless 'em
Votes for Women! but you bet—
If there's one we'd do without,
She's the Suffragette.

ARREST OF MRS. PANKHURST, MISS PANKHURST, AND MRS. DRUMMOND.
MR. JARVIS READING THE WARRANT AT CLEMENT'S INN, OCTOBER 13, 1908.
The National Women's Social and Political Union, 4, Clements Inn, W.C.

marching band), the offices and staff, arson attacks and imprisonment. In addition to broadcasting WSPU activities to outsiders, postcards also provided a communication line within the movement. As the main 'collectables' of the time, they allowed members to feel part of a greater system and to build up their own record of the movement, which they invariably did. Even the poorest could have a little piece, or souvenir, of the campaign events.

The mouthpiece of the Union, and an important source of finance, was its newspaper *Votes for Women*, which began as a monthly and quickly grew into a weekly that included material about matters as diverse as politics and fashion. It was publicized and sold by a wide variety of means, and members were even encouraged to leave copies on seats in public transport – to be scanned or read by the next traveller, leading perhaps to a casual conversion to 'the cause'.

All of these devices underpinned and gained recruitments for the WSPU's ongoing militant activities, which initially included 'pestering' politicians at their homes, at work or wherever possible, canvassing against the (Liberal) government candidates at all elections, demonstrating and creating disturbances outside the House of Commons, heckling politicians (including the Prime Minister) at public meetings, chaining themselves to railings, smashing windows of government offices and commercial properties, stone-throwing and sending deputations to the King and the Prime Minister. Most of these actions resulted in outbreaks of violence with the police, arrests and, inevitably, imprisonment. The imprisoned suffragettes' hunger-strikes provoked the government's retaliatory tactic of forcible feeding as early as 1909, colouring all WSPU strategies thereafter.

The other main sphere of WSPU activity, corporate image-building, continued alongside the militancy. Its main instrument was an innovative propaganda campaign that embodied an extremely modern concept: the design of a corporate identity and its use for political purposes. The WSPU's visual design owed much to the artistry of Sylvia Pankhurst, in her four logos and in many other design elements. But it was the Pethick-Lawrences who possessed a brilliant talent for fund-raising schemes, so vital to the campaign's success, and a vision for marketing and public relations. Emmeline Pethick-Lawrence devised the tricolour scheme of purple, white and green (purple for dignity, white for purity and green for hope). She introduced the scheme in 1908 in preparation for 'Women's Sunday', the WSPU's first mass demonstration in Hyde Park, and promoted it both within the ranks and without. The use of colours was not in itself new; it had roots in the military, and in a similar manner the WSPU 'army' would use its colours to define identity and allegiance. (Colours had even been adopted by liberation groups before this time, for example, by the Jacobin women of the French Revolution.) The innovation was, in fact, in the marketing strategy. Emmeline Pethick-Lawrence realized the power the colours would have if co-ordinated – not just as banners, but as fashion on parade. They would make a popular impression on the public, the press and the commercial world, simultaneously promoting the political and stylish acumen of the movement. In her attempts to popularize and co-ordinate their use on Women's Sunday, she even wrote that, 'If every individual woman in this union would do her part, the colours would become the reigning fashion.' And sure enough, they led astute business minds to see suffragettes as a commercial market. It wasn't long before leading stores, as well as small shops, were stocking everything from tricolour underwear to coats and hats – all sporting the 'suffragette look'. Merchandising boomed; individual entrepreneurs and businesses made specially designed clothes, or adapted existing designs, and a wide range of accessories and goods, including jewellery, leather belts, handbags, soaps and teas. These businesses also bought advertising space in *Votes for Women*; in return the magazine encouraged its readers to patronize supportive firms, and lavished special praise on suffragette entrepreneurs.

The WSPU quickly adopted the idea of the 'suffragette uniform' – a short skirt of purple or green, a white golf jersey, simple hat of purple or green, and the regalia (sash)

A LANCASHIRE LASS IN CLOGS AND SHAWL BEING "ESCORTED" THROUGH PALACE YARD.

CHORUS

Take me back to Palace Yard, Palace Yard, Palace Yard, that's where I long to be
With the friends so dear to me; the tall policemen smiling, bland, to gently take me by the hand
For "Women's Rights" anything we will dare; Palace Yard, take me there!

not much like our policeman. Y. H.

worn over the right shoulder and fastened under the left arm; there was even a 'full dress uniform' – a white frock with regalia and colours. Members were instructed when to wear them and given advance warning. The uniform was required for special occasions, such as the breakfast parties held for freed prisoners, rallies or demonstrations, while 'full dress' seems to have been reserved for large processions. Suffragettes were actually encouraged to wear the colours at all times, as a sign of their allegiance and commitment to the cause – and, as with any army, for the strength and solidarity to be had in being part of a greater force.

The WSPU's combination of style and 'spectacle' (the use of processions, marches, mass demonstrations and smaller rituals including breakfast parties and other ceremonies) served other purposes too, well beyond commerce and fashion. Apart from their value as a marketing tool, they were very much a psychological ploy, designed to create a public image of the suffragette in terms of dignity, grace, conviction and femininity, thus softening the effects of their conduct on a generation unused to seeing women operate outside the domestic sphere, let alone marching in the street or heckling politicians. Most particularly, the use of style and spectacle helped to combat the continual onslaught of anti-suffrage attitudes, which painted all suffragettes as ugly, unsexed, unwomanly, over-emotional or hysterical harridans. Hence processions were a matter of strategy as much as presentation. The suffragettes made very calculated decisions about their manipulation of fashion and femininity, and the effect it would have on the public and the press. They also remained attentive to their political effectiveness; for it was increasingly obvious that the later processions were becoming more a form of popular entertainment than a political statement.

As time went on, spectacle and ritual became important opportunities for WSPU members to parade their martyrdom and support those who had suffered or were suffering. Women in parades carried long poles or sticks topped by broad arrows to signify they had been imprisoned; they marched wearing medals of honour as a tribute to their courage, accompanied by banners that carried the names of hunger-strikers. These were solidarity devices aiming to sustain morale within the ranks, as well as to impress the public with their courage, while gradually generating a sense of injustice.

Yet another area of visual propaganda that was important to their image-building, particularly for its use of humour, was merchandising. Suffragette entrepreneurs and sympathetic manufacturers created a wide range of special or customized items to be sold through WSPU shops both in London and around the country – a grand show of enterprise that seemed to pay off handsomely. The WSPU founded The Woman's Press (its publishing imprint) in 1908, handling weekly production of *Votes for Women*, sales of Woman's Press literature, and also stocking a wide range of products and novelties in 'the colours'. Business was so good that in May 1910 they expanded into additional premises with a shop at the impressive central London shopping location of 156 Charing Cross Road. Indeed, for the period 1907–14, no fewer than twenty-two WSPU shops were listed for London alone.

The range of products handled by WSPU shops was astonishing, and must have made a brilliant display in variations of the colours. For allegiance and decoration, there were badges, brooches, scarves, ties, hatpins, 'Emmeline' and 'Christabel' bags, and of course 'the uniform'. Only a limited stock of clothing was kept, as a whole suffragette fashion industry awaited customers in shops and stores throughout London. There were games and toys: kites, suffragette dolls, specially devised puzzles, card games and board games; and, for the more sedate, postcard albums, writing papers, books and pamphlets. Foods included specially packaged teas, chocolates and jams. Most impressively, suffragettes exploited their notoriety and that of the events surrounding them, and did so with a sense of humour that must have won them popular appeal and

The campaign persisted despite increasing violence and arrests:
1   Postcard showing the arrest of Emmeline and Christabel Pankhurst and 'General' Flora Drummond at the WSPU offices in Clement's Inn on 13 October 1908. Published by the WSPU.
2   Postcard (probably) showing an incident at a demonstration in October 1907 outside the House of Commons in London, which was protesting against the earlier failure of W H Dickinson's Bill. The card is also unusual for carrying an image of a working woman.
3   Famous photograph of the arrest of Mrs Pankhurst on 21 May 1914 while trying to present a petition to King George V. During this particularly volatile WSPU demonstration, 200 women attempted to break through a line of 1,500 police surrounding Buckingham Palace.
4   Postcard showing a church burnt by the suffragettes, 1913.

gone at least some way towards disarming their critics. For example, according to the instructions of the card game 'Panko', playing with anti-suffragist friends presents no problem: 'If you begin by amusing them with "Panko" you can convert them afterwards'.

By all accounts, the merchandising and other aspects of image-building were extremely successful. It was in the political sphere that there was a turn for the worse. With the failure of a third Conciliation Bill in 1912 and hopes of the vote becoming increasingly distant, the WSPU's political campaign became even more militant. By that time, a great deal of suffering had been endured in the name of 'the cause'. There had been injuries at demonstrations; imprisonment and force-feeding had led to cases of broken health. The martyrdom had escalated: 700 prisoners, or their proxies, had marched in the Women's Coronation Procession alone.

In the final two years, 1912–14, the WSPU wound down its fashion, marketing and merchandising activities and put all its energy into 'political activities': attacks on property, such as window-smashing, setting fire to pillar boxes and burning houses (specifically unoccupied houses – the suffragettes never threatened human life). The Woman's Press cut many of its novelty products and concentrated on selling the WSPU colours, propaganda literature and its new militant magazine The Suffragette, launched late in 1912. The increasingly violent policies caused the Pethick-Lawrences to leave the WSPU membership, although they continued to publish Votes for Women. Emmeline and Christabel now worked with steely resolve. All opposition was purged; even Sylvia Pankhurst was forced to leave.

These final two years were the most violent of the campaign, making the suffragettes increasingly unpopular with the public. Despite that, The Suffragette sustained its sales and was even sold abroad. Some loyal firms and manufacturers withdrew their advertising and services, but even at the last and most intense stages of activities in 1914, thirty-five companies were claimed to be doing business with the WSPU and advertising in The Suffragette. Public tolerance may have waned, but commercial tolerance had not. To the bitter end, suffragettes were seen as a lucrative market. Then came the outbreak of war in August 1914 and, suddenly, it was all over.

Wars, patriotism and post-war domestic prisons: the First World War (1914–18)

The militant suffrage campaign did not achieve the vote, but it provided the stepping stones towards it. Above all else, those last few decades of campaigning had transformed the expectations of women. They now moved about and operated in the public realm as never before, earned money, were educated and spoke for themselves. An attitude of confidence and self-determination had been the achievement of those suffragette years. And women now put it to use in the war effort.

With the outbreak of war, Millicent Fawcett (NUWSS) and Emmeline Pankhurst (WSPU) both called a halt to their suffrage crusade, encouraging women to back the government and support the war effort. Emmeline and Christabel Pankhurst, in particular, encouraged women to work in munitions factories and men to enlist in the armed forces. The Suffragette was renamed Britannia, bearing the slogan 'For King, For Country, For Freedom'. Sylvia Pankhurst worked to help alleviate war hardships among the poor in the East End of London, and campaigned for better working conditions and equal pay for women doing war work in factories.

Governments on both sides of the Atlantic set a broad range of both student and professional commercial artists to work on selling and sustaining the war to their respective publics through the most popular current advertising medium – the poster. For mass communication and persuasion, it had no equal; film and radio were still too young, and

AT LAST!

Reproduced by kind permission of the Proprietors of "Punch," from the cartoon of January 23, 1918, and published by the National Union of Women's Suffrage Societies, 62, Oxford Street, W.1.

1 A postcard published by the NUWSS that celebrates obtaining the franchise (the vote), with a drawing of Joan of Arc taken from Punch, 23 January 1918, Britain.
2 Recruitment poster by artist Joyce Dennys for the VADs, or Voluntary Aid Detachments, who were sent to the fronts overseas. Britain, 1914–18.

FRANCE
ITALY
MALTA
GIBRA'
SALO'

EGYPT
MESOPOTAMIA
HOLLAND
SWITZERLAND
RUSSIA

V.A.D.
NURSING MEMBERS . COOKS . KITCHEN-MAIDS.
CLERKS . HOUSE-MAIDS . WARD-MAIDS.
LAUNDRESSES, MOTOR-DRIVERS, ETC.
ARE URGENTLY NEEDED
APPLICATION TO BE MADE TO

newspapers were still the province of a literate minority.

In both Britain and America, posters were produced in large quantities to recruit men and to raise money from war loans. Images of women often appeared in these posters in a variety of stereotyped nurturing and supportive roles: as nurses, guardian angels, mothers and homemakers. Britain, in particular, focused heavily on poster recruiting, since conscription wasn't introduced until 1916. British poster publicity played especially on feelings of shame and horror in its audience, insinuating their cowardice in the face of much-advertised enemy atrocities; and representations of women were central to this imagery. Posters sometimes appealed directly to women to get their men to enlist (see the poster addressed 'To the Young Women of London' above). More often, however, it was a matter of using images of women to induce guilt and persuade. Hence, 'Women of Britain say – Go!' in E Kealey's poster; even little girls say go – in Savile Lumley's renowned 'Daddy, what did YOU do in the Great War?'. The diatribe was at its strongest in Britain within the first eighteen months of the war, and seems to have been very successful in engaging recruits.

Once the USA entered the war in 1917, the US government issued a massive number of posters in an attempt to unite the public behind the war effort. Women appeared as nurses, angels, mothers, as Columbia and the Statue of Liberty, and even as sex objects, as in Howard Chandler Christy's eroticized girls (see page 62). But the Americans too were subject to sensationalized themes of atrocity, showing women and children being bloodied or dragged off by the animalistic Hun.

However, there was another role for women to play, which brought further promises of liberation and a new graphic culture surrounding women and work. From the very start, British women, including the suffragettes, were quick to volunteer for war work. The VADs, or Voluntary Aid Detachments, called for volunteer labour (partially trained or untrained workers) to serve as stretcher bearers, medical attendants, cooks, laundresses and, in later years, even ambulance drivers. VAD units were sent to the fronts overseas, as were a growing number of trained nurses.

The country also needed armaments and food. Women were trained to work in munitions factories making shells, bullets, cartridges, fuses (often handling dangerous substances). Rising casualties and enlistment opened up more jobs for women. Wartime ministries, local government and local industries employed women as clerical workers, plumbers, carpenters, technicians, fire fighters, chimney sweeps, police – almost any job necessary to keep trades, industries and communities running. By 1917, various women's agricultural committees were drawn together into the Women's Land Army, which organized women into uniformed units to work on farms around the country. Also at that time, women began to enter the armed services, replacing men in non-combatant roles such as cooks, drivers, clerks and accountants, or undertaking skilled jobs such as engineers, fitters and electricians. The last two years of the war saw the creation of the WAACs (Women's Auxiliary Army Corps), the WRAF (Women's Royal Air Force) and the WRNS or 'Wrens' (Women's Royal Naval Service). Women serving in the military received official commendations and medals of honour; the large mass of working women did not.

Working women did, however, receive a very different kind of glory, as they were depicted in popular graphic culture. Recruitment posters for the Land Army or munitions work showed women in an independent and assertive mode and often in clothing such as trousers and uniforms, which would have been unthinkable before the war. Postcards and other ephemera, such as cigarette cards and savings stamps, honoured their drive, energy and capabilities in an astounding range of jobs. Land Girls and Munitions Girls found their way into books, novels and comic postcards, sub-

4

In World War I the British recruitment tactics of inducing shame or guilt often made manipulative use of women to convey their message:
3 'To the Young Women of London', recruitment poster , Britain, c1915.
4 'Women of Britain Say – Go!', poster by E Kealey, Britain, 1915.
5 'Daddy, What Did You Do in the Great War?', poster by Savile Lumley, Britain, 1915.

5

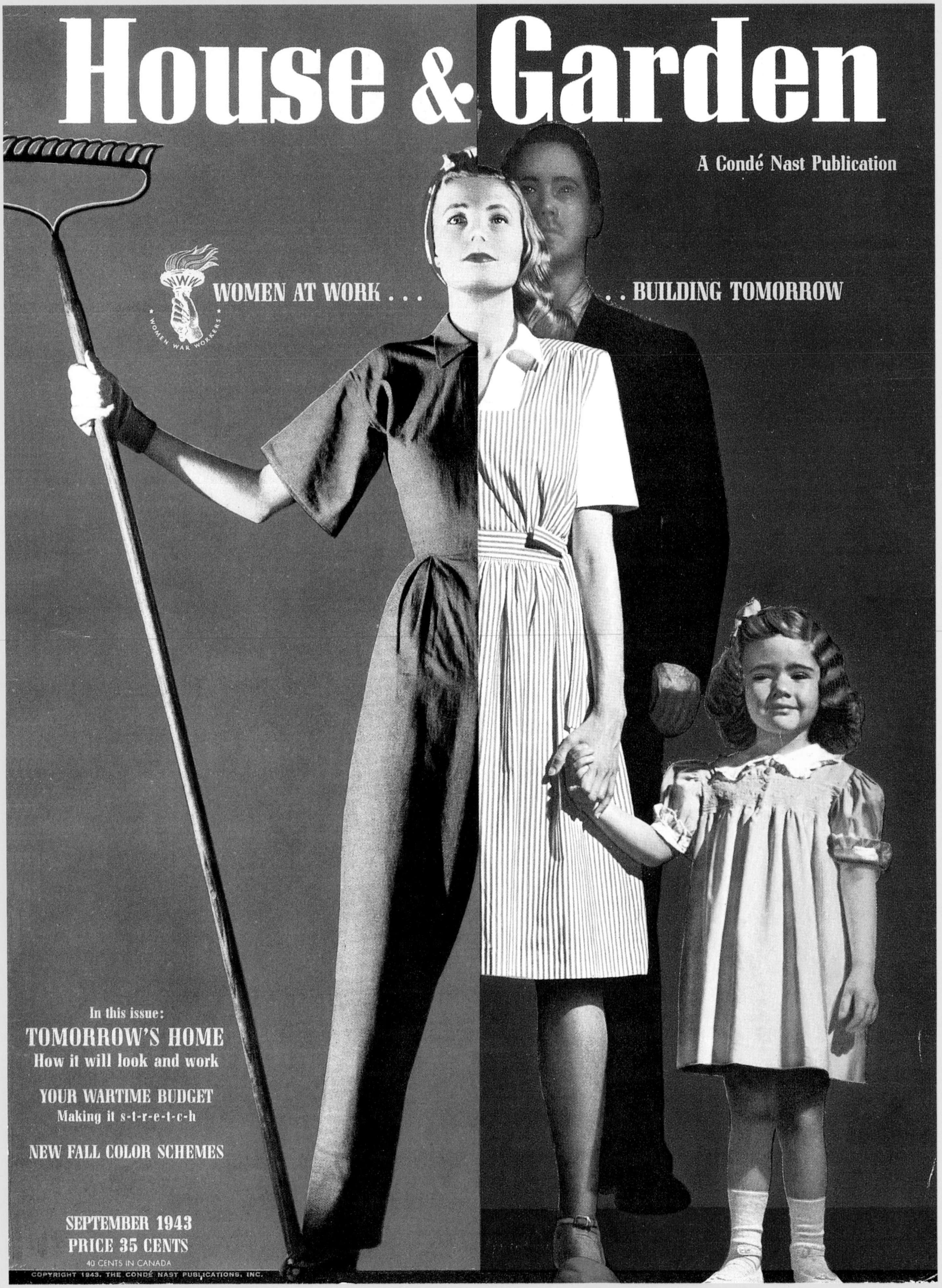

House & Garden

A Condé Nast Publication

WOMEN AT WORK . . .   . . . BUILDING TOMORROW

In this issue:
TOMORROW'S HOME
How it will look and work

YOUR WARTIME BUDGET
Making it s-t-r-e-t-c-h

NEW FALL COLOR SCHEMES

SEPTEMBER 1943
PRICE 35 CENTS
40 CENTS IN CANADA
COPYRIGHT 1943, THE CONDÉ NAST PUBLICATIONS, INC.

1 Cover of House & Garden magazine, USA, September 1943, which uses the split-woman image discussed on page 84.
2 'Women of Britain Come into the Factories', World War II poster by Philip Zec, Britain, c1942.
3 Trans: 'Emancipated Women, Build Socialism', Soviet poster by Adolph Strakhov, 1920. (This offset reproduction is by Bread and Roses Bookshop, California, USA.)

ject to the usual crass jokes, while the highly popular group photographs on postcards and in other graphic media celebrated the camaraderie of munitions workers and volunteer groups. For many women, it was a great moment of personal independence; and for some, their first taste of economic independence.

There was of course a darker side to it all, in addition to the destruction caused by the war itself. Behind the smiles lay reports of the dangerous working conditions, long hours and poor pay of many of the factory workers. Munitions workers in particular were in danger of TNT poisoning through inhalation or absorption through the skin, which could be fatal. Yet the press joked about the 'yellow girls' working with TNT, whose skin had become dyed in the process.[1]

The cheery faces also belied the die-hard prejudices that working women faced from certain groups, such as farmers – prejudices that were gradually overcome. There was the usual criticism that, by working, they were betraying motherhood and becoming 'unsexed'; more realistically, the unions and the general public were worried that the women might push men out of their jobs. Women were therefore constantly reminded that the situation was only 'temporary', and of how glad they would be to give it all up when the boys came home (see the cigarette cards on page 65).

Indeed, the establishment – the government, councils and industries – made sure that this happened. For as soon as the war was over, women were forced to give their jobs up to the returning war heroes and were sent back to their 'rightful place' in the home. The pressure on women to be capable, productive and equal to men was removed as quickly as it had been created. Promises of liberation and equality had been a manipulative con: the value of women's labour and their right to independence had only been recognized as long as they were of use to the male ethic and the operations of war. And it would happen again, within the same generation, in the next world war.

Women had, however, gained a new sense of achievement and freedom, and had been depicted in a newly assertive and independent manner. They had also won a more concrete victory. In 1916, on the strength of the contribution women were making to the war effort, the ever-determined Millicent Fawcett quietly began to push the government once again for women's suffrage. This time it received support from public, press and politicians. After some agonising over age restrictions and other details, the vote was granted in 1918 to British women over thirty (see also page 23).

After the revolution

With the success of the Bolshevik revolution in 1917, the members of the Russian avant-garde art movement known as Constructivism committed themselves to creating a utilitarian role for art and design in the new Soviet future. Constructivism's visual language pulsated with boldness and energy. Comprised of the flat, abstract geometric shapes of Suprematism and a highly dynamic sense of composition, it was applied across a broad range of applied arts and design including industrial design, furniture, textiles, theatre sets and graphics. Women maintained a lively visual presence in the graphics of this period, as typified by the graphic design work of Alexander Rodchenko. His wife Varvara Stepanova, and Liubov Popova (both painters), applied Constructivism's graphic shapes and dynamic configurations to textiles and clothes design, and remain the most visible of all the artists working in this area. They also created theatrical costumes and played highly influential roles in the Constructivists' revolutionary approach to fashion, particularly the creation of professional clothes and sportswear for a society of new freedoms and new activities. Both Popova and

3

Stepanova worked on designs of clothing for everyday wear in the work-place, encompassing all professions – from factory worker to doctor – and all created with a functional view to convenience of movement, cleanliness and economy.

Hence women occupied an equal place as comrades and workers in the Constructivist vision of a productive future, and this was reflected in their bold, assertive presence in the imagery of the time. But this period of artistic experimentation and intense creativity didn't last long. Stalin saw the avant-garde style as decadent and set about repressing it in the years after Lenin's death in 1924. By the early 1930s, it was replaced by the heroic art and stalwart workers of Socialist Realism. Women remained comrades: they were promised freedom from the decadence and corrup-tion of the past, largely symbolized by religion, and a productive work-ing role in the Soviet future. But under Stalin, such promises of freedom were just one more aspect of Kremlin rhetoric. As the State's control over the arts, the media and general conduct became more rigid, imagery became more reg-imented and formulaic, and pictures of happiness more absurd. Nevertheless, the opti-mistic depictions and bold poses of emancipated working women in early (and even later) Soviet imagery are still borrowed and pastiched by graphic designers today.

The Second World War (1939-45)

In the Second World War, women in both Britain and the USA were con-stantly targeted by governments in their graphic campaigns to join the armed services, register for war work, save supplies and economize at home, cope with the shortages of food and clothing rationing, and basical-ly keep things running. The poster still played a key role in this process of mobilization and maintenance, although other media, such as radio and film, had also come into play.

America entered the war in 1941 and posters continued to present women as angelic Red Cross nurses, wives or home-makers in their appeals for money or war loans. But images of a new, tougher, self-assured woman also appeared on posters call-ing on women to enlist in war work or join the military in such divisions as the US Women's Army Corps and the US Marine Corps. In addition, there was a considerable change in tone: the softer plea of 'Your Country Needs You' became the hard bark of 'Be a Marine!'. Women therefore transformed the profile of the American workforce, pouring into factories and plants in a variety of industries in order to cover the man-power shortage. New employment opportunities arose for women in non-traditional and skilled (as well as highly paid) jobs, and new groups of women were drawn into the workforce, including black women, married women and women over thirty-five. Women were trained to be shipbuilders, welders, riveters, steel workers, munitions workers and machine operators of all sorts – giving rise to the popular heroine 'Rosie the Riveter', a recruitment figure as well as a household name for the new women fac-tory workers. By 1945, women made up a third of the whole US workforce.[2]

With Britain suffering a constant and real threat of invasion from 1939 onwards, it demanded much greater commitment from its women, over a longer period of time. Although volunteering was popular, in 1941 women aged twenty to thirty were con-scripted into the armed forces or industry; in 1943, it became ages eighteen to fifty (with various qualifiers attached). As in the First World War, women covered a wide range of duties: support jobs in the armed services, such as the ATS or (Women's) Auxiliary Territorial Service, working as drivers, couriers and radar operators; protecting against bombing raids in the civil defence and the fire brigade; working in industry – munitions and factory work; working on the farms for the Land Army; and helping out in the Women's Voluntary Service, which did everything from darning socks to running

The Chef does everything but cook – that's what wives are for!

nurseries. Women were constantly 'doing their bit', shoulder to shoulder, equal to men. By the end of the war, there were 460,000 women in the armed services, and over 6.5 million in civilian war work.[3]

In both Britain and the USA, women made up a substantial percentage of their country's workforce (approximately one third) as the war rolled on, and made an even greater contribution than the women war workers in the First World War. But as it all drew to a close, they suffered exactly the same fate as their working sisters before them. Most of them lost their jobs at the end of the war, to make way for the conquering heroes, and were unceremoniously shoved back to where they came from – unskilled labour or the kitchen sink.

As before, the shoulder-to-shoulder ethic vanished: the patriotism of war had been used to push women into determined action and capability, and then right back into their domestic prisons. Once again, though, there were some gains: for both American and British women, the war had opened up opportunities for independence, money and freedom. They had progressed further along the line of self-assertion, and although they suffered a set-back at the end of the war, there had been a profound and irreversible change. They had invaded non-traditional sectors of the workforce, defeated stereotypes and shown capability and strength – and these qualities had been recorded and reflected in a tougher graphic image that pounded through recruitment material, appeals for industry, ads for domestic products, and other aspects of graphic culture. To be sure, pre-war stereotypes of femininity and domesticity would continue regardless, but there were new roles to add to the mix and new expectations for women themselves.

Post-war consumerism and the fifties

In the years after the war, higher education opened up for women in Britain and the USA. But post-war consumerism brought intense psychological programming for women – through magazines, films, radio, and the new broadcast medium of television. The highest feminine aspiration was pitched as marriage to Mr Right, a home and children. After that came the acquisition of 'labour-saving' household technology, the right soap powders, the right cleaning liquids, and so on; in short, the management of the 'ideal home'.

In America a higher percentage of women had gone to college or university, and then given up careers for marriage. By the end of the 1950s the average marrying age had fallen as low as twenty and continued to fall. By the mid-1950s, sixty per cent of the women in higher education were dropping out to marry or because too much education might deter potential husbands.[4] Once married, American culture told women that their only fulfilment should come from being wives and mothers; they didn't need (or shouldn't want) careers, education or political rights – all the freedoms and opportunities that the early feminists had fought so hard to win. US advertisers found many ways to tell the 'happy housewife' to cook, clean, decorate, sew – and buy their products. And it wasn't long before the image began to come apart at the seams. In her 1963 bestseller *The Feminine Mystique*, Betty Friedan pointed to the isolation and dissatisfaction felt by many American women who were suffocated by society's expectations, calling it 'the problem that has no name'.

Suddenly, a new atmosphere of change began to brew, for women had come full circle. Just as before, in the early part of the century, they had become locked into their homes; viewed as the possessions of their husbands, to be seen but not heard; prettied-up, corsetted, and treated as mindless, passive childbearers – to be trapped forever in their domestic prisons. Once again, it was time to break out.

Elizabeth Cady Stanton – Susan B. Anthony
1815–1902 (seated)   1820–1906 (standing)
"Our trouble is not our womanhood, but the artificial trammels of custom under false conditions."
Suffragettes / Lecturers / Editors • Founders of suffrage and equal rights associations, Lyceum Lectures, co-edited History of Woman Suffrage.

1, 2 Advertising for domestic products in the 1950s and 60s placed women firmly back in the house again:
1 Advertisement for a washing machine, USA, 1950s.
2 Advertisement for a food processor, Housewife magazine, Britain, June 1961.
3, 4 A new wave of Women's Liberation in the 1960s and 70s found inspiration in the early suffragists:
3 Poster with photo of Elizabeth Cady Stanton and Susan B Anthony, **founders of the nineteenth-century US suffrage movement. Designed by Maria Jensen, published by Les Femmes, USA, 1973.**
4 Cover and inside spread of the influential book Shoulder to Shoulder, a documentary by Midge Mackenzie (1975) which also provided the basis for a BBC television series on the battle for Votes for Women.

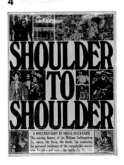

The WSPU: corporate identity and militancy

SYLVIA PANKHURST.

1   Postcard of Sylvia Pankhurst, Britain (probably) c1914.
2   Ribboned badge with portrait of Emmeline Pankhurst, head of the WSPU, c1908.
3   WSPU postcard showing Christabel Pankhurst addressing an audience at Trafalgar Square in London, October 1908.

Founded in 1903, the Women's Social and Political Union (WSPU) embodied the new spirit of militancy in the British women's suffrage movement, and its members became popularly known as 'the suffragettes'. Its main organizers included Mrs Emmeline Pankhurst, her two daughters Christabel and Sylvia, the Pethick-Lawrences (Emmeline and Frederick), Annie Kenney and 'General' Flora Drummond. Militancy and direct action demanded an army-like structure; Mrs Pankhurst ruled as the undisputed leader and policy-maker, and complete loyalty and allegiance was required of all members. They were crusaders on a holy mission: to obtain the vote.

For nearly a decade, from 1906 to the onset of war in 1914, the WSPU organized its activities (both political and image-building) along lines similar to a modern-day corporate identity, all of it underpinned by visual propaganda. A variety of media and communications strategies were employed to reinforce their military tactics and put across their message, including handbills, pamphlets and public speeches, as well as postcards (one of the most popular media of the time) and their newspapers, *Votes for Women* and later *The Suffragette*.

The innovatory aspects of the WSPU's propaganda campaign embodied an extremely modern concept: the design of a corporate identity and its implementation for political purposes. Then, as now, corporate identity did not consist merely of surface image or decoration; it involved a co-ordinated programme of communications strategies that would allow the organization to operate effectively, both internally and externally in their interface with the public. Corporate image-building and visual identity rested to a great degree on Sylvia Pankhurst's artistry. But it was Emmeline Pethick-Lawrence's device of the tricolour scheme (the purple, white and green, signifying dignity, purity and hope), her vision to push for its use as the identity of the movement, and her attempts to relate it to marketing and fashion, that gave birth to the 'suffragette look', forging links between the suffragettes and the commercial world which would continue up to the outbreak of war. Meanwhile, Frederick Pethick-Lawrence's genius for all manner of fundraising guaranteed that the Union kept afloat throughout all the manoeuvring.

2

MISS C. PANKHURST AT TRAFALGAR SQUARE INVITING THE AUDIENCE TO "RUSH" THE HOUSE OF COMMONS ON OCTOBER 13.
The National Women's Social and Political Union, 4, Clements Inn, W.C.

3

4

5

6

4 Catalogue and enquiries stall (showing prominent display of Sylvia Pankhurst's logo) at the WSPU 'Women's Exhibition and Sale of Work in the Colours', Princes' Skating Rink, Knightsbridge, London, May 1909 – one of many WSPU fund-raising activities.

5 Three of the four logos designed by Sylvia Pankhurst for the WSPU. Left to right: the angel trumpeter; a woman emerging from prison and stepping over broken chains; and a woman sowing the seeds of women's suffrage.

6 Postcard showing the front of the WSPU shop at 39 West Street in Reading, Berkshire, 1910.

1   Poster by Hilda M Dallas, advertising Votes for Women, the official newspaper of the WSPU from 1907 to 1912. The woman depicted is wearing the 'suffragette look'.

2   A bevy of leading WSPU personalities sporting the 'suffragette look'. Front row, centre to right: Mary Gawthorpe (dark dress), Christabel Pankhurst, Emmeline Pethick-Lawrence (dark dress) and Annie Kenney, c1908.

3   Standard-bearer Daisy Dugdale wears 'the uniform' and leads a procession to meet Mrs Pankhurst and Christabel on their release from Holloway Gaol, 19 December 1908.

4   Assorted pins and badges used by the WSPU, 1908–14.

5   Silk scarf in the WSPU colours of purple, white and green, 1908.

6   The banner of the Hammersmith branch of the WSPU, showing the WSPU motto 'Deeds Not Words'. (Reversible, using a mixture of machine stitching, crewel stitch embroidery, and appliqué. The hammers and horseshoes are painted on fabric placed over card.) Britain, c1911.

3

The creation of the 'suffragette uniform' and its co-ordinated appearance in processions, pageants and other forms of spectacle – amidst waves of purple, white and green paraphernalia – brought the movement's dignity and, above all, femininity to the public eye. This shrewd and manipulative use of fashion and femininity challenged the stereotype of the hysterical, ugly suffragette, and gained the movement support from both press and public.

Such image-building tactics were continued alongside the on-going siege of militant incidents, which included demonstrations, stone-throwing and violent clashes with the police. Even when suffering imprisonment and force-feeding, the suffragettes paraded their dignity and martyrdom in processions before the crowds. However, after the failure of the third Conciliation Bill in 1912 (with no further hope for the vote in sight) the Union declared war, and concentrated almost solely on violent political activities, including window-smashing, arson attacks and house-bombings.

5

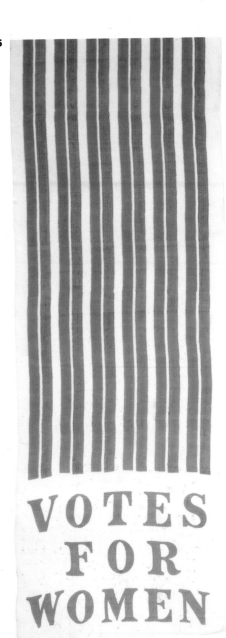

4

6

WSPU newspapers

In autumn 1906 the WSPU set up a national headquarters at 4 Clement's Inn in London, and in autumn 1907 it launched its newspaper *Votes for Women*, co-edited by the inimitable Emmeline and Frederick Pethick-Lawrence. Originating as a monthly, the paper quickly grew to weekly status, and was sold by newsagents all over the country.[5] With the continued success of the newspaper, The Woman's Press was launched the following year, acting as the publishing imprint and distribution house for *Votes for Women* and other WSPU publications.

Votes for Women itself played a variety of roles. It was used to put across the WSPU political message and discuss current topics or crises. It carried news of forthcoming processions or events, and instructions on appropriate dress – 'the uniform'. It carried fashion features and advertisements from entrepreneurs, leading stores and all manner of businesses which, along with sales, were an important source of revenue. The weekly production, packing and dispatching of the newspaper were in themselves focal points of activity and publicity for the campaign, involving both salaried staff and a growing army of volunteers.

There were lively sales drives and sales competitions. Horse-drawn 'press carts' were used to distribute to pitches all over London or to sell on-the-spot. Another well-known distributor and mobile advertisement was the 'suffragette bus', plastered with advertising posters and sporting both a suffragette driver (a woman driver: shocking!) and conductor, as well as a trumpeter on the roof to attract attention. There were 'parasol parades' of suffragettes walking in a line to advertise the newspaper; as well as 'poster parades' which involved carrying sandwich boards (apparently a very difficult exercise, as it was impossible to see the pavement or kerb underneath when walking). Street sellers were also based around transport stations and other vantage points.

When the last and worst stage of militancy struck in 1912, the new and more militant newspaper *The Suffragette*, edited by Christabel Pankhurst, replaced *Votes for Women* as the WSPU's main organ. (*Votes for Women* was, however, still published by the Pethick-Lawrences; both newspapers were sold abroad, spreading news of the movement internationally.) Once again, heavy publicity and sales tactics helped to keep sales of *The Suffragette* rising steadily. Faith in suffragette purchasing-power, meanwhile, kept major companies advertising – even in the final, most violent stages of the campaign (mid-1913 to mid-1914) when suffragette unpopularity with the public was at its height.

1 Advertising in Kingsway, London with the Votes for Women omnibus, October 1909.
2 Front page of Votes for Women, August 1910.
3, 4 Advertisements from the pages of Votes for Women, June 1911, in preparation for the upcoming Women's Coronation Procession on 17 June.
5 Poster by Hilda Dallas advertising the more militant WSPU newspaper The Suffragette, 1912.

WSPU merchandising

In addition to its publishing activities, The Woman's Press acted as a focal point for WSPU merchandising, selling a wide range of novelties and products. Initially based at 4 Clement's Inn, by 1910 it had expanded into additional premises (including a shop) at 156 Charing Cross Road. Indeed, business must have boomed, for from 1908–12, goods were sold from WSPU shops based all over London and around the UK. (However, with the onset of the worst militancy in 1912, the WSPU wound down its merchandising and concentrated solely on hard-core propaganda and violent political protests.)

The WSPU was one of the earliest political organizations to use merchandising for propagandist purposes. (Although it was certainly preceded and possibly influenced by the American political parties: for example, in 1904 Republican Teddy Roosevelt's campaign for the Presidency made use of a 'teddy bear', and created teddy pins, medals and buttons.) But the most impressive thing about the WSPU's approach was the way in which it relayed and even extended its political message and solidarity through employing a variety of expressive modes, including instructional or educational (literature), entertaining (games), decorative (tea sets), communicative (stationary, postcards), ephemeral (greetings cards) – and of course devotional, for it offered 'the uniform', tricolour badges, sashes, pins, ribbons, and all the demonstrative trappings necessary in order to show allegiance and to be part of the cause.

This collection of products and artefacts owed much of its visual impact to Emmeline Pethick-Lawrence's tricolour scheme of purple, white and green, as well as Sylvia Pankhurst's logos and designs. (In particular, her angel trumpeter logo, which first appeared in 1908, was used heavily on a wide range of objects, from printed handbills to jewellery.) But the collection also

1 WSPU postcard showing the exterior of The Woman's Press shop at 156 Charing Cross Road, 1910.
2 WSPU postcard of the interior of The Woman's Press shop on Charing Cross Road, 1910. Close inspection of this photo will reveal some of the merchandise mentioned in this chapter.
3 China teaset bearing Sylvia Pankhurst's 'angel' logo, first manufactured in 1909.

PANK-a-SQUITH

4 'Pank-a-Squith', a board game that promised to keep its players amused while also helping to spread the movement. It involved a suffragette's attempt to journey from her house to the Houses of Parliament, while overcoming all manner of difficulties. First available in 1908.

5 Metal 'suffragette' playing pieces for Pank-a-Squith, c1909.

6 Cover of songsheet, drawing by Margaret Morris, 1911.

4

5

owed much to the love of pictorial illustration and decorative style passed from Victorians to Edwardians, as well as the creativity and invention of the large number of entrepreneurs and businesses involved. Many would have been sympathizers, and some not – but all knew a lucrative market when they saw one.

Perhaps most surprising and impressive of all was the good-natured wit and humour involved – unexpected in a movement so stridently and passionately committed to its cause. No doubt a product of shrewd psychology, it gave the movement a wonderful element of fun and a human face. Yes, suffragettes could even laugh at themselves: an endearing quality which helped to enhance their popularity and disarmed the barbs of critics who described them as cruel, harsh harridans.

6

Dedicated to THE WOMEN'S SOCIAL AND POLITICAL UNION.

VOTES FOR WOMEN

THE MARCH OF THE WOMEN
(Popular Edition in F. To be sung in Unison)
By ETHEL SMYTH, Mus.Doc.
Price: One Shilling & Sixpence net.

To be had of THE WOMAN'S PRESS, 156 Charing Cross Rd, London W.C. and BREITKOPF & HÄRTEL, 54 Gt Marlborough St, London W.

WSPU regalia, imprisonment and martyrdom

2

3

An army honours its own. So too did the WSPU, which fashioned itself as an army of crusaders, complete with uniforms and regalia. Hence it operated an elaborate support system to sustain morale among the troops and honour sacrifice.

There were Holloway (prison) badges and brooches, and medals of honour for hunger-strikers. These sometimes had an extended ribbon with additional metal bars or 'stripes', inscribed with dates of imprisonment or force-feeding on the back. Many of the badges and medals were personalized: initials or names were inscribed on the back, or printed on the protective cases. Hand-calligraphed names appeared on the Emancipation Certificates: illuminated addresses acknowledging imprisonment, designed by Sylvia Pankhurst and signed by Emmeline Pankhurst. All such items were a symbolic representation of the commitment and fervour needed to undertake militant actions, and an important acknowledgement of the pain and suffering endured. For prison conditions were terrible, and personal testimonies of force-feeding describe it as a terrifying process: accounts of the bleeding, wretching and body-breakdown involved do not make for pleasant reading. To undergo voluntarily such hellish procedures required far more than everyday courage; and deserved more than passing thanks.

Great attention was also paid to ritual and ceremony. Released prisoners were met by delegations or welcomed with breakfast parties, often accompanied by a marching band. As the militant activities escalated over the years, the WSPU also used processions as an opportunity to parade their martyrdom, displaying banners that listed the names of hunger-strikers. Those who suffered imprisonment often carried long poles topped by broad arrows. Such measures must have had a stunning effect as numbers of victims increased; 617 'prisoners' marched in the 'From Prison to Citizenship' procession shown on page 45. Shrewd as ever, the WSPU even managed to turn its pain and misery to its advantage as brilliant propaganda. Such symbolic displays of suffering drew sympathy and admiration from the crowds and the press.

4

5

1

6

1 Former suffragette prisoners dressed in replica prison clothing and badges in an open-top vehicle, October 1908.

2 Prison badge, inscribed on reverse: 'M M' 28 October, 28 November 1909. (Probably awarded by the WSPU to a suffragette who had endured a prison sentence.)

3 Hunger-strike medal (silver, attached to a purple, white and green silk ribbon). Awarded by the WSPU to suffragettes who endured hunger-strikes or force-feeding while imprisoned. Name and date usually inscribed on the back; more silver bars sometimes added to signify force-feeding (with dates usually engraved on the back). This medal is inscribed 'For Valour / Hunger Strike / Kate Eleanor Cardo', dated 1912.

4 Medal stating 'Sacrifice for Women's Rights' and embossed with an image of a woman being force-fed (similar to poster on page 52), dated 1914.

5 Holloway brooch (silver, with a convict's broad arrow in purple, white and green enamel on a silver portcullis, designed by Sylvia Pankhurst), awarded by the WSPU to suffragettes who had endured a prison sentence, c 1908.

6 Handkerchief embroidered in Holloway Gaol by Jane Terrero (charged on 1 March 1912 for causing wilful damage – smashing windows) with a photo of Christabel and Emmeline Pankhurst attached, 1912.

7 Illuminated WSPU certificate acknowledging imprisonment for the cause of women's emancipation; designed by Sylvia Pankhurst, 1908.

The use of spectacle by suffrage societies

Although the WSPU presents a particularly interesting case study in terms of corporate design and visual propaganda, it sits within a broader context of activities undertaken by all the suffrage societies – activities which represent the single-mindedness and determination of the entire movement.

The use of spectacle – by means of large-scale demonstrations, marches, parades or processions – was one of the most dramatic and effective ways in which suffrage societies could show allegiance to their cause and the strength of their movement (at least in the early days). Processions, for example, were heavily orchestrated and by most accounts an administrative nightmare to plan and prepare, but they offered wonderful opportunities for artistic and symbolic display.

The NUWSS in particular made spectacular use of embroidered or appliquéd banners, many of them designed and made by the Artists' Suffrage League or by its founder Mary Lowndes, who was passionate about the possibilities of women's political needlework. Meanwhile, the WSPU saw marvellous marketing opportunities in parading their tricolour scheme; exploited the performance opportunities (such as marching a number of processions to a termination point in time to shout 'Votes for Women' at five o'clock); and paraded their imprisonment as martyrdom, often accompanied by the militant Women's Freedom League (WFL). Furthermore, the success of the WSPU's use of colours led other societies to follow suit: the NUWSS adopted red, white and green, and the Women's Freedom League (WFL), green, white and gold – thereby introducing an important design and identification element into the processional display.

All the societies were keen to benefit from the public image exercise which the processions offered: challenging the Edwardian attitudes that kept women locked up at home, and defiantly marching through the streets with dignity and grace. It was an opportunity to charm the public and override stereotypes of harsh, 'unsexed' women, and rampaging suffragettes. It was also unfortunately an opportunity for the societies' inevitable divisions to surface. From the very start – namely, the NUWSS 'Mud March' of 1907 – there were intense arguments over the wisdom of constitutionalists and militants marching together, hence the WSPU was not officially invited to join the march. Many subsequent attempts to organize joint demonstrations also failed. The NUWSS was constantly worried about being asso-

THE WOMAN MILITANT: LEADERS OF THE SUFFRAGIST PROCESSION AND THEIR SYMBOLIC BANNERS COMMEMORATING GREAT WOMEN OF ALL AGES.

1 A page reporting on the NUWSS demonstration of 13 June 1908 and illustrating 23 of the 'heroine' banners designed by the Artists' Suffrage League, taken from the Illustrated London News, 20 June 1908. The top centre portrait is of the dynamic Charlotte Despard, leader of the Women's Freedom League (WFL).
2 'General' Flora Drummond in a boat on the Thames, inviting MPs to attend 'Women's Sunday' (demonstration in Hyde Park, 21 June 1908).
3 Tickets for 'Women's Sunday', 21 June 1908.

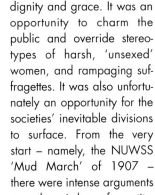

MRS. DRUMMOND OPPOSITE THE TERRACE OF THE HOUSE OF COMMONS ADDRESSING M.P.'S, INVITING THEM TO THE HYDE PARK DEMONSTRATION.

2

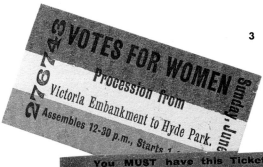

3

VOTES FOR WOMEN Procession from Victoria Embankment to Hyde Park. Assembles 12-30 p.m., Starts 1

You MUST have this Ticket to remind you that next Sunday, June 21st, is Suffrage Sunday, and that you must join the Procession to Hyde Park, to be present at the great Demonstration at 3-30 p.m., to shout VOTES FOR WOMEN, at 5 o'clock.

ciated with the militant WSPU and 'tarred with the same brush'. The only united procession, able to claim the peaceful participation of all the major societies, was the Women's Coronation Procession of 1911. But correspondence relating to the design of NUWSS banners and decorations shows that there were still worries, and great care was taken to make them appear as different from the WSPU ones as possible.

There were many marches and demonstrations, both large and small (and construed for a variety of purposes), but among the most prominent were: the NUWSS 'Mud March' of 9 February 1907 (its first public open-air demonstration); and the Spring demonstrations of 1908, comprised of the NUWSS procession to a mass meeting at the Royal Albert Hall on 13 June, and the following week, the massive WSPU demonstration known as 'Women's Sunday' on 21 June (with seven processions culminating in Hyde Park) – which also saw the introduction of their colours. The WSPU/WFL 'From Prison to Citizenship' procession followed on 18 June 1910, with both militant societies marching. The last great procession, the largest and most united, with no political protest, was the Women's Coronation Procession of 17 June 1911. This was headed by a costumed Joan of Arc (the suffragettes' patron saint) on a horse leading at least twenty-eight women's organizations.

The subsequent introduction in November 1911 of a (suffrage) Reform Bill giving more votes to men – but none to women – drastically changed the nature of the societies' campaigns from then on, and brought on the most intense stages of WSPU militancy. One final WSPU public procession took place: the funeral of Emily Wilding Davison who ran under the hooves of the King's horse at the Derby races, and in doing so became a martyr for the cause. But by that time, the days of the great processions were really over. They had become a triumph of planning and organization, evolving from 3,000 marchers in 1907 to 40,000 marching in the Coronation Procession. They had also given the early days of the cause one of its most potent political tools – but inevitably, as time went on, they lost their political effect.

4 Procession moving through Fleet Street, 18 June 1910, with suffragettes (ex-prisoners) carrying broad arrows on staves.

5 The WSPU's Official Programme and Souvenir for 'Women's Sunday' (21 June 1908), showing the platforms in Hyde Park and the women chairing them.

5

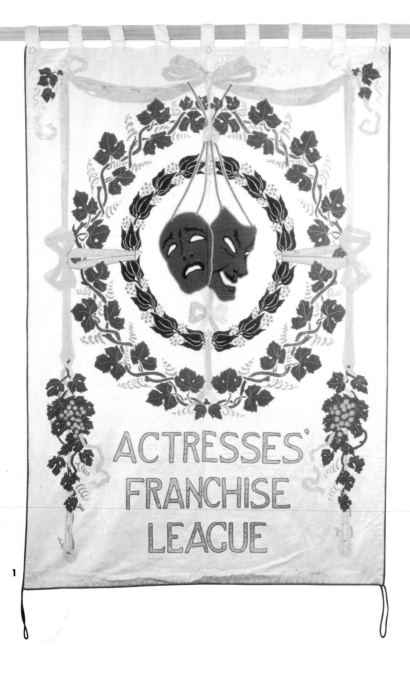

1　The banner of the Actresses' Franchise League, whose colours were pink, white and green, c1911. (Materials: cotton sateen, appliquéd pink silk embroidery, gold and green paint.) The AFL performed and published suffrage plays.
2　The Actresses' Franchise League and their banner, waiting for the Women's Coronation Procession, 17 June 1911.
3　The Women's Coronation Procession, with its elaborate floats and costumes, moves along Piccadilly in London.

VOTES

HANDICAPPED!

CARL HENTSCHEL LTD 182, 183 & 184 FLEET ST E.C.   PUBLISHED BY THE ARTISTS' SUFFRAGE LEAGUE

Artists and studios of the suffrage campaign

The graphic and artistic needs of the three suffrage societies were met largely by professional women artists, working both as individuals and in organized groups. (Interestingly, a substantial number of women, trained as artists in the late 1800s, were attempting to earn a living with their art at the start of the century.)[6] Women artists, particularly those attached to the suffrage movement, tried to confront a number of challenges and prejudices at that time, such as the argument (still familiar to us today) that their sex had produced no geniuses or Michelangelos. At the same time they were asserting a new image of the skilled, independent, professionally competent woman, and contesting the traditional (and limiting) representations of women. To this end, they designed and produced political material ranging from needlework to printed posters and postcards; designed and orchestrated major demonstrations and schemes of banners, costumes and graphics; lent their studios for meetings; and contributed to a variety of other activities such as exhibitions and bazaars.

The Artists' Suffrage League, chaired and organized by Mary Lowndes (and usually convened in her studio), was founded in 1907 to help with the NUWSS 'Mud March'. It was a group of professional artists (both fine artists and illustrators) keen to use their skills for the cause of woman's suffrage – but not all necessarily 'suffrage artists', for it is obvious that some had a customer workload which competed with their suffrage activities. Nevertheless, they produced pictorial propaganda in the form of posters, postcards and leaflets (used both in Britain and the USA); designed and produced an enormous number of banners for NUWSS branches and special groups; and organized decorative schemes for major demonstrations and meetings. In 1909 the League also organized a competition for a poster to be used by the NUWSS at election time, which yielded Duncan Grant's 'Handicapped' as one of the winners. All-in-all, the group produced a body of poster work – all coloured lithographs and commercially printed – that contains some of our best-known suffrage images. Mary Lowndes herself was a major contributor to both poster and (above all) banner work.

Justice – at the door: I, SURELY AM NOT EXCLUDED

Miss Jane Bull : "Give me a bit of your Franchise Cake, Johnnie."
Master Johnnie Bull : "It wouldn't be good for you."
Miss Jane Bull : "How can you tell if you won't let me try it ? It doesn't hurt those other little girls."

Printed and published by the Artists Suffrage League. 259 King's Road, Chelsea.

ANTI-SUFFRAGIST TYPES.
(Dedicated to the A.S.S.)
The man who thinks that "Women have no right to Vote because they can't defend their Country."

TYPES OF ANTI-SUFFRAGISTS.
(Dedicated to the A.S.S.)
The gentleman who thinks that women ought not to work, and therefore under-pays his typist.

TYPES OF ANTI-SUFFRAGISTS.
(Dedicated to the A.S.S.)
The Parliamentary Candidate who thinks "that the women would be sure to Vote for the handsomest man!"

1 'Handicapped', poster by Duncan Grant, published by the Artists' Suffrage League and joint winner (with a poster by W F Winter) of the ASL poster competition in 1909.
2 'Justice at the Door', poster by Mary Lowndes, head of the Artists' Suffrage League. Published by the NUWSS, 1912. A reminder that to exclude women from the Reform Bill debate was to exclude Justice itself (normally depicted as a woman).
3 Postcard commenting on the international women's suffrage scene and showing Britain to be lagging behind. Published by the Artists' Suffrage League, Britain, post-1907.
4 'Types of Anti-Suffragists', three postcards from a series of twelve ('Dedicated to the ASS' or Anti-Suffrage Society), created by Louisa Thomson-Price, Britain, 1909–10. Thomson-Price was originally aligned with the constitutional suffragists (NUWSS). She left to join the militant Women's Freedom League (WFL) and produced this series of controversial cartoons for the WFL's newspaper, Vote.

3

4

Artists and studios of the suffrage campaign

The members of The Suffrage Atelier, established in 1909, saw themselves as 'an arts and crafts society' working for women's suffrage. They did this in a wide variety of ways including designing, exhibiting and selling posters and postcards; contributing to pageants and decorative schemes; and organizing fund-raising, recruitment and studio space for meetings. The group printed all its own designs, chosen from members or by competition, and exploited the cheapness and immediacy of hand-printing processes. It was consequently more prolific than the Artists' Suffrage League, and its work has a more raw and urgent power.

Of particular interest, however, is the Atelier's attempt to teach its members (all professional and skilled artists) the appropriate drawing methods and hand-printing processes necessary to produce their own publications (via stencilling, etching, wood-engraving, wood or lino-cut etc). Most of the Atelier's posters and postcards were in fact block prints, such as woodcut or lino-cut, in black and white or with colour added by hand. Its other great contribution was to offer women artists an opportunity to experiment in other media and learn new processes. To this end, it operated as an educational centre with a regular programme of activities that included instruction in life-drawing, painting, designing, embroidery and banner-making, and printing; as well as exhibitions, lectures and design criticism. It also trained women in drawing for the new, more sophisticated photo-mechanical reproduction processes – essential for commercial survival, as hand-engraving had seen its day.

Although the Atelier had been founded as a non-party organization aiming to work impartially for all societies, it was in reality closely affiliated to the WFL, designing processional schemes, posters and postcards, and 'pictorial supplements' to the WFL newspaper, *Vote*. In its aim to provide what it called 'picture propaganda' for the suffrage, the Atelier produced some of the most expressive, almost avant-garde, statements – by essentially archaic methods. It also excelled at information design strategies, such as producing informative statements on its postcards and posters, which used simple language and 'conversations' in an attempt to educate people about the injustices in the legal system.

THE PREHISTORIC ARGUMENT

THE PRIMEVAL WOMAN – 'Why can't I go out too and see the world?'

THE PRIMEVAL MAN – 'Because you can't. Woman's proper sphere is the cave'

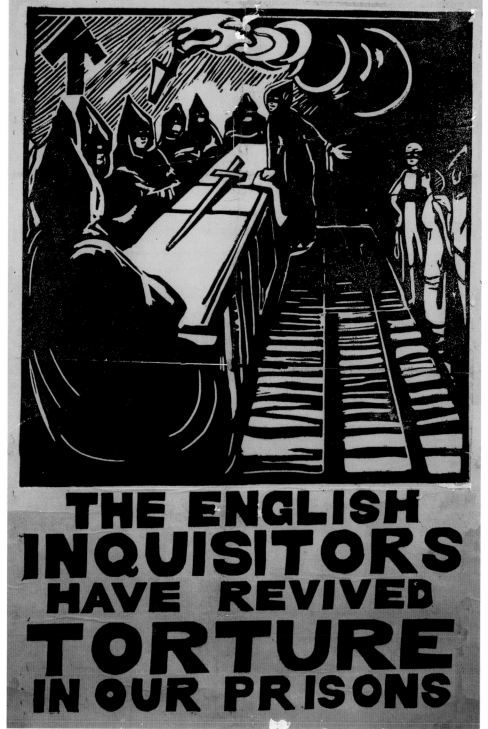

THE ENGLISH INQUISITORS HAVE REVIVED TORTURE IN OUR PRISONS

1 'The Prehistoric Argument', poster and postcard by Catherine Courtauld, published by the Suffrage Atelier, 1912.

2 'What a Woman May Be...', anonymous poster and postcard, published by the Suffrage Atelier, c1912.

3 'The English Inquisitors', anonymous poster and postcard, published by the Suffrage Atelier, c1912. The torture referred to is force-feeding.

4 Two posters (and postcards) designed by 'MaC', published by the Suffrage Atelier, 1909. Both were part of a series on how the law discriminated and ruled against women.

5 'The ASS as Portrait-Painter', postcard (probably) by Catherine Courtauld, published by the Suffrage Atelier, c1912. The Anti-Suffrage Society was referred to as the ASS in a number of postcards 'lampooning the antis'.

THE ANTI-SUFFRAGE SOCIETY AS PORTRAIT-PAINTER

"THE A·S·S·— This, my dear Mrs Britannia, is a true & authentic portrait of yourself if ever you get the vote."

HOW THE LAW "PROTECTS THE WIDOWER

WIDOWER: "My wife has left no will"
LAW: "Then all her property is yours, had you died, she would only have got a third of your property."

HOW THE LAW 'PROTECTS THE WIDOW.

WIDOW: "Can nothing alter my husband's will?"
LAW: "No Madam, a man may leave his money to whom he likes but you must maintain your children, that is one of the laws of England."

Artists and studios of the suffrage campaign

Graphically speaking, the WSPU seems to have concentrated on photographs, postcards, spectacle and other devices – and published comparatively fewer poster designs than the other societies. Designs also tended to come from a few individuals. For example: Hilda Dallas and Mary Bartels provided advertising posters for the newspapers, *Votes for Women* and *The Suffragette*. Meanwhile, Alfred Pearce (aka 'A Patriot') provided political cartoons for the pages of *Votes for Women*, as well as posters and postcards. Having said that, what little that did exist in poster form either carried a colourful impact, or a fair amount of controversy.

Two of the WSPU posters shown here are noted for their use of violence. One, by an unknown artist, was inspired by the commonly-termed 'Cat and Mouse Act'. (Devised by Home Secretary Reginald McKenna in 1913, this act allowed the release of prisoners suffering from ill health through hunger-striking or force-feeding, and then re-arrested them on recovery in order to finish their sentence.) The other poster, by Alfred Pearse, presents the force-feeding of a hunger-striker. There was an obvious attempt to turn this group pose, or configuration of people, into an icon, because it appeared in various forms: as a photographic reconstruction, on a poster (shown here), and even embossed in metal on a WSPU medallion of honour (shown on page 43).

1

2

But the WSPU's use of violent imagery posed problems, and carried the danger of playing into the hands of its critics. It demanded an emotional response – which might fuel the overriding view of women as hysterical and over-emotional; presented women as victims (again, critics could harp on about women being weak and defenceless); and, most horribly, would allow more sadistic viewers to enjoy seeing women 'get what they deserve'. In the posters shown here, the use of a stylized, symbolic tone works in their favour (particularly as they are aimed at members, sympathizers or concerned individuals). But the worry becomes more pertinent on taking a broader graphic view – for the postcards on page 56 show that sadistic jokes and tasteless comments were part of the general milieu.

1 'Votes for Women: the People Not the Commons Must Decide', poster and postcard by 'A Patriot' (Alfred Pearse) and published by the WSPU for use in the General Election of December 1910. It mimics a well-known contemporary Ripolin paint advertisement. Pearse also produced many cartoons for the front page of Votes for Women.
2 'The Modern Inquisition', poster by 'A Patriot', published by the WSPU in 1910, for the General Election of January 1910.

3 'The Right Dishonourable Double-Face Asquith', poster and postcard by 'A Patriot', published by the WSPU in 1909, and targeting the General Election of January 1910. Asquith is shown championing constitutional rights, but then denying them to women.
4 'The Cat and Mouse Act', anonymous poster, published by the WSPU, 1914. Referring to the Act that demanded the rearrest of hunger-strikers (once recovered) who were released early due to ill health.

The graphic environment

Because the suffragettes offered the most extreme behaviour – and the Pankhursts, in particular, were vibrant personalities – they were colourful targets for caricature and graphic treatment. In one sense, caricatures and graphic portraits served the movement well; if viewing items from The Woman's Press, there is no lack of humour. The suffragettes poked fun at politicians, the police, the law, themselves, and even their imprisonment. But this was only a small part of a much broader arena of graphic debate. Women's demand for the vote had become a part of current affairs (and thanks to the suffragettes, one of the burning issues of the day). Consequently, the suffrage societies and their activities became part of one of the most active print environments of that period. They were grafficked in magazines, photo-documented in newspapers, chastised on press hoardings, and so on. The WSPU in particular knew the value of press coverage and manipulated it at every opportunity, while all the societies benefited indirectly from the press publicity of the militant actions (even if, in the case of the NUWSS, they considered it bad publicity).

Within this scenario, a fairly distinct, declared argument developed between certain groups and societies. A counter-movement of anti-suffragists was mobilized in 1910 as the National League for Opposing Women's Suffrage (NLOWS).[7] A number of NLOWS graphic statements emanated from an (unknown) artist named Harold Bird, but the NLOWS unfortunately also enjoyed the enthusiastic talents of John Hassall, one of the best-known posters artists of the period. Nevertheless, the suffrage artists retaliated: sometimes in direct response, as in Louise Jacobs' poster 'The Appeal of Womanhood', a parody of and reply to Harold Bird's creation, or as part of the on-going process of 'lampooning the antis', typified by the series of Atelier postcards directed at the Anti-Suffrage Society (ASS).

However, just as damaging – and far, far more prolific – was the anti-suffrage (and indeed, anti-woman) imagery produced on an unofficial or popular basis, by commercial postcard publishers or anyone else out for commercial gain, such as toy manufacturers. Within the misogynistic Edwardian climate, the graphic environment proceeded to cough up a multitude of 'anti' themes, repressive stereotypes and representations – many of which seem shockingly modern-day in their content. (The postcard on page 56 stating 'It's not a vote you want – it's a bloke' finds its jeering modern-day equivalent in 'what you need is a good fuck'.) The gallery of postcards shown provides a range of the popular anti- themes of the time, including the neglectful housewife and mother; militant viragos and 'the shrieking sisterhood'; the masculine woman; and the ugly or 'unsexed', unfeminine woman.

1 'A Suffragette's Home', poster (and post-card?) by John Hassall, published by the National League for Opposing Woman Suffrage (NLOWS), 1912. Not only a comment on the neglectful wife, but a play on the erosion of masculine (working-class) labour and the subjection of men to women.

2

But five policemen
Now have met
The ramping, tearing
Suffragette.
They do not faint,
Nor yet turn pale;
But grab and haul her
Off to jail.

Now here are some
Who want their rights
You see they all
Are perfect frights!
Their feet are huge,
Their stockings blue—
The Press says so:
It must be True.

2 Pages from Beware! A Warning to Suffragists, a book of rhymes lampooning the antis, by Cicely Hamilton and containing sketches by C Hedley-Charlton and others. Published by the Artists' Suffrage League, c1912.

3 'No Votes Thank You', poster and postcard by Harold Bird, published by the NLOWS, 1912; pitting the 'womanly' woman against the shrieking suffragette in the background.

4 'The Appeal of Womanhood', poster and postcard by Louise Jacobs, published by the Suffrage Atelier, 1912. A direct response to Harold Bird's poster (fig 3), where the 'womanly' woman wants the vote in order to stop white slave traffic, and address poverty and other issues.

3

4

"Automatic Suffragette Exterminating Pillar-Box"
(patent NOT applied for).

IT'S NOT A VOTE YOU WANT
—IT'S A BLOKE

THIS IS "THE HOUSE" THAT MAN BUILT,

AND these are a few of the women of note Who say that they want, and they will have the vote; And think that they ought, To have Man's support: Even although HE should have to go short, The sly Suffragette Who is all on the get And wants all, in THE HOUSE that man built

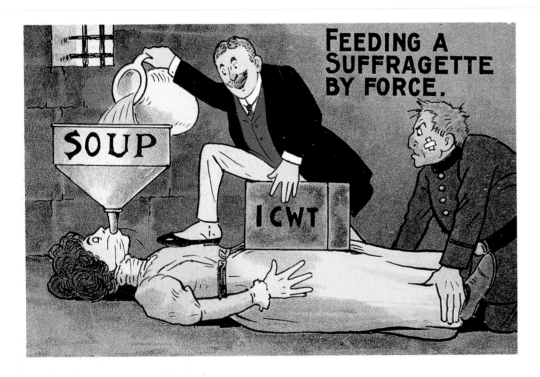

FEEDING A SUFFRAGETTE BY FORCE.

SOUP

I CWT

SUFFRAGETTES WHO HAVE NEVER BEEN KISSED.

Votes for Women

While in the act of voting, Mrs Jones remembers that she has left a cake in the oven!

A gallery of anti-suffrage abuse in the form of commercially-produced postcards, plus a few examples using cats which might be read both ways, 1908–14.

We Demand The Vote.

An Advocate for Woman's Rights.

I want my Vote!

THE "SUFFRAGETTE."
DOWN WITH THE TOM CATS.

I WANT A VOTE

GIVE ME A VOTE AND SEE WHAT I'LL DO!

"A perfect woman, nobly planned
To warn, to comfort & command"

Mummy's a Suffragette,

Is your wife a Suffragette?

1   Anti-suffragette symbolism rendered in the form of transfers, Britain, 1908–14.

2   'Suffragettes', sheet music with illustration by Reginald Rigby, Britain, 1913.

3   'One of the Striking Features of Kew Gardens', a postcard referring to suffragette window-smashing, sometimes done with toffee-hammers or other tools, 1908–14.

4   A jack-in-the-box toy containing a suffragette wearing a feathered Tyrolean type hat (a hat often used in cartoon caricatures of the early suffragist Lydia Becker), c1913.

5   'Elusive Christabel', a push-pull 'vanishing card' game, referring to Christabel Pankhurst's secret escape to Paris to avoid arrest, 1912.

International suffrage: the USA and Britain

Even in its early stages, the move towards women's suffrage was international. At the turn of the century, the USA had a women's suffrage movement half-a-century old which, through the energies of Elizabeth Cady Stanton, Susan B Anthony, Lucy Stone and others, had resulted in the formation of the National American Woman Suffrage Association (NAWSA, f 1890). Four states had already achieved the vote for women. The American movement was then subject to fresh energy from 1910–13, adopting militant propaganda techniques from the British campaign and thereby adding five more states to the roll call.

The influence of the British campaign was understandable. There was a long tradition of transatlantic relations between the leading feminists of both countries. The American press avidly followed the campaign in Britain, viewed as the epicentre of the worldwide movement; while both of the WSPU newspapers (*Votes for Women* and *The Suffragette*) were sold in New York around 1913–14. The visits of British suffragists, such as Emmeline Pankhurst, to the USA received wide acclaim; and there were many other women on both sides of the Atlantic who participated in campaign activities when visiting the other country.

This led to the American societies adopting the British use of colours, as well as pageantry and decorations. Furthermore British posters, from both the Artists' Suffrage League and the Suffrage Atelier, were apparently used in American campaigns (on issues of common ground) as there were no equivalent artists' organizations in the USA. On the whole, the USA produced fewer posters and tended to use a gentle form of art nouveau 'goddess', or homely motherhood approach – steering clear of tough images of working women or the harshness of some of the Atelier comments.

1

2

1 'Votes for Women', poster by B M Boye, USA, c1913.
2 'Votes for Our Mothers', anonymous poster, USA, c1915.
3–5 American suffragette parades in New York City, 1912–15.

6 Suffragette Headquarters in Cleveland, Ohio, 1912. The President of the organization, Belle Sherwin, can be seen in the centre holding the suffrage flag.

The First World War (1914–18): women and war work

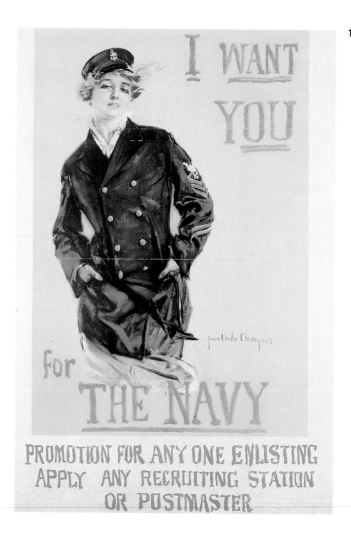

With the outbreak of the First World War in 1914 (and the vote still not achieved), British women mobilized themselves in order to back the war effort. Both in Britain and later in the USA (which entered the war in 1917), posters were produced in vast quantities to recruit men and raise money through war loans – and images of women appeared in a variety of supportive roles: as angels, nurses, mothers and home-makers. But with no conscription in Britain until 1916 (and therefore total reliance on a volunteer army), early British recruitment posters often resorted to shaming and guilt-inducing techniques – implying loss of honour or cowardice – or scare tactics using atrocity themes. Both approaches involved, through words or images, the manipulation of women and their motives. Hence women were used as a means of inducing guilt, or were seen to be ordering men off to war, or were depicted as innocents who needed protection from 'the ravaging Hun'. America's populist approach, on the other hand, veered towards nurses and angels for the most part, and extended the range to the use of sexual enticement with the 'Christy girl' posters, shown here. The Americans, however, were also capable of using atrocity-related themes and sensationalism, exemplified by Fred Spear's poster 'Enlist'. Germany's posters centred on masculine courage and sacrifice in war and seldom depicted women at all, except to recruit them for industrial work when desperate, or ask them to salvage materials.

1 'I Want You for the Navy', World War I recruitment poster by Howard Chandler Christy, USA, 1917.
2 'Women's Royal Naval Service', World War I poster by Joyce Dennys, Britain, c1915.

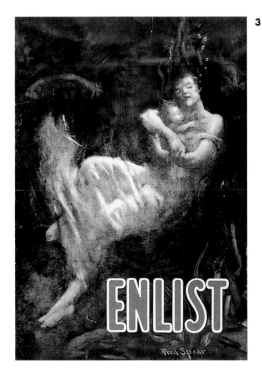

There was, however, another role for women to play (most crucially in Europe), and that was in war work. In Britain, graphic campaigns encouraged and applauded women's contributions to volunteer medical services (shipped to the front), munitions work, the Land Army and its agricultural work, and a wide range of public services, trades and industries. Thus war workers entered popular graphic culture (and were now even seen wearing trousers) in posters, books, postcards, stamps and even cigarette cards. But the push to be capable, productive and equal to men (the carrot of liberation and equality) was snatched away with the end of the war. They were forced out of their jobs, and pushed back into the home.

However, there were some very critical gains. For they had now obtained the vote because of their efforts; they had experienced a new sense of achievement, freedom and camaraderie with other women; and they had brought into existence a new, tough graphic image of a working woman: assertive, capable and equal to any man.

Frauen und Mädchen!
Sammelt Frauenhaar!
Abnahmestelle jede Schule
Ortsausschuß für Sammel- und Helferdienst
Töpfergasse 33

3   'Enlist', World War I poster by Fred Spear, USA, 1915. The sinking mother and baby made an evocative reference to the German torpedoing of the Lusitania in 1915.
4   Trans: 'Collect combed-out women's hair', World War I poster by Jupp Wiertz, Germany, 1918. For a Red Cross campaign, which collected women's hair for the war effort (used as a substitute for leather and hemp in drive belts and insulation).
5   'Help America's Sons Win the War', World War I poster by R H Porteous, USA, 1917/18.
6   'The Greatest Mother in the World', World War I poster by Alonzo E Foringer, USA, 1918. One of the most popular US posters, and used again by the Red Cross in World War II.

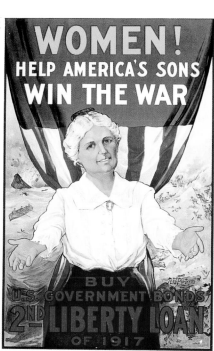

1   'National Service, Women's Land Army', World War I poster by H G Gawthorn, Britain, 1917.
2   'Expecting a Rise Shortly', postcard by Reg Maurice of a British 'munitions girl' sitting on a powder keg, Britain, 1914–18.
3   'Munitions Workers', postcard, Britain, 1914–18.
4   'Getting in the Flax Crop', postcard, Britain, 1914–18.
5   'Food for the Guns', postcard, Britain, 1914–18.

THESE WOMEN ARE DOING THEIR BIT

LEARN TO MAKE MUNITIONS

6

6 'These Women are Doing Their Bit', World War I poster by Septimus E Scott, Britain, c1917.

7 Covers of various books show 'munitions girls' as part of popular culture in Britain, 1916/17.

8 Selected Black Cat cigarette cards, Women on War Work series, Britain, 1916. A series showing the versatility of women's war work and applauding their abilities, while also telling them (in the small print on the back) to leave it all to the men again after the war.

7

8

After the revolution: early Soviet images of women

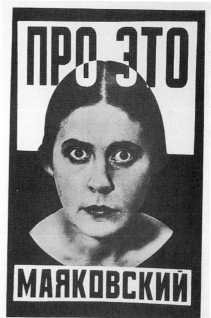

The later years of the First World War brought revolution to Russia (1917), accompanied by the Constructivist art movement, which placed art and design in the service of the new Soviet future. Constructivism applied bold colours, flat geometric shapes and dynamic composition across a broad range of applied arts and design: from industrial design, furniture and theatre design to textiles and graphics. It also started off a growing mass of early Soviet imagery which depicted women as active comrades and emancipated workers, producing graphic models and poses that are inspiring even today.

Women occupied a lively place in the Constructivist vision of a productive future; their dynamic presence is particularly underlined in the graphic and photographic work of Alexander Rodchenko. Also, their contribution to Constructivist experimentation and vision was embodied in the work of Liubov Popova and Varvara Stepanova, both of whom applied the art movement's

3

4

visual language to textile and clothing design. Popova and Stepanova were also responsible for a revolutionary, new approach to fashion and dressing, designing costumes for everyday wear in the workplace as well as for sports activities – and all based on requirements of movement, cleanliness and economy.

But as time went on, and Stalin rose to power, the avant-garde movement was repressed. By the late 1920s, the regimentation of industrialization had replaced the energy of the art experiments. In later years, women retained their optimistic pose as productive members of the bright Soviet future, but in truth they merely became one of many fixtures in Central Party propaganda, covering over the harsh and often terrifying realities of Stalin's oppressive regime.

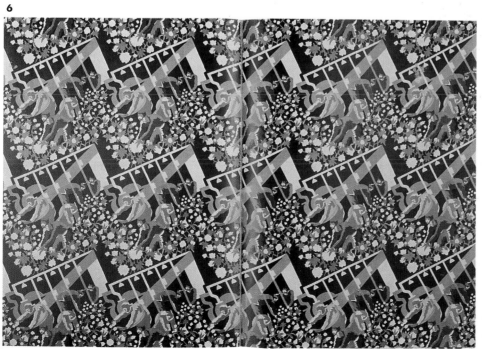

5

6

1   Cover of Pro Eto, a book of poems by Mayakovsky, designed by Alexander Rodchenko, Soviet Russia, 1923.
2   Trans: 'Books!', window poster by Alexander Rodchenko, Soviet Russia, 1925.
3   'Literacy for All', woven cotton, designed by Marya Nazarevskaya, manufactured by the First Factory of Printed Cotton in Moscow, late 1920s.

4   Designs for a costume for a working woman (ink and gouache on paper), by Varvara Stepanova, Soviet Russia, 1924.
5   Spread from the post-Revolution Constructivist book LEF (Left Front of the Arts) showing Stepanova's designs for sportswear on the left page, and Rodchenko's logo designs on the right, Soviet Russia, c1917.
6   'Red Army Soldiers Help with the Cotton Harvest', furnishing satin, designed by Marya Nazarevskaya, manufactured by the First Factory of Printed Cotton in Moscow, 1932.

Chapter 1 *Early Soviet images of women*

1 Trans: 'Working woman in the struggle for socialism and the struggle against religion', poster by B Klinch and Koslinskii, USSR, 1931. The dark past of religious superstition and drunken domestic brutality of women is depicted as overtaken by a shining modern socialist society where women are productive workers and no longer subservient to men or suffering at their hand.

2–5 Soviet posters encouraging women to play an active role in the socialist state. Originally published by the State Publishing House for the Fine Arts (figs 2, 4, 5) and the Moscow Committee of the All Union Communist Party (fig 3), in the early 1930s, and 1942 (fig 5), and reproduced by the Plakat publishing house, Moscow, 1980s.

6 Trans: 'Women delegates, be in the front [of collectivization]', photomontaged poster by anonymous artist, USSR, 1931.

The Second World War (1939–45): women and war work

1

Women made an even greater working contribution to the Second World War than they had to the First. In both Britain and the USA, graphic campaigns and other media (such as film) called upon women to join the armed services, register or volunteer for war work, save supplies, cope with shortages and rationing, and keep families and communities running. And, as in the First World War, their graphic image underwent a transformation.

America's entry into the war in 1941 brought with it the more predictable poster images of angelic Red Cross nurses, or pert, pretty housewives, in appeals for money or war loans. But it also introduced a 'dynamo' in the form of Rosie the Riveter: the popular recruitment heroine (with muscle) who came to represent the vast number of women pouring into factories in order to cover the man-power shortage, and handling everything from welding to ship-building. In addition, a sterner mission was offered to women in joining the military, shown in the recruitment poster for the US Marines on page 75.

Britain had to rely on women over a much longer period (from 1939 onwards) and by 1941 was conscripting them into the armed forces or other war work. All manner of printed media encouraged them to join up with the auxiliary services, civil defence, the fire brigade, factory work and Land Army work. Morale-boosting was another all-important role taken up by government campaigns telling women how to skimp, save and make-do without. It was also an inherent part of the popular graphic environment, in the form of product advertisements, magazines and all manner of graphic ephemera, as the general public closed ranks to help fight the war on home ground.

Nevertheless, in both Britain and the USA, women lost their jobs at the end of the war and once again were pushed back into the home. But although independence, money and freedom had vanished into thin air (and post-war consumerism would try to convince them that that was the way things should be), their strength and determination throughout the war had been recorded in a graphic legend – to be drawn upon in generations to come.

2

1 Women factory workers during World War II, USA, 1942–5.
2 'Even a Little can Help a Lot – NOW', World War II poster asking people to buy war bonds, with illustration by A Parker (originally from Ladies' Home Journal). It shows an idealized view of a woman's place at home. But the reality was often more similar to the photograph above. Published by the US Government Printing Office, 1942.

3 'Rosie the Riveter', World War II poster bearing the popular character used to recruit women for war work, published by the War Production Co-ordinating Committee, USA, 1942–5.

1

For a healthy, happy job
Join the
WOMEN'S
LAND
ARMY
For details:
APPLY TO NEAREST W.L.A. COUNTY OFFICE OR TO W.L.A. HEADQUARTERS 6 CHESHAM ~~PLACE~~ STREET LONDON S.W.1
Issued by the Ministry of Agriculture and the Ministry of Labour and National Service

1 'Join the Women's Land Army', World War II recruitment poster, artist unknown, published by the Ministry of Agriculture and the Ministry of Labour and National Service, Britain, 1940/41.
2 'It All Depends on Me', World War II cigarette card depicting munitions worker. Produced by Ardath tobacco company, Britain, 1940.
3 British war-time press advertisement for Tampax tampons (invented in America in the mid-1930s).
4 'Join the ATS', well-known recruitment poster by Abram Games which was banned for giving the Auxiliary Territorial Service an image that was too 'glamorous', Britain, 1941.
5 'Don't Take the Squander Bug...', World War II poster by Phillip Boydell, published by the National Savings Committee, Britain, 1942.

2

3

4

5

ATS **CARRY THE MESSAGES**

The motor cyclist messenger, roaring across country from Headquarters to scattered units is now an ATS girl

1

2

SERVE IN THE WAAF
WITH THE MEN WHO FLY

BE A MARINE...
Free a Marine to fight
U.S. MARINE CORPS WOMEN'S RESERVE

3

1 'ATS Carry the Messages', World War II recruitment poster for the Auxiliary Territorial Service, by Beverley Pick, published by HM Stationery Office, Britain, 1940.
2 'Serve in the WAAF...', World War II recruitment poster for the Women's Auxiliary Air Force, by Jonathan Foss, Britain, c1942.
3 'Be a Marine...', World War II recruitment poster for the US Marine Corps Women's Reserve, USA, 1945.
4 Two US nurses hold a Red Cross 'Uncle Sam Needs Nurses' poster for which they posed, New York, 1941.

4

Post-war consumerism: 'the happy housewife'

The Saturday Evening
POST
September 19, 1959 – 15¢

Does it Help to Swap Visits With the Russians?

Although educational opportunities opened up for women in Britain and the USA after the war, it wasn't long before the new climate of 1950s consumerism began to place extraordinary new pressures on women – through magazines, films, radio and the new broadcast medium of television. Women were programmed to centre their ambitions on the search for a husband, marriage, having children and running the 'ideal home' – all a prelude to purchasing the latest domestic technology and household products.

The cultural brainwashing was most intense in America, where many of the new breed of educated women had given up careers in order to marry. Fast approaching its commercial height, the USA was busily constructing the American Dream of suburban family life with all modern conveniences. 'The happy housewife' was the cornerstone, assaulted by media messages and images on all sides telling her to cook, clean, sew and buy lots of new products – and to seek fulfilment only as a wife and mother. Forget about careers, education and political rights.

It wasn't long before the image of the perfect homemaker (with no thoughts beyond which washing powder to buy) began to show signs of discontent. In 1963, Betty Friedan's best-selling book *The Feminine Mystique* took the lid off the isolation and disillusionment felt by a whole generation of those 'happy housewives', and lit a spark of revolution.

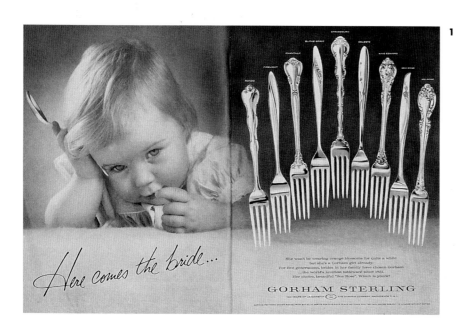

Here comes the bride...

GORHAM STERLING

love story

Once every blue moon or so, a household idol comes into your life and you strike up a beautiful friendship. It happens quite often with people like you and a Parnall and it's very, very satisfying. The Parnall Spinwasher de luxe does all the work: you merely look doting (so becoming).

We burn to tell you the *facts* about the truest of true romances; meanwhile, just a few tender words . . .

ONE TUB does everything. Do you really want to hump wet washing from one tub to another? Size – only 22 inches square.

CHOOSEABLE AUTOMATION. You make the decisions – set switches – and dote.

CLEAR-FLO RINSE – thorough continuous rinsing.

SUDS SAVER. Hot sudsy water is saved for the next wash load – and you save pounds.

SERVICE. Well made things work better for longer. Parnall Spinwashers are beautifully engineered. But of course we have a nation-wide service organisation.

ABOUT MONEY. Parnall Spinwasher costs more than the ruck. (So do your clothes.) It also does more, does it better and for years longer. Prices: £88.4.0 with heater £84.0.0 without.

Let us send you some convincing literature

PARNALL
Spinwasher de luxe

Awarded the British Electrical Approvals Board mark of safety — A RADIATION PRODUCT

Electrical Showrooms & dealers everywhere. In London, visit the RADIATION DOMESTIC APPLIANCE CENTRE, 59 BAKER STREET, W.1
ELECTRICAL DIVISION OF RADIATION LIMITED · Radiation House · North Circular Road · N.W.10

1   Double-page advertisement for silverware, taken from McCall's magazine, May 1961 issue, USA.
2, 3   Front cover (with gatefold, shown below) of The Saturday Evening Post, 19 September 1959 issue (USA), which makes flippant reference to what was soon to become a burning issue – womens' disillusionment with idealized notions of marriage and the role of the 'happy housewife'. Illustration by the artist Alajálov.

4   Cheer washday detergent advertisement, USA, 1953.
5   Advertisement for a washing machine, Britain, 1965.
6   Advertisement for luxury scatter rugs, Britain, 1962.

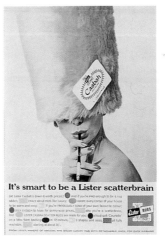

It's smart to be a Lister scatterbrain

The Women's Liberation Movement, or Second Wave Feminism (1960s and 1970s)

THE FEMININE MYSTIQUE
Betty Friedan

Today a family and a home constitute the twin heights of feminine ambition. But one looming problem remains to be solved.... The problem that has no name...

1

O f all the stages of feminism this century, the Women's Liberation Movement – the 'second wave' of feminism – was the most acute in its analysis of the masculine hold on power. Its fundamental aim was no less than the transformation of society. Women challenged the entrenched patriarchy with its binary oppositions – the public sphere defined as male and of high value, and the private/domestic sphere as female and of low value – and searched for new cultural perspectives, putting new value systems in place. Most crucially, they redefined 'politics' in their own terms. 'The personal is political' became one of the foundation stones of the new radical vision (declaring that even our most personal concerns are influenced or controlled by a broader political context). The great achievement of this period was therefore a revolution in thinking, a change in perceptions and attitudes – even though the realities of change have often been slow to follow, or in some instances non-existent.

AMAZON ODYSSEY
THE FIRST COLLECTION OF WRITINGS BY THE

POLITICAL PIONEER OF THE WOMEN'S MOVEMENT
TI-GRACE ATKINSON

2

The great strength of the Movement was in its methods. Networking built up the notion of sisterhood and connectivity, as well as extending the Movement's vision to an international scope. Attention was paid to raising women's consciousness through education and self-discovery. Direct action forced issues and feelings into the arena of public debate. Celebrations of heroines and activities both past and present not only brought a sense of continuity with past struggles, but also encouraged a new vision of creativity and culture in the present, opening the way for a renaissance of women's writing, art, craftwork and so on. Cultural critiques (perhaps better called power critiques) revealed the extent to which prejudice and sexism were at the root of the visual field. Critical examinations of such topics as representations of women in art and advertising, and language use (defining sexism in language, reclaiming words, inventing new words) became part of the revolution's massive redefinition and revaluation process.

Graphic formats, such as posters, magazines and postcards, and the imagery they carried were integral to the revolutionary process. The images often played an iconic or symbolic role: intended to shock their audience into a greater awareness, they sprang from a common source in women's collective experience. More often than not, they aimed to connect – to convey to women that they belonged to a network. A visual language developed that expressed women's struggles and concerns. Created by amateurs and professionals, it marked the beginning of a more democratic use of art and design as communications tools.

The graphic formats themselves operated as the conductors of the Movement. Posters, newsletters, magazines and other forms of multiples encapsulated the messages and emotions of the revolution and spread them far and wide, propagating the developing 'women's culture' expressed in a visual vocabulary. This process of exchanging information and imagery (even by the most basic methods such as the post) initiated an

Radical texts from the revolution:

1   Betty Friedan's The Feminine Mystique, published simultaneously in Britain and the USA in 1963. This British edition dates from 1968.

2   Amazon Odyssey, a collection of speeches and essays from 1967 to 1972 by Ti-Grace Atkinson, one of the pioneers of radical feminism. With chart drawings and book cover by the artist Barbara Nessim, USA, 1974.

3   The Female Eunuch by Germaine Greer, first published in Britain in 1970. This paperback version with its memorable cover appeared in 1971.

4   'What is Male Supremacy?', poster for a meeting of the Revolutionary Feminist London Region Conference, with a drawing by Alison Fell, Britain, c1973.

5   Everywoman newspaper 'centerspread', designed by Sheila Levrant de Bretteville, USA, 1972. The 'Cunt Cheerleaders' of the Feminist Art Program at Fresno State College appear in the background.

6   Poster reproduction of Monica Sjöö's painting God Giving Birth, Britain, 1968. The image came under threat for 'obscenity and blasphemy' and became an important feminist icon.

3

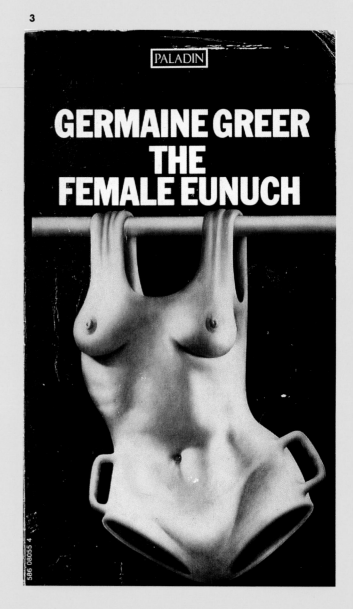

PALADIN

GERMAINE GREER THE FEMALE EUNUCH

4

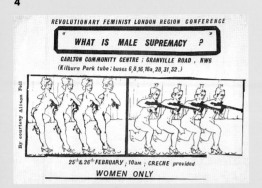

REVOLUTIONARY FEMINIST LONDON REGION CONFERENCE

" WHAT IS MALE SUPREMACY ?

CARLTON COMMUNITY CENTRE ; GRANVILLE ROAD , NW6
(Kilburn Park tube ; buses 6,8,16,16a,28,31,32.)

By courtesy Alison Fell

25th & 26th FEBRUARY ; 10am ; CRECHE provided
WOMEN ONLY

international communications network that has been growing ever since, making use of new formats and new technologies to connect women worldwide.

The Movement's analysis and methods were also prompting new perspectives in the fields of graphic and communication design, and a questioning of the values and 'control ethic' of current design practice. Issues such as democratization and inclusiveness, interactivity and participation, networking and information sharing, and design as politics (or an expression of personal politics and awareness) would gradually transform design and its motives throughout the 1980s and 1990s.

In the beginning: scenarios and influences

The social climate of the USA in the 1960s was volatile. Amidst civil rights protests and other signs of social unrest, a new generation of young people rebelled against traditional authority. They 'dropped out' and went underground, creating an alternative culture that espoused an ethic of peace and love, while expressing itself through sex, drugs and music. Protests and demonstrations were staged against the Vietnam War, student unrest brought bloodshed to college campuses and cries of police brutality, adding to the general instability and malaise. Towards the end of the 1960s, anti-Establishment feeling was at an all-time high; there was an undeclared war between the generations and their values; between races and classes; between Left and Right. It was the time for change: to fight for liberation, power and rights. Sexual liberation, black liberation, gay liberation – and Women's Liberation. For within the turmoil, radicalized women had found that the politics of the New Left and the so-called revolution contained the same old sexist values, devaluing women's demands and depriving them of a voice. So they organized: and the Women's Liberation Movement was born.

Warning shots had been fired throughout the decade. Betty Friedan's *The Feminine Mystique*, viewed as signalling the oncome of the Movement, appeared in 1963. By 1966, Friedan had founded the National Organization for Women (NOW), serving as its first president. But it was the 1967 National Conference on New Politics in Chicago, at which issues of women's liberation were described as unimportant, that shocked the new political movement into action. Its first nationally recognized protest was staged against the Miss America Contest in Atlantic City, New Jersey in September 1968. This was the event which led the news media to invent the myth of 'bra-burning'. Although bras, girdles and other items of oppression were being symbolically thrown into a bin entitled the Freedom Trashcan, nothing was burnt. Not long after, the first American National Women's Liberation Conference was held in Chicago. Interestingly, both of these founding events included representatives from Canada. The Movement had already burst national borders.

By 1970, Women's Liberation was a mass movement whose small groups and collectives, already numbered in the thousands, were multiplying at a tremendous rate. Major names were beginning to emerge: Gloria Steinem, one of the founding editors of *Ms.* magazine (f 1972); Robin

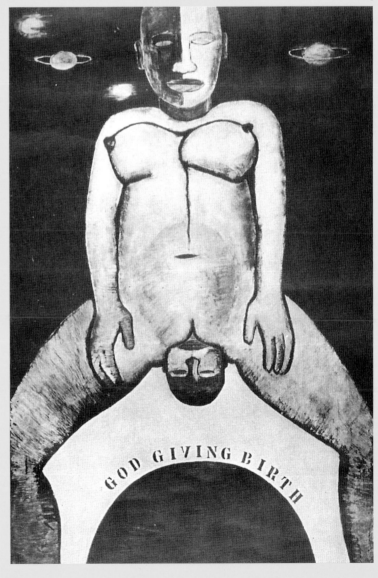

GOD GIVING BIRTH

Morgan, writer and poet; Kate Millet, the author of the key text *Sexual Politics* (1970); Mary Daly, feminist philosopher; Susan Brownmiller, who analysed rape in *Against Our Will* (1975); and Andrea Dworkin, who focused on pornography in her polemics on violence against women.

The new movement's tremendous diversity soon produced conflict and distress. Some felt that it wasn't addressing their needs, hence the formation of splinter groups, and new pathways for black feminists (having to cope with both sexual and racial oppression) and lesbians, to name just two. The splinter groups grew stronger and more directed in themselves, building up their own distinctive cultures as time went on.

Lesbianism provides a good case in point. In 1969, Betty Friedan apparently referred to lesbians as a 'lavender herring', while others claimed lesbianism would discredit the Movement. Feeling as oppressed within the Women's Liberation Movement as anywhere else, about twenty lesbians formed the group known as The Lavender Menace, and agitated for lesbianism to be recognized and discussed. But from 1970–2, the division between heterosexual and lesbian feminists threatened to split the American movement. Such explosions marked an important point when American society slowly shifted from its white middle-class (male) orientation, and began to recognize a diversity of colour, sexual orientation and other groupings.

The creative and visual influences affecting these early days of the Movement were just as diverse and energetic. Underground youth culture, emanating from the West Coast, had developed a visual identity of its own. Rebellion came in the form of an anti-Establishment look: long hair, jeans, t-shirts, no-bra, flowing see-through fabrics and gypsy-like jewellery. All were a reaction against the Eisenhower crewcut, business suit and tie; or the cast-iron bras and girdles, and bondage-like skirts and high-heels of *Vogue* and *McCall's* magazines. Decorative patterns and logos adorned textiles, posters, graphics, buildings, cars, and were even painted or tattooed onto bodies. The style was a mix of art nouveau, art deco, pop art, prints of the Far East and other decorative forms. But the colour palette of the underground was derived from pop art and 'psychedelia', which dazzled the eyes by twisting bright or Day-Glo colours into complex patterns reminiscent of drug experiences.

The 'popular arts' flourished in posters, cartoons and underground comics and newspapers. The iconography was produced by both amateurs and professionals in the collectives, art projects and progressive publishing groups which grew out of the alternative culture's search for co-operative work structures and communal living. Keen to disassociate themselves from mainstream media, the new art and media forms aimed to shock and provoke in their language and imagery. This climate of intense self-expression and popular creativity energized all the new movements of the time, including Women's Liberation, as well as affecting the youth cultures of other countries.

1

2

1   *'Protest': poster protest relating to beauty contests and women's objectification, by See Red Women's Poster Collective, Britain, mid-1970s.*
2   *Women in Springfield, Illinois, May 1976, marching for the Equal Rights Amendment (ERA) – a unifying issue in American feminism throughout the 1970s.*

Europe was primed to follow, and caught up in its own war between the new generation and the old social order. The 1960s found Britain, in particular, undergoing a transformation with the younger generation attacking the government, the monarchy and the class system. The underground press brought across the ocean an exhilarating wave of news, discussions and visual arts from America's counter-culture. It is therefore difficult to say exactly which spark lit the feminist powder keg.

Disillusioned by the sexism in the underground's vision, many women felt the revolution had little to offer them. The underground press's objectification of women was a particularly sore point, leading to the creation in 1972 of the alternative women's magazine *Spare Rib*. *Oz* was one of the few underground magazines to carry news of the new women's movement: its most blatant statement being the 'Cuntpower' issue guest-edited by Germaine Greer. Even so, the magazine's ultimate aim was to shock, and some of the erotic pictures of naked women in other issues were more likely than not to be called sexist. Anna Koedt's revolutionary article 'The Myth of the Vaginal Orgasm', which was written for the First American National Women's Liberation Conference in Chicago in 1968, arrived in England in 1969. In ascribing the female orgasm to the clitoris, it pronounced vaginal orgasm a male myth, liberating women from assumptions about the nature of sexuality. Germaine Greer's extremely witty and outspoken writing and philosophy emerged in alternative publications such as *Oz* and *Suck*, and in her brilliant polemic *The Female Eunuch* (1970), in which she vigorously attacked the institutions and burdens of womanhood.

In 1970, the first conference on Women's Liberation held in Oxford marked the founding of the British movement, and throughout the decade the Women's Liberation Movement established itself as a major political force across Europe and North America. France, Germany, Holland and Italy all saw heavy activity, as did Denmark and other countries. But women also played a strong role in revolutionary movements and in the fight against dictatorships through Latin America, South Africa, the Middle East, and elsewhere. Thus, by the 1980s, the modern feminist movement had spun a network of groups and organizations around the world, bringing a new reality to the concept that 'Sisterhood is Global' (see Chapter Five).

New methods, new messages

The Women's Liberation Movement was less a unified structure than an umbrella over a wide range of philosophies and activities with the common aim of doing away with the oppression of women. To this end it devised its own methods. It explored new work structures, such as collective working and co-operatives, rejecting the notion of isolated, male genius, and refusing to adopt male power hierarchies and 'leaders'. Graphics and the visual arts – both processes and products – were vital and inextricable parts of this machinery of change. They held the Movement together, and made visible the process of change and politicization.

The Movement was fortunate to be able to claim a brilliant graphic symbol – the female biological sign – as its popular emblem, which embodied identity, presence and strength. Acting like a battle standard or rallying cry, the symbol's great value lay in its simplicity, for it could be scribbled or drawn by anyone, anywhere (and by practically any means). Furthermore, it was manipulated into a multitude of artistic variations, often quite intricate, and was given endless personality traits. But its most intimate and endearing function was as a signature mark at the end of letters, often accompanied by the words 'in sisterhood': the symbol was like a code for a secret society or an underground network. Shifted into a more public mode (but still retaining the secret society feel), it was also used as an anonymous signature mark in graffiti sprayed onto buildings or billboards.

3 **Images from early days in the Movement showing variations on the Women's Liberation symbol.**

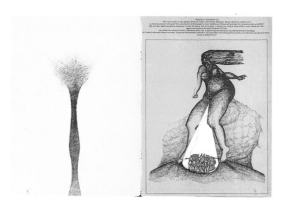

Above all, the symbol identified feminism in the public eye. On both sides of the Atlantic, direct action took many forms – demonstrations, strikes, mass meetings, marches – and more often than not, the Movement's symbol appeared on banners, placards and other forms of 'demo-graphics'. Alternatively it was worn on badges or pins as a mark of pride and personal commitment. However and wherever it was rendered, it served to tie the Movement together. Transcending languages and cultures, it became the visual password for feminism around the world, remaining one of the most heavily reproduced political symbols of modern times.

Consciousness-raising was the Movement's main instrument for analysing women's oppression and how to end it, and was viewed as a process of education and self-discovery. It involved members 'rapping' or speaking from personal experience on predetermined topics, such as marriage or sexuality. The aim was to offer women a supportive environment in which to explore how they themselves could become politicized, and help to bring about change.

Out of such discussions flowed the main concerns of the Movement, issues which were central to women's experience and at the core of their oppression. These gradually became known as 'women's issues', and included such matters as reproductive freedom (including abortion and birth control), health and self-help, a woman's right to express her own sexuality, divisions of labour, equal opportunities and equal pay at work, and violence against women. Furthermore, the questions and discoveries poured out of the discussion groups and straight onto graphic formats of all types. In this fashion, a large amount of writing, recording, documenting and street/amateur publishing and presswork began, which gradually grew into a vast network of journals, newsletters and other periodicals. Women everywhere had suddenly 'found a voice'.

Networking in itself became a crucial tool. More than just a system of contacts, it actually involved the sharing of information and experiences, passed on through women's groups, organizations and presses. It also underpinned the notion of 'sisterhood', in which all women – friends or strangers – bonded together in solidarity, as an acknowledgement of shared oppression and the need to work together for their liberation. The network spread across countries and continents, adding symbolism and globality to posters, magazine covers and other formats carrying graphic imagery.

The Movement also brought celebrations: the discovery and acknowledgement of heroines, past and present, and the revaluation of women's culture and art. So while connecting across cultures and continents, there were also many attempts to connect with the past. The Women's Liberation Movement looked back to the first wave for inspiration and a sense of continuity with the fight. There were direct actions and great sacrifices to be admired; there were also graphic elements to be borrowed or appreciated. The visual propaganda of the earlier British suffrage societies and the militant suffragettes, for example, inspired a revival of women's bannermaking and political needlework; the use of rituals and large-scale 'spectacle' by performance artists such as Suzanne Lacy (USA); the creation of poster workshops and the reprinting of early suffrage posters by various organizations; and the start of a growing number of women's presses and publishing companies around the world, producing books and other publications, postcards and ephemera. Indeed, the discovery of first wave writing and publishing did much to foster the second wave notion that women find a voice through writing, publishing and presswork.

All this was accompanied by a broader investigation into the contribution that women had made to world history itself. This brought up new names and a different storyline, producing calls for a view of history from a woman's perspective (women's

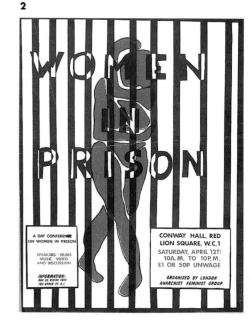

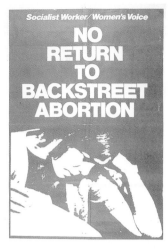

Socialist Worker/Women's Voice
NO RETURN TO BACKSTREET ABORTION

3

1 Cover and inside spreads from the 'Cuntpower' issue (no 29, July 1970) of Oz magazine, guest-edited by Germaine Greer, Britain.
2 Poster for a one-day conference on Women in Prison, organized by the London Anarchist Feminist Group, Britain, late 1970s.
3 'No Return to Backstreet Abortion', poster by the Socialist Worker Party, Britain, mid-1970s.
4 'Women's Liberation IS the Revolution!', poster by Pen Dalton, Britain, 1975.

history, or 'herstory'). There were studies of the longstanding denigration of women's work, and celebratory promotions of feminist or female values. It was felt that for too long human culture had been male orientated, while women's interests and experiences had been ignored, denied or trivialized. The need to define 'women's culture' produced a renaissance of work by women writers, poets, playwrights, novelists, philosophers, art historians, fine artists and textile artists, and a celebration of traditional women's arts or crafts, such as needlework or quilt-making. Alternative institutions were sought out, including schools, courses, galleries and exhibition spaces. Most crucially, the search for 'women's culture', in both its present and past forms, was conducted as a multi-disciplinary exploration, an emphasis which proved fruitful in many areas of education, publishing and the creative arts.

One of the most popular projects to emerge from this period of exploration was Judy Chicago's *The Dinner Party* (1973–9), which created place settings at a dinner table for thirty-nine women from history. Created in Los Angeles over six years with the involvement of hundreds of women, it impressed not only for its sheer scale but also for the breadth of its statement. For it produced a massive homage to women's achievements throughout history; a showpiece of such traditional women's arts as china-painting and needlework; and an example of collaboration on a large scale. The project's symbolic (and highly graphic) handling of visual forms, its multi-disciplinary base (incorporating a mixture of 2D and 3D forms and materials), and its accompanying graphics and books (so wonderfully designed by Sheila Levrant de Bretteville) all meant that it made an impact across a whole range of artists and disciplines.

Another valued product of this period was the Helaine Victoria Press, which researched women's contributions to history and culture and then presented them through the original and particularly accessible medium of the postcard. Co-founded in 1973 by Jocelyn Cohen and Nancy Poore, the Press combined archival photographs and potted-history captions of its subjects into a uniquely intimate educational experience – celebrating groups of women, important events, and particular individuals such as Sojourner Truth and Susan B Anthony. Poore left in 1982, but Cohen carried on for a further decade developing many series of postcards on themes such as Women in the American Labor Movement (1886–1986), Suffrage, Frontierswomen, and Black and Afro-Americans. Valued as inspirational icons and very distinctively designed, Helaine Victoria postcards spanned the globe by post and became one of the Movement's best-loved institutions.

The attempt to create a new culture based on feminist values also brought a period of questioning that slowly began to deconstruct the social programming inherent in existing culture. John Berger's *Ways of Seeing* (1972) looked at the representation of women in art, while new readings of advertising and its imagery were offered in *Gender Advertisements* by Erving Goffman (1976) and *Decoding Advertisements* by Judith Williamson (1978). All unsettled our relationship with the graphic environment, and were the first step towards educating the general public to recognize oppressive stereotypes and offensive denigration of women in visual forms and the media. Concern was also directed at the programming inherent in educational courses and illustrated books used at school (which depicted boys as engineers and girls as nurses or housewives); all such issues were beginning to be deliberated by artists, designers and publishers everywhere.

Language itself underwent scrutiny for the value judgements embed-

4

ded within it. This brought about a large number of alterations (chairman to chairperson or chair, mankind to humankind or humanity); newly invented words (sexism, ageism); new titles (Ms); new phrases (reproductive freedom, gay rights, sexual harassment at work, battered women); replacement terms (homemaker replaced housewife); and the reclaiming of words (bitch, dyke) or phrases (cunt art or cuntpower) for positive purposes. All became part of an attempt to make language more gender-free (or at least less gender-oppressive) and more expressive to the new groups and new philosophies in existence. This gave graphic designers, as visual communicators of messages in both private and public formats, quite a lot to deal with. For the psychology of their 'palette' had changed dramatically, and the sensitivities of their audiences had come into focus as never before, developments that worked their way into discussions and critiques taking place in design education.

Here we are at home, says Daddy.

Peter helps Daddy with the car, and Jane helps Mummy get the tea.

Good girl, says Mummy to Jane.

You are a good girl to help me like this.

Good good girl

1

2

Judith Williamson

DECODING ADVERTISEMENTS

Ideology and Meaning in Advertising

3

A collective iconography

The questioning that started the creation of 'women's culture' also manifested itself in a form of visual exploration. In rejecting a world defined by a male vision, women began to search for a vision of their own – a vision that had women's experience at its centre.

Artists, designers, poster collectives and other groups attempted to produce a new kind of imagery that related to the collective experience of women. Themes that had for years represented the belittling or devaluing of women's experience, suddenly became its strength. In the poster 'A Woman's Work is Never Done' by See Red Women's Poster Collective on page 86, the image of a woman divided or split was used to represent a number of issues: the arguments raging at that time over the 'double shift' (the double strain of women who worked outside the home as well as working within it, raising children etc); the devaluing of women's work and especially domestic work; and the ability of women to cope with multiple tasks and round-the-clock home responsibilities. The split-woman icon also had an equivalent in the multi-armed woman, which seemed to have been favoured around the world. Poster versions are shown here produced by the Spanish Women's Liberation Movement (page 85), as well as the Speak Collective in South Africa (see Chapter Five, page 195).

Other symbols and metaphors began to filter through the art and design world, often taking very private concepts and forcing them into public symbols, turning years of intimidation and embarrassment into power. The shape and form of female genitalia, for example, was explored in 'cunt art' – in its very earliest phase, a subversive and often fun series of multi-media experiments involving images of female sex organs, generated by Judy Chicago and her students at the Fresno Feminist Art Program (1970). They not only represented a search for a new form of expression, but were also intended as a blatant, loud and up-front gesture of defiance, aimed at confronting women's social intimidation. The experiments also led into performance: students dressed up as 'cunt' cheerleaders and would do 'pussy cheers' and 'cunt cheers' to welcome visiting feminist lecturers to the course – all marvellously indicative of the defiant mood of the times. Chicago herself went on to show, through the brilliant example of *The Dinner Party*, how such an intimate part of the body could be artistically manipulated into a powerful political statement or icon. The transfer of genitalia from private intimacy to public icon also represented the further destruction of the rigid divisions between the

4

WAYS OF SEEING

JOHN BERGER

Seeing comes before words. The child looks and recognizes before it can speak.

But there is also another sense in which seeing comes before words. It is seeing which establishes our place in the surrounding world; we explain that world with words, but words can never undo the fact that we are surrounded by it. The relation between what we see and what we know is never settled.

The Surrealist painter Magritte commented on this always-present gap between words and seeing in a painting called The Key of Dreams. The way we see things is affected by what we

5

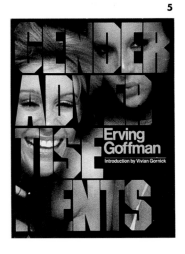

private and the public spheres; a process taken to its ultimate stage in the 1990s by Diane Gromala's work, where private and public merge and become one as we travel through her body in an experimental project using virtual reality (see Chapter Four, pages 157 and 185–7).

Yet another variation on the genitalia theme, and one used even more publicly, involved the symbol created by holding both hands together to make the shape of female genitalia – this was, and still is, used as a sign of Women's Liberation and sisterhood all over the world. The inverted triangle, representing the shape of a woman's pubic hair, also saw a fair amount of use (again, in Judy Chicago's *The Dinner Party*, the dinner table is triangular). Moons, goddesses and depictions of cosmic forces alluded to fertility and the menstrual cycle, another hush-hush subject which was suddenly visualized on posters and in books, and calendared as never before. Objections to the way women were treated and depicted appeared in the imagery too; the headless body (similar to the one shown on the cover of Germaine Greer's *The Female Eunuch*, page 78) became a statement about women's treatment as brainless, inconsequential sex objects. Their objections were now given a visual form.

All in all, the way that women used their bodies to create symbols and metaphors was only one aspect of a broader move to reclaim their bodies for themselves and for their own expressiveness. As their bodies were the crux of so many stigmas and arguments waged against them, they now used them in a variety of ways to make political statements. For instance, their nudity – and its shock value – was used to express strength, new ideas and new freedoms, in posters (such as Monica Sjöö's on page 79) and presswork. In order to gain control of their health and reproductive freedom, knowledge of their bodies became one of the mainstays of the Women's Health Movement (page 108). They created their own body imagery for feminist learning purposes, and diagrams and depictions relating to contraception, childbirth, self-examination and other matters of health became commonplace in feminist information material.

Even the use of colour became political. The significance of colour in relation to women, and the gender programming of women as soft, pretty and pink, was explored in eloquent terms in Sheila Levrant de Bretteville's early poster 'Pink' (page 91). In the hands of de Bretteville and many of the women artists and designers after her, pink became an extremely proud and radical colour. In Britain, it came close to being the identity colour of the Movement. By the 1980s, its associations with feminism had pushed it to the intensity of Day-Glo pink or rhodamine red.

The concepts of liberation, freedom and release were often symbolized by the breaking of chains, the blossoming of flowers or the release of birds. Such symbols became part of an international vocabulary that crossed cultural and language barriers as many of the posters and pamphlets travelled the world. Literary and historical sources, such as the legendary woman warrior, supplied the material for images of struggle and battle, and met their real-life equivalent in the gun-toting women engaged in national liberation struggles in Africa and South America, depicted on posters that made their way to Europe and North America. Such images were highly inspirational to women in the West, and did much to contribute to a solidarity among women around the world. Other images served to continue the struggle: the spinning of webs, a symbol of women connecting and standing together in solidarity, outlasted the 1970s to appear in the 1980s as one of the prominent symbols of the Women's Peace Camp at Greenham Common.

6

1 Page from a reading book for young children showing traditional sexist gender stereotyping, Britain, 1975.
2 Poster protesting such stereotyping in educational material, by See Red Women's Poster Collective, Britain, late 1970s.
3–5 The climate of social critique brought analyses of advertising and all manner of imagery:
3 Judith Williamson's rigorous text Decoding Advertisements offered an analysis of the images and values of advertising, London, 1978.
4 Ways of Seeing by John Berger: a book of essays exploring ways of reading images and how their use and context can change their meaning, London, 1972.
5 Gender Advertisements by Erving Goffman offered yet another critical view of advertising and its subtexts, London, 1979.
6 One of many reminders that the Movement had a global reach. Poster from the Spanish Women's Liberation Movement showing the popular image of the multi-armed woman, 1977.

Feminism, design and education: a design revolution

A search for the nature of women's expressiveness was going on in educational terms too. The West Coast of the USA had become a well-established haven for sixties' radical ideas, and consequently became the birthplace for educational experiments in relating feminism to art and design processes.

In 1970, Judy Chicago formed her Feminist Art Program at Fresno State University and developed an innovative approach to exploring feminist issues in art by applying consciousness-raising to the creative art-making process, within a course program.[1] She soon joined forces with Miriam Schapiro and together they planned a new programme and transferred it to California Institute of the Arts (CalArts) the following year; it opened in autumn 1971 with both co-directing. The programme's first and best known project was 'Womanhouse', which placed performances and site installations within a seventeen-room condemned mansion in a Los Angeles neighbourhood. The installations centred on themes relating to the everyday house-wife, all derived through consciousness-raising methods. Its impact was phenomenal. Open for only one month, it was visited by over 9,000 people, achieved world renown through television and the press, and remains one of the key reference points for feminist art of that period. At the same time, de Bretteville initiated her Women's Design Program at CalArts, aiming to explore feminist issues in design. Concentrating on graphic and communication design (as opposed to product-orientated design), it brought together a search for female values, the use of personal experience as an inspirational source, and an emphasis on co-operative work methods – planting the seeds for a later redefinition of the design process itself.

The call for 'participatory, non-hierarchical and non-authoritarian relationships between the designer and the user' brought to many (de Bretteville first, then many women designers to follow) the realization that existing design definitions were in fact about the opposite. As de Bretteville pointed out, in order to introduce 'participation' it was necessary to relinquish control, in terms not only of process but also of the final form. A revaluation of form and aesthetics was consequently in order, whose implications threatened to subvert existing notions of quality and standards, as well as the styl-

The Judgment of Patricia Hearst
by Kathy Barry

Women and Nature
by Susan Griffin

Original Art
by Mary Beth Edelson

Catalog of Healing Resources

Freud and the Sexual
Abuse of Children
by Florence Rush

Poetry
by Audre Lorde, Honor Moore,
Adrienne Rich

Interview with Joan Snyder
by Ruth Iskin

Fiction
by Deena Metzger

Redesigning the Domestic
Workplace
by Dolores Hayden

Reviews
by Frances Jaffer, Leah Fritz

a magazine of women's culture

Chrysalis

No. 1

The image of a split or divided woman became symbolic of women's diversity, as well as the dualities they faced in their lives with regard to work and the home.
1   'A Woman's Work is Never Done', an early poster by See Red Women's Poster Collective, Britain, 1976.
2   Cover of the first issue of Chrysalis, the feminist cultural magazine (edited collectively), designed by Sheila Levrant de Bretteville, USA, 1975. De Bretteville also designed the magazine's logo, format and promotional materials, and was a member of the Editorial Board, 1977–9.
3   Cuban poster reprinted by the Chicago Women's Graphics Collective, USA, 1972–3.
4   Assorted badges from the Women's Liberation Movement, 1970s and early 1980s. Note: The WAVAW badge refers to the British network of groups known as Women Against Violence Against Women (first national conference in 1981). Also note the badge with the 'labrys' or double-bladed Amazonian axe, a symbol associated globally with radical feminism and/or lesbianism. Above the labrys is the Star of David (symbol of Judaism) and, within it, the word 'Life' in Hebrew.

istic principles of elegance, simplicity and purity, which were so dear to Bauhaus hearts. For all had been generated according to male value-constructs. Thus began the search for an alternative vision of design which has, in many ways, continued ever since.[2]

Having fostered new alternative paths for women and their creativity, it wasn't long before Sheila Levrant de Bretteville, Judy Chicago and Arlene Raven together founded 'a public center for women's culture' known as The Woman's Building, which opened in 1973. The Woman's Building offered an alternative space for the making and exhibiting of work, housing a variety of organizations and activities including galleries and theatre groups. Among its occupants were The Feminist Studio Workshop, an alternative school combining art and feminist education within the broader activities of the women's community, and the Women's Graphic Center, founded by de Bretteville, which offered an educational programme and laboratory facility to women (many of them new to design). The Center's aim was to connect the private/domestic sphere (women's personal 'voices' or home experiences) with the public sphere and its professional systems. To this end, print technology in the form of offset litho, letterpress and silkscreen was on offer for experimentation. The Center proved to be very successful and by 1980 included a fully-equipped graphics studio publishing books, posters and cards.

In both her educational and professional work, de Bretteville continued to explore the idea of 'feminist design strategies', casting new light on old graphic design tools and traditions. Seeing design as a dialogue or exchange, she introduced strategies for participation by the viewer – such as the use of a grid as a non-hierarchical way of presenting different viewpoints (allowing the viewer to decide on a reading order, and associations to be made), as in her poster 'Pink'. Her strategy of 'asking a question without providing an answer' invited viewers to join a discussion, and emphasized that their opinion mattered. She tried to provide imagery or views of a subject that had multiple readings, allowing viewers to ascertain their own meaning, and relinquishing some of the designer's authority. Text and image were sometimes put together in a contradiction intended to set the viewer thinking. For example, the See Red poster on page 100 states 'My Wife Doesn't Work', and then sets about illustrating hour by hour how she does – an invitation for the viewer to agree, disagree, or at least think about it. Such explorations proposed a new purpose for design as an inclusive process, aiming to connect, or engage.

De Bretteville's experiments and writings were at the cutting edge of a surge of graphic art and design work carried out by feminist poster collectives, magazines, presses and publishing houses, as well as individual designers and educators. All were involved in the process of rejecting former educational and creative frameworks; making new statements; reassessing design aims and processes; and exploring new working methods. Add to this a rush of developments from the art world – fine artists, performance artists, art historians – and it amounts to a substantial body of work that contributed to (if not originated) a questioning and transformation process in art and design that still goes on today.

In the end, the second wave's revolution was far-reaching in creative terms, and its multi-disciplinary experiments became a springboard for new, expressive pathways for women. It set the modern precedent of women as activists: a legacy that would be developed in both the 1980s and 1990s. It expressed and promoted the value of women's work and women's ideas. It introduced new working methods and strategies of democratization and collaboration, participation and inclusiveness, collective inspiration (a rejection of male genius), networking, and the ongoing attempt to eliminate barriers between the public and private spheres, and the values attached to them.

All of these issues proposed a shift in vision: a different set of (female) values for the design process, based on connectivity and interaction – and a leaning towards lateral, non-hierarchical structures. This new vision would develop and come into its own in the 1990s, when notions such as connectivity have become crucial to the way in which women are beginning to take on new technology and use it to empower themselves through networks, webs and other structures, redefining them in their own terms.

1

Women in Design: the next decade, a conference for women who work with public visual and physical forms, March 20 & 21 at the Woman's Building, 743 South Grandview, Los Angeles, California 90057

Women's Liberation: early days in the USA

2

3

4

The 1960s brought social revolution to the USA: a new generation of young people 'dropped out' to form an underground counter-culture, while civil rights protests and anti-Vietnam War demonstrations threatened to tear the country apart. Within this volatile climate of change, a movement of young radicalized women organized to bring an end to their oppression, and demanded the right to voice their own views. The Women's Liberation Movement called upon all women to challenge the existing politics of male/female power relations. The first nationally recognized protest took place at the Miss America contest in Atlantic City, New Jersey in 1968 (also famous for creating the media myth of 'bra-burning'). By 1970, Women's Liberation was a mass movement with small groups and collectives forming daily.

The Movement's machinery for bringing about direct change included consciousness-raising, networking and direct action, as well as the use of celebrations to promote women's achievements. Graphics and the visual arts were integral to this machinery, holding the Movement together and making the process of change and politicization visible.

Graphic formats such as posters, magazines and postcards carried the new messages and ideas to an international audience. All became part of the search for a new visual language that grew out of women's experience, and expressed women's struggles and concerns. Some of the most renowned graphic statements in the USA came from Sheila Levrant de Bretteville and the Women's Graphic Center (based at the Woman's Building in Los Angeles), and the Chicago Women's Graphics Collective, as well as from a variety of radical poster groups covering a broad range of liberation subjects; for example, Inkworks of Oakland, California or the Student Strike Workshop at Massachusetts College of Art. Equally interesting statements were created further afield in Britain and Australia, and all became part of the new, developing visual aspect of 'women's culture'.

1 Diazo poster for the 1975 conference on 'Women in Design: the next decade' held at the Woman's Building (Grandview St site) in Los Angeles, designed by Sheila Levrant de Bretteville.
2 Badge showing the symbol of the Women's Liberation Movement, Britain, 1970s.
3 Badge demanding freedom for the imprisoned Black Panther activist Angela Davis, and others, USA, c 1971.

4 Front cover of the graphic design magazine Print, USA, 1970.
Early actions from the Movement:
5 Robin Morgan throwing away a bra as part of the protest staged at the 1968 Miss America Pageant in Atlantic City, New Jersey.
6 Gloria Steinem, editor of Ms. magazine, at a press conference in December 1977.

6

5

Copyright 1972 by Women's Graphics Collective 1100 n. Southport, Chicago IL 60657

1

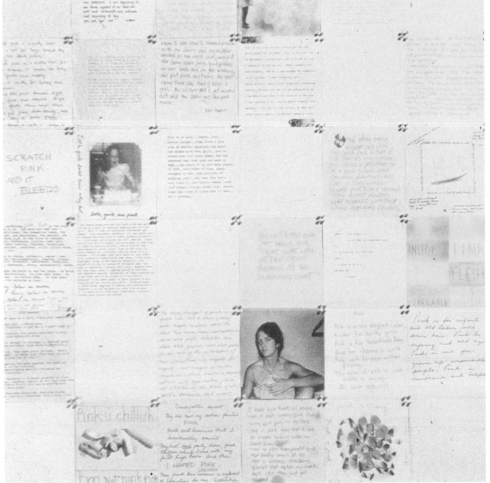

1 'Women are not Chicks', one of the earliest posters by the Chicago Women's Graphics Collective, USA, 1970–1.

2 'Sisterhood is Blooming', poster by the Chicago Women's Graphics Collective, USA, 1970–1.

3 'We Celebrate Women's Struggles; We Celebrate People's Victories', poster designed by Susan Shapiro and produced by Inkworks in Oakland, California, 1975, in support of the Women's Movement and shortly after US troops pulled out of Vietnam.

4 'Women Working', poster by the Chicago Women's Graphics Collective, USA, 1970–1.

5 'Pink', poster by Sheila Levrant de Bretteville, USA, 1974.

A feminist perspective in design: education and resources

The USA's West Coast was a haven for radical ideas and educational experiments in relating feminism to art and design. At the California Institute of the Arts in autumn 1971 (at the same time that Judy Chicago and Miriam Schapiro started their Feminist Art Program), Sheila Levrant de Bretteville initiated her Women's Design Program, focusing on graphic and communication design. The programme combined a search for female values, the use of personal experience as an inspirational source, and the use of co-operative work methods in an attempt to explore alternative, female perspectives in design.

In 1973, Sheila Levrant de Bretteville, Judy Chicago and Arlene Raven founded the Woman's Building, a public centre for women's culture which offered an alternative space for feminist studies, and the making and exhibiting of art. It housed a variety of organizations and activities, including the Women's Graphic Center founded by Sheila Levrant de Bretteville, which offered teaching and print facilities to women, many of them new to design, as a way of making their own personal 'voice' or experiences visible. The poster shown here by de Bretteville encapsulates the liberating possibilities of graphics; a splodge of printing ink represents communications potential – words not yet spoken, or the desire to be vocal.

The Woman's Building also supported women's networks, literary events and readings, exhibitions, and conferences, such as the first National Women in Design Conference in 1975. Lasting well into the 1980s, this hive of activity very much represented the multi-disciplinary and collaborative characteristics of a feminist perspective, in which art and design activities overlapped and informed each other in the attempt to develop an alternative to male-dominated culture.

If this were your Broadsheet, what would you say?

Women's Graphic Center

3

4

5

6

7

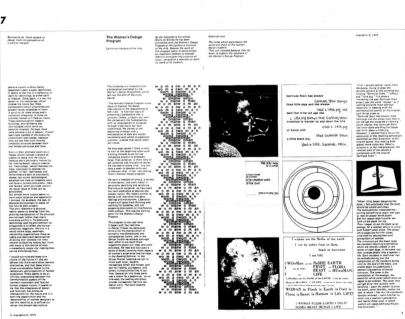

1   Poster/brochure publicizing the Women's Graphic Center, by Sheila Levrant de Bretteville, 1973.
2   Poster/brochure invitation to visit the Woman's Building (Grandview St) in Los Angeles, by Sheila Levrant de Bretteville, 1973.
3   Entrance signage to the Woman's Building (Spring St site) in Los Angeles, by Sheila Levrant de Bretteville, 1975.
4   Fifth birthday celebration poster for the Woman's Building, drawing by Phranc, design by Sheila Levrant de Bretteville, 1978.

5   Women's Graphic Center poster, designed and printed collectively at the Woman's Building, by Helen Alm, Sheila Levrant de Bretteville, Cindy Marsh, Linda Norlen, and Phranc, 1975.
6   Exhibition installation at the Woman's Building on 'Posters Books Postcards by Women', created by Sheila Levrant de Bretteville, 1975.
7   Description of The Women's Design Program based at the California Institute of the Arts, which accompanied de Bretteville's article 'Some aspects of design from the perspective of a woman designer', Icographic 6, London, 1973.

Resurrections and new discoveries

iewed as a process of education and self-discovery, 'consciousness-raising' brought political awareness and suggestions as to what women could do as individuals to bring about change. But in addition to discovering their own, and one another's, personal histories, women gradually enlarged the search to include an examination of history itself. Thus began a process of uncovering women's contributions and achievements throughout the ages, and in all walks of life, as well as tracing the historical de-valuing of women's work and traditional women's arts or crafts, such as needlework and quilt-making. This provided the foundation for the creation of a new and developing 'women's culture', a multi-disciplinary exploration which unleashed new messages through education, publishing and the creative arts, and which seeded itself in countries around the globe.

One of the best known graphic comments on this process (and a popular feminist icon) was artist Mary Beth Edelson's offset poster 'Some Living American Women Artists/Last Supper' (1971). It struck simultaneous blows to both the patriarchal structuring of organized religion, and women's cultural and historical exclusion; for one of feminism's great cultural critiques was that women had virtually been written out of art history – a claim substantiated by merely picking up the nearest reference book on the subject, which was sure to be full of men.

1   'Some Living American Women Artists/Last Supper', poster by Mary Beth Edelson, USA, 1971.

Postcards celebrating women's achievements from Helaine Victoria Press (f 1973):
2   Lucy E Parsons (1852–1942), US free speech and labour leader.
3   Trackwomen working on the Baltimore & Ohio Railroad in 1943.
4   Children marching to abolish child labour, in the 1909 May Day Parade in New York City.
5   Woolworth Workers' Sit Down Strike of 1937.
6   Josefina Villafañe de Martínez-Alvarez, M D (1890–?), Puerto Rican doctor, suffragist and feminist.
7   Zora Neale Hurston (1901?–1960), US novelist.

1

SOME LIVING AMERICAN WOMEN ARTISTS

Lucy E. Parsons

Defiance towards the exclusion of women's achievements brought about the cultural search for 'hidden heroines', as practised by the well-loved Helaine Victoria Press which published concise mini-histories of both ordinary and extraordinary women within the ingenious format of the postcard. The treasuring of women and their work was also the subject of many poster artists and collectives, including the skilled postermakers of Australia whose work during this period inspired a larger new wave of young Australian women to turn to feminist postermaking in the 1980s.

SIT-DOWN
WOOLWORTH
WORKERS
STRIKE
HELP US WIN
40 HR. WEEK

ZORA NEALE HURSTON
Novelist, Folklorist, Anthropologist & Adventurer
She once claimed she was arrested for crossing against a red light, but escaped punishment by exclaiming that "I had seen white folks pass on green & therefore assumed the red light was for me." In this way she personalized traditional stories.

1, 2 'History I' and 'History II', posters by Toni Robertson (Earthworks Poster Collective), produced at The Tin Sheds, University of Sydney, Australia 1977.

3 'Mothers' Memories, Others' Memories', poster by Toni Robertson and Vivienne Binns publicizing an influential women's art/politics project, produced at The Tin Sheds, University of Sydney, Australia, 1979.
4 'Adelaide Railway Station', poster by Mandy Martin, Australia, 1974.

3

Resurrections and new discoveries

Women's historical exclusion also provided the basis for Judy Chicago's phenomenal large-scale project *The Dinner Party*, which created place settings at a triangular dinner table (48 feet on each side) for thirty-nine women from history, all set on a white tile floor inscribed with 999 women's names. Six years in the making, from 1973–9, it was extraordinary for the breadth of its statement, encompassing historical research, a showpiece of traditional women's arts and crafts, such as china-painting and needlework, and collaboration on a massive scale, involving over four hundred people. It also created and reinforced a range of graphic symbols that were then embedded into the consciousness of the Movement, including variations on the theme of female genitalia, the use of the inverted triangle as a symbol of the pubic region, and the fluidity and central focus of spirals, scrolls and concentric circles. The multidisciplinary nature of its statement – incorporating both two- and three-dimensional forms and materials – assured its popularity and enjoyment across a wide range of art and design disciplines. Additionally, it engendered graphic publicity and documentation in the form of programmes, postcards, and most importantly two books, which were equally renowned for Sheila Levrant de Bretteville's unique layout and graphic design.

JUDY CHICAGO
THROUGH THE FLOWER

The Women's Press, 124 Shoreditch High Street, London E1 6JE

1   Poster promotion by The Women's Press, London, for Judy Chicago's autobiography Through the Flower: My Struggle as a Woman Artist (first published in the USA in 1975).
2, 3   Cover and spread from Embroidering Our Heritage and The Dinner Party by Judy Chicago (USA 1980 and 1979 respectively), two books documenting the creation of The Dinner Party and both designed by Sheila Levrant de Bretteville.

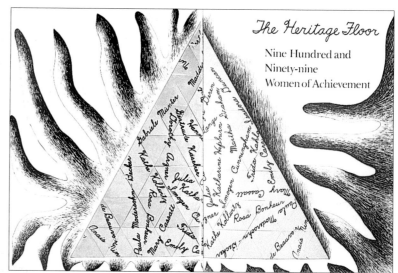

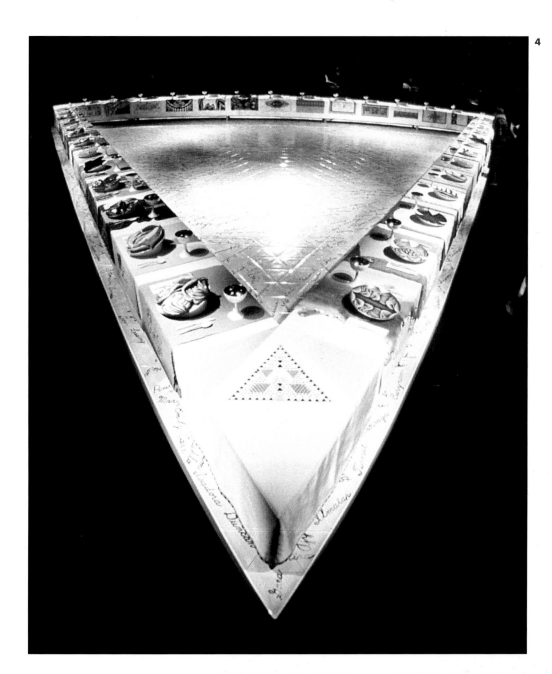

4

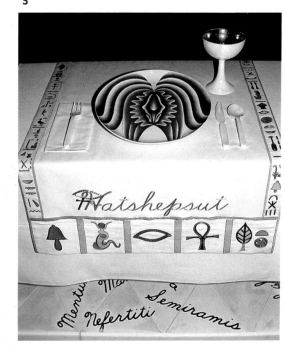

5

6

4　Postcard showing an overview of Judy Chicago's large-scale art project The Dinner Party, USA, 1979. Photo by Michael Alexander.

5　Postcard of the placesetting for Hatshepsut (1503–1482BC), the Egyptian Pharaoh of the XVIII Dynasty, from The Dinner Party, USA, 1979. Photo by Michele Maier.

6　Placesettings for the American religious figure Anne Hutchinson (1591–1643) and Sacajawea, the Native American heroine (1787–1812) from The Dinner Party, USA, 1979.

Early days in Britain: feminist posters

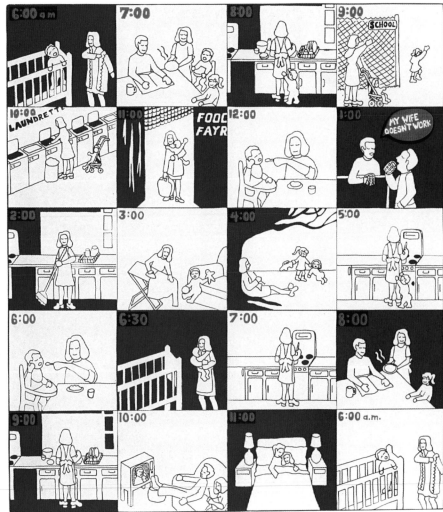

The British Women's Liberation Movement spawned a large number of postermakers, collectives and short-lived *ad hoc* groups, producing images of remarkable simplicity and grit. Many of the earlier posters were marked by a spareness of look, due to a lack of money or facilities, and were often hand-drawn or made from hand-cut screen stencils. They still had an angry potency and energy, however, which, in its more vibrant forms, could border on rage.

Artist and writer Monica Sjöö produced some of the most familiar and powerful images of the early movement, including the landmark *God Giving Birth* (page 79), a painting created in 1968 (and a feminist icon in poster form) depicting the goddess as the great cosmic and creative power, giving birth to all life. It offended patriarchal establishment views of religion and decency, and its public exhibition led to Sjöö being threatened with prosecution for 'obscenity and blasphemy'. Subsequently, in venues around Britain, it was removed by police and banned from exhibition. Meanwhile, posters of her 'Great Mother Sphinx' spread spiritual fury through the hallways of art colleges and other radical haunts. These were revolutionary images; and they were deeply shocking to the arch-conservative attitudes that prevailed.

Another dynamic source of international renown was the See Red Women's Poster Collective, active in London from 1974–89. See Red occupied a unique place in radical postermaking in that it concentrated on issues relating to women's daily lives, such as housework or domestic politics. It also placed women's oppression in a wider political context, as in protesting about the conditions of Irish women in Armagh Gaol. Dedicated to keeping its posters cheap, accessible and a positive alternative to commercial advertising stereotypes, it kept producing images throughout the 1980s (despite continual financial worries) and closed shop at the end of the decade.

WOMEN HOLD UP more than HALF THE SKY

BITE THE HAND THAT "FEEDS" YOU

A 'Service' a day and he'll work, rest and play....

1–5 Posters from See
Red Women's Poster
Collective, Britain,
1970–80.
6   'Parity Begins at
Home', poster (probably)
by Pen Dalton, Britain,
mid-1970s.

1 'The Women's Army is Marching', poster, Britain, 1974–5.
2 Poster promoting equal rights for Iranian women, artist unknown, Britain, 1970s.
3 'Free Castration on Demand', poster, Britain, 1970s.
4 'Great Mother Sphinx', the highly controversial poster by Monica Sjöö, Britain, 1969.

WOMEN ARE THE REAL LEFT. WE ARE RISING WITH A FURY OLDER THAN ANY FORCE IN HISTORY. THIS TIME WE WILL BE FREE OR NO ONE WILL SURVIVE.

Power to all the people or to none

WOMEN'S LIBERATION

Finding a voice: magazines and journals

The discussions and concerns of the Women's Liberation Movement were carried around the world by a vast network of newsletters, magazines and journals which originated in the 1970s and has continued to grow and change ever since. By means of this massive communications web – dedicated to the sharing of information, stories, events, news and images – the smallest statement, even the tiniest voice, could claim to have an international reach. This notion of international networking and global 'sisterhood' became one of the great hallmarks of second wave feminism.

The magazines or periodicals themselves were often ground-breaking in their nature. They were traditionally low budget and often crudely produced, but as conductors of energy and inspiration they had no parallel. They carried new ideas and attitudes relating to 'women's issues' such as women's health, reproductive freedom (abortion and birth control), sexuality, labour divisions, equal opportunities and equal pay at work, violence against women, and so on. They carried news of strikes or political actions and events and provided platforms for new writers and journalists. They defied mainstream media prejudices that rendered certain groups invisible – it was common for feminist magazines, for example, to interview or refer to older women for their historical perspective, opinions and political sense, as well as underlining their hardships.

Feminist periodicals opened up the world to women, carrying news from every continent, reports from conferences, and writings by women banned from publishing in their own countries. Feminist periodicals and their creators were also subject to the political contexts in which they sat. In some countries, they were viewed as a threat. Editors and writers, as outspoken people and activists, were therefore punishable – as shown by the poster in Chapter Five, page 209 relating to political prisoners in South America (one being the editor of a feminist magazine).

1

SHREW

Evidence of an early feminist press in Britain:

1   Cover of Spare Rib, Britain's most long-standing feminist magazine, 1980.

2   Poster publicizing Shrew magazine, by Sarah Beazley, Britain 1976. Shrew was the monthly magazine of the Women's Liberation Workshop, a federation of a number of different groups (f 1969). The magazine was produced by a different group each month.

3   Dishtowel, sold to raise funds for Spare Rib magazine, c1981.

4   Badge from Feminist Arts News (FAN).

5   Badge from Spare Rib.

6   Front and back cover of Bloody Women, a publication from the Cambridge Scarlet Women: a Women's Liberation group in and around Cambridge University, c1971.

Finding a voice: magazines and journals

A sample of magazines from the Women's Liberation Movement around the world, and an indicator of the importance of 'finding a voice' and establishing sisterhood through networking and print media. In alphabetical order: Bad Attitude, London, Britain, 1995; Banshee, Dublin, Rep of Ireland, 1976; Big Mama Rag, Denver, Colorado, USA, 1975; Broadsheet, Auckland, New Zealand, 1977; Chrysalis, Los Angeles, USA, 1975; Courage, West Berlin, German Federal Rep, 1979; Echo, Assoc of African Women for Research and Development (AAWORD), Dakar, Senegal, 1987; Emma, Cologne, German Federal Rep, 1988; FAN/Feminist Art News, regional collectives, Britain, 1985; From Women, Cape Town and other locations, South Africa, 1981; Heresies, New York, USA, c1985; Isis, Rome, Italy, 1976; Kinesis, Vancouver, BC, Canada, 1988; Labrys, Athens, Greece, 1982/3; Manuela, Breña, 1988; Manushi, New Delhi, India, 1986; Ms., New York, USA, 1993; Mujer/Fempress, Santiago, Chile, late 1987; Off Our Backs, Washington DC, USA, 1988; On The Issues, Forest Hills, New York, USA, 1987; Outwrite, London, Britain, 1988; Red Rag, London, Britain, 1973; Rites, Toronto, Canada, 1988; Sash, Mowbray, South Africa, 1990; Sauti Ya Siti, Dar Es Salaam, Tanzania, 1992; Shrew, London and other locations, Britain, 1971; Spare Rib, London, Britain, 1980; WIN News, Lexington, Massachusetts, USA, 1987; Woman Speak!, University of the West Indies, Barbados, 1988.

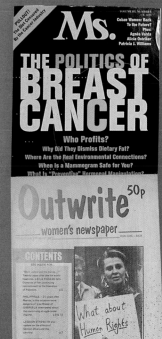

broadsheet

ASSEMBLY LINE BABIES
WOMEN DON'T PROTEST UNLOADED ANYMORE

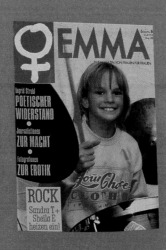

EMMA

Ingrid Strobl
**POETISCHER
WIDERSTAND**

Journalistinnen
ZUR MACHT

Fotografinnen
ZUR EROTIK

ROCK
Sandra T +
Sheila E
heizen ein!

off our backs

$1.50 a women's newsjournal

Lesbian
Break-ups

Panama

Grace
Paley

Women

MANUSHI

A JOURNAL ABOUT WOMEN AND SOCIETY

WIN NEWS

WOMEN'S INTERNATIONAL NETWORK

FRAN P. HOSKEN EDITOR

ALL THE NEWS THAT IS FIT TO PRINT BY, FOR & ABOUT WOMEN.

CONTENTS

Page
- EDITORIAL
3-6 WOMEN AND THE UNITED NATIONS
6-13 WOMEN AND DEVELOPMENT
14-18 WOMEN AND HEALTH
19-25 FEMALE CIRCUMCISION: GENITAL AND SEXUAL MUTILATION
26-27 WOMEN AND VIOLENCE
22-34 WOMEN AND MEDIA
39-46 REPORTS FROM AROUND THE WORLD: MIDDLE EAST AND AFRICA
47-57 REPORTS FROM AROUND THE WORLD: ASIA AND PACIFIC
58-66 REPORTS FROM AROUND THE WORLD: EUROPE
67-73 REPORTS FROM AROUND THE WORLD: AMERICAS
79-80 INFORMATION OF INTEREST: INTERNATIONAL
WOMEN'S INTERNATIONAL NETWORK NEWS

WIN NEWS

WOMEN'S INTERNATIONAL NETWORK

FRAN P. HOSKEN EDITOR

manuela

III CONVENCIÓN
DE FEPOMUVES

"Estamos
avanzando
en la
organización"

Nº 28
MARZO
1988

8 de marzo
DÍA INTERNACIONAL DE LA MUJER
No solo queremos dar a la vida
sino también cambiarla

RADICAL WOMEN'S NEWSPAPER   QUARTERLY   ISSUE 7

BadAttitude

Still alive in 95!

POLICE

- Mexico
Zapatista Women Tell All

SASH

JUSTICE · PEACE · DEMOCRACY

THE BLACK SASH

RECONSTRUCTION: A VISION IN THE MIDST OF CONSTRAINTS
CHANGING THE GUARD AT PLYMOUTH, OR LIBERATION FOR ALL?
SOCIAL WELFARE: EXPLORING THE POSSIBLE
BREAKING THROUGH THE MYTHS OF LAND OWNERSHIP

THIS COVER EXPLOITS WOMEN

From
Women

August 1981

RED RAG

price 10p

RATHER THAN
GIVE YOU MORE
MONEY I WOULD
PUT A MAN ON
YOUR MACHINE

INSIDE
UNIONS, ORGASMS AND MORE

35c

March, 1979

Big Mama Rag

Vol. 3-A; No. 2

Inside:
Sterilization Policy
Jane Alpert Interview
Dalkon Shield Returns
Personal/Political Politics Examined

Western Women's Journal

"Who needs Charlie Brown?"

RiTES

for lesbian and gay liberation

- AIDS Activism
- Lesbian Herstory
- George Smith Takes On Stan Persky

4th Anniversary Issue

Playing the Relationship Game

aktuelle frauenzeitung 9

Courage 9

September 1979, 4. Jahrgang, 2 DM, A 1700 EX

Frauendienst
im Militär

Feministische Partei in Spanien • Sylvia Plaths Briefe
Schularbeiten • Protest im Bayerischen Funk • Mongolismus

Η ΛΑΒΡΥΣ

Λεσβιακος Λογος

Τευχος 3   Δρχ 120

The Women's Health Movement

Women's Liberation brought a radical move towards self-awareness, and, with it, the need for women to regain control of their bodies and their lives. Thus began the Women's Health Movement, and the text most credited with starting it all was *Our Bodies, Ourselves* published in 1971 by the Boston Women's Health Book Collective. It not only set out to help women learn more about their bodies, but also placed women's health within a context of relationships, self-image, violence, and other essential issues. Still published in the 1990s, it remains one of the most liberating books on women's health in existence.

In an attempt to confront the taboo of women's bodies, encourage learning, and end women's reliance on a predominantly male medical profession, the Women's Health Movement generated new information, new demands and new attitudes, designing and illustrating an endless number of pamphlets, posters and leaflets. These emanated from a wide variety of sources, including women's groups, charities, health associations and eventually government bodies. Informational graphics such as diagrams and instructional drawings provided new imagery for the self-help aspect of the Movement – self-examination of the vagina using a speculum, breast examination, and so on – bringing to women a new knowledge of their bodies and a sense of personal control.

BY THE BOSTON WOMEN'S HEALTH BOOK COLLECTIVE

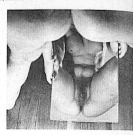

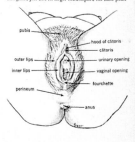

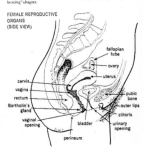

1, 2 Front cover and inside pages from the book Our Bodies, Ourselves, the classic text of the Women's Health Movement by the Boston Women's Health Book Collective, USA, 1971.

3 Poster for Broadsheet, a feminist magazine from New Zealand, 1977.

4 Poster promoting self-examination of the breasts, for the Women's National Cancer Control Campaign, Britain, late 1970s.

5 'Take a Pill Mrs Brown', poster cautioning women against taking tranquillizers by underlining the influential role played by overly busy doctors and profit-minded drug companies. By See Red Women's Poster Collective, Britain, c1980.

6 Poster showing Wonder Woman brandishing a speculum (used for self-examination of the vagina) and challenging the male-dominated medical establishment. Cartoon by C Clement, USA, mid-1970s.

Self-examination was first demonstrated in the USA in 1971, and by 1975 the Women's Health Movement had carried it to a dozen other countries.

The Movement further developed a sharp-shooting attitude towards the prescription of drugs to women, the side-effects of certain methods of contraception, and other issues. The subject of contraception in itself tended to generate graphic innovations in Britain, as seen in the classic 'Pregnant Man' campaign of 1970–1 by agency Cramer Saatchi (for its Tanzanian equivalent see page 225), or in the pioneering use of a comic-strip technique to introduce birth control to young people in the Family Planning Association campaign 'Too Great A Risk' (1972), written and designed by Gillian Crampton Smith.

(for its Tanzanian equivalent see page 225)

3

6

4

5

FREE SAFE VASECTOMY
ON DEMAND

Would you be more careful if
it was you that got pregnant?

1   'A Stitch in Time
Saves Nine', original
poster design by Marie
McMahon (Earthworks
Poster Collective), printed
at The Tin Sheds,
University of Sydney,
Australia, 1979. This
version was reprinted by
Fly Press for the London
Anarchist Feminist
Group.
2   Poster for a cam-
paign to promote contra-
ception, by advertising
agency Cramer Saatchi
for the Health Education
Council, Britain, 1970.

3   Badge, Britain,
c1975.
4   'Too Great a Risk',
cover and illustrations
from a leaflet on contra-
ception which pioneered
the use of a comic-strip
format to introduce
family planning to
young people. Written
and designed by Gillian
Crampton Smith, pub-
lished by The Family
Planning Association,
Britain, 1972.
5   Poster offering help
and information on birth
control, designed by
Bartholomew, Britain,
late 1970s/early 1980s.

5

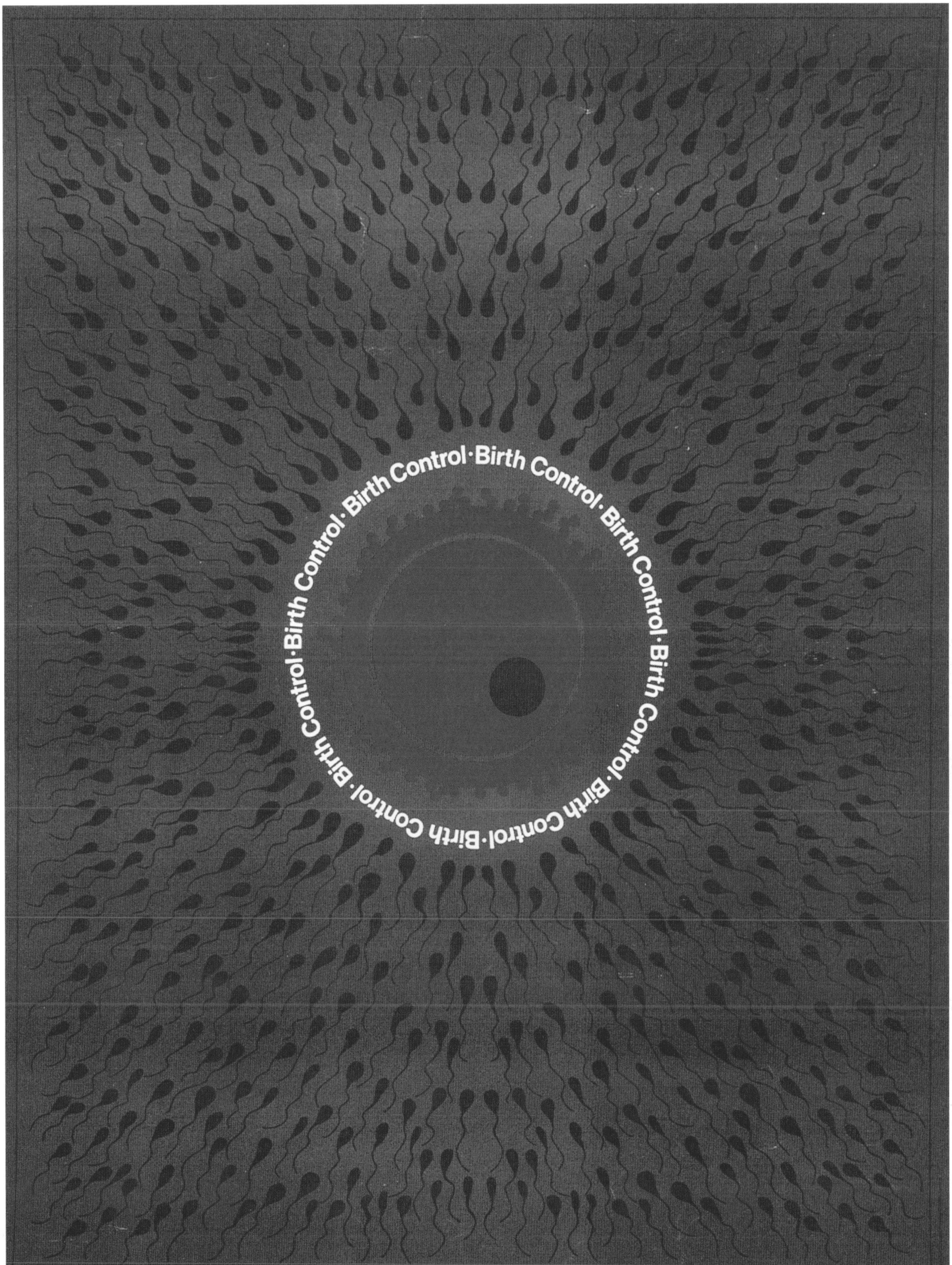
Birth Control · Birth Control · Birth Control · Birth Control · Birth Control · Birth Control · Birth Control

Reclaim the night: combating violence against women

Another major concern of the Women's Liberation Movement was confronting the issue of violence against women. In defining such abuse as 'violence', they thereby rejected traditional notions of masculine dominance and female submission, fighting the social acceptance of violence against women and insisting on the recognition of all its forms – rape, domestic violence, intimidation, sexual harassment at work, pornography (as a woman-hating device), and so on. Such confrontations went on in many countries and produced many graphic statements on the subject, ranging from announcements for demonstrations to stickers noting telephone numbers for rape crisis hotlines.

Important demonstrations took place. On 30 April 1977, women staged simultaneous night-time demonstrations in towns all over West Germany, protesting against all forms of violence against women – as symbolized by their fear to walk the streets at night. Britain followed, with a night-time demonstration staged simultaneously in five cities later that year, and 'Reclaim the Night' became the rallying cry and title for many night-time marches. These sometimes directed anger at sex shops and pornography, or responded to a particular incident of violence or assault. In the USA in November 1978, a rally entitled 'Take Back the Night' saw 3,000 chanting women march through the streets of San Francisco at night in protest against pornography and other forms of violence against women.

In all three countries mentioned, subsequent demonstrations were staged: in Britain they carried on into the 1990s. All such night-time marches tended to be visually spectacular with floats, banners, blazing torches, lanterns or candles. Another common element was the all-important use of sound – shouting, chanting and percussion, ranging from drums to saucepan lids – as a way of letting antagonists know that women meant business.

5

6

7

Reclaim the Night

Women Demand an end to male violence + the right to walk alone without fear. Join us - all women welcome Friday 20th July 9.30 pm kingsmead Square bring lights + noise

1 'Women Against Rape Unite!', poster announcing meetings of the Women Against Rape Collective, France, 1970s.
2 'Twice Battered', poster announcing a public forum on ending violence against women, by Chicago Women's Graphics Collective, USA, 1979.
3 Graffiti in front of the Chiswick Women's Aid Centre (f 1971), the first refuge for battered women, Britain, 1975.

4 Handbill summoning demonstrators to a mock-trial of government officials accused of violence against women, to be held in London's Trafalgar Square. By the group Women Against Rape, 1977.
5, 6 Badges, Britain or USA, 1978.
7 Poster announcing a 'Reclaim the Night' march, Britain, c1978.

Activism and Backlash (1980s)

Throughout the 1970s the second wave of feminism had created a massive change in consciousness, attempting to redefine politics and culture in all their manifestations by challenging the control structures of patriarchy, and by introducing female values and experience as an alternative. Most crucially for women, consciousness-raising and the great experience of 'sisterhood' had brought recognition of an inner strength that (when connected, from woman to woman) represented not power, but empowerment of a new kind. Consequently, when the following decade brought the spirit of feminism up against a brick wall of conservative politics, it didn't just vanish into thin air – it transformed itself. It took on new personalities and new faces, and responded to the climate of the times, picking up new tools and techniques. It became highly commercial; it went underground; it exploded onto large-scale environmental art formats; it donned disguises (including gorilla suits); it formed activist groups; it went global as never before. This was the decade in which international feminism was truly consolidated.

There were strong cultural and visual forces acting upon feminism in the intervening years. As the seething anger of liberation and anti-Vietnam War movements of the 1960s began to diminish, an urban revolution rose up from the energy of the streets. Punk brought exhibitionist social critique and nonconformism expressed through music, fashion, fanzines and other forms of street publishing. It also introduced a new generation of women with a tough, self-defined attitude and a powerful form of delivery. In the years thereafter, girls would become grrrls; dykes would become queers (and in the

1990s, Lesbian Avengers); women would become 'angry', activists, Greens, Greenham women, power-bitches and techno-feminists – and it was all happening 'in your face'.

The 1980s was also the decade in which both girls and women pitted themselves against the commercial media and cultural institutions that dominated and fashioned their lives – often appropriating traditional communication formats, such as signs and billboards, to put across new messages. The effects were substantial: battles with the media, conducted both underground and overground, meant that sexist imagery would forevermore be subject to protest or public outcry from one direction or another. Battles with museums, meanwhile, through the street-postering of statistical information by the Guerrilla Girls in the USA, did much to expose the discriminatory attitudes of the New York art world, and began a slow process of change. Their activism marked the birth of a new breed of cultural watchdog that would sink its teeth into the health system, the government, and other institutions in the 1990s in the form of WAC (Women's Action Coalition) and other activist groups.

Needless to say, a myopic press and media continued to report throughout it all that feminism was 'dead' or defunct. Then lightning struck: the Pro-Life/Pro-Choice disputes, simmering beneath the surface of America throughout the decade, exploded into view in the late 1980s and brought all of feminism's new faces (and quite a few old ones) back to the frontline in a show of force. They rallied over the issue of 'a woman's right to choose' in an attempt to stop the erosion of a number of the women's rights gained over recent decades. Susan Faludi's bestselling book *Backlash*, published in 1991, confirmed 'the undeclared war against women' and set the scene for a new era of retaliation.

Women stand up for their rights in the 1980s:
1   A poster protest against a particularly sexist advertising campaign for a brand of women's underpants entitled No Knickers, by artist Julia Church, Australia, 1985. The campaign included 3D billboards featuring a giant pair of plastic buttocks, barely covered by a real fabric skirt which blew up in the wind. They were regularly paint-bombed by irate women – as suggested by this image.
2   Women's Liberation Movement postcard, Britain, mid-1980s.
3   'Do women have to be naked to get into the Met. Museum?', poster by the feminist art activist group Guerrilla
Girls, USA, 1989. Originally a billboard design that was rejected by the Public Art Fund in New York, it then became a self-funded bus ad and street poster.
4   Calendar page, Britain, 1986.
5   Cover of issue 10 of Shocking Pink, the highly irreverent London-based feminist girls' magazine, c1990.

1

at the age of five
I decided to stop serving him

With hindsight, a glance back over the 1980s reveals that the Women's Liberation Movement may have ceased to exist as a mass political force – but feminism, networking and women's activism had been going strong the whole time and, furthermore, had developed new forms of graphic expression that were unconventional, street-bound and highly varied. All matters on which, in the end, even the press agreed: for with the arrival of the 1990s, there were shudderings in the media that the 'f-word' was back.

Global issues and a socially committed role for design

The angry years of Conservatism were dominated by the politics and economics of the 1980s, although in spirit they extended well beyond the borders of the decade. The pendulum of Western politics swung to the right, with Margaret Thatcher elected in 1979, and Ronald Reagan in 1980 followed by George Bush in 1988. It was a time of inflated wealth, enterprise and commercialism – the decade of the Me Generation, the decade of youth and young wealth. It was also however, in social terms, a period of growing divergence between rich and poor.

Along with the swing to the Right, the alternative politics of the Left rose with a vengeance, and women maintained a highly visible and active profile. Developments in communications media and technology meant that the ordinary person in the street could be in touch with the world as never before. Not only could people be more informed of struggles and protests taking place in other parts of the world, they could also take action and be involved, through international solidarity movements. 'Act Local, Think Global' became the slogan of the day, and a true reflection of the zeitgeist.

NATO re-armament and the deployment of short- and medium-range missiles in Europe activated the international peace movement, and established the Women's Peace Camp at Greenham Common in 1981. With the rise of the anti-nuclear lobby came the rise of the Greens: feminist Petra Kelly founded the German Green Party, *Die Grünen*, in 1979, and in 1984 they made their significant move into the European Parliament. Environmental issues and animal rights have remained part of the modern-day protest agenda ever since. Protests against official and unofficial violence (the crisis in the Falklands, Britain's 'troubles' in Northern Ireland, US interference in Central America) as well as the anti-apartheid movement and other human rights campaigns were just a few of the issues addressed by women artists and designers, or women's groups (see Chapter Five). Advances in communication also meant that the international feminist network grew stronger. Groups such as Isis International, the women's information and communication service, were starting to bring together information that would gradually construct an overall picture of how women around the world were living their lives.

But on the homefronts of the Western world – in cities and in small communities – tensions between the rich and the poor were central to a whole decade of social re-definition and change. Europe and the USA were gradually forced to acknowledge the large-scale social problems underlying their 'prosperity', including alcohol and drug abuse, crime and urban poverty. This was also the decade that dispelled our traditional picture-construct of society. Reports were beginning to show that happy, long-lasting, fairy-tale marriages and 'the nuclear family' were fast becoming a myth. Although the media would

2

3

4

1   Postcard by Carole Wilson and Barbara Miles of the Jillposters collective, Australia, 1985.
2   'Nuclear Family, No Thanks!', badge, Britain, mid-1980s.
3, 4   Badges from the women's peace movement, Britain, mid-1980s.
5   Chrissie Hynde (of The Pretenders), Vivienne Westwood, and Jordan (shown centre to right) pose with body graffiti inside 'Sex', the shop run by Westwood and Malcolm McLaren in King's Road, London, 1974. In 1976 they renamed it Seditionaries: the first Punk clothing shop.

5

continue to propagate the ideal of heterosexual marital bliss (as typified by Princess Diana's wedding), it was countered by the alternative media and activists who energetically dismantled gender stereotypes and traditional concepts of marriage and family. They also began to campaign against domestic brutality, rape and other forms of violence against women. The campaign against the AIDS crisis brought the caring qualities of the gay and lesbian communities to the fore. It also introduced, through the work of art activist groups such as Gran Fury, a new up-front visual profile for lesbians. The coy metaphors of the past – flowers clinging together, cats playing on the doorstep, women smiling 'knowingly' but never touching – were suddenly replaced with visual reality. Lesbians – kissing, loving and just being themselves – became part of the graphic environment, and in the 1990s they would achieve an even greater public presence.

So by the end of the decade, the visual portrait of modern society had changed dramatically. For while conservative policies and power institutions had become more firmly entrenched (and more restrictive to women and other groups), the alternative realities of the protest culture had become stronger and more vocal. Women had developed their own world view through a wide range of communications and protest formats, including environmental signs, billboards, fanzines, performance art and flyposting, and had joined the combative street culture. In Europe, one of the key influences in the creation of this alternative view of society had been Punk, which had provided a new visual language of social critique.

The British Punk legacy: attitude, individuality and street publishing

After the underground revolution of the 1960s, the next era of revolution for British youth was Punk: a movement which arose in the mid-1970s from the counter-cultures of the city streets. Although not a movement for social or political change, it was intensely anti-Establishment. In the midst of a severe economic depression, with high unemployment, there was a mood of disillusionment in Britain, and anarchy and subversion were seen as creative forces. Punk preached subversion and rejection of nearly all social conventions: employment, materialism, tradition, the family, the home, religion and so on. It also targeted and defaced their visual icons, such as the Queen, the British flag and the

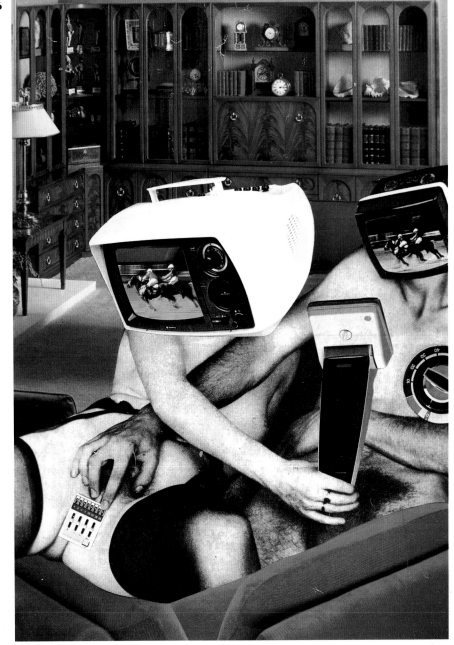

6

7

6 Feminist statements within a Punk context: one of the graphic collages of Manchester-based artist Linder, Britain, 1977.
7 Inside spread from i-D, the style magazine created by Terry Jones and heavily influenced by Punk fanzines, where street fashions (such as 'my dad's vest' or outfits from charity shops) appeared next to labels such as Bodymap or Fiorucci. Britain, 1983.

Crucifix, enacting a social commentary within the visual dimension, and often eliciting public disgust.

Punk's inspiration came from the street, maintained by the enterprise and energy of adolescence. It drew its graphic vocabulary from sources such as comics, magazine advertising, newspapers, and the packaging in supermarkets, using a modern palette of bright, garish colours, aggressive cut-out shapes, and chaotic layout, typified by the graphics of Jamie Reid, art director of the Punk band the Sex Pistols. Beginning from a milieu of drugs, sex and club music, and at first aiming principally to shock or provoke, Punk grew gradually into a highly creative cultural movement that encompassed art, music, graphics, fashion and photography.

Self-expression, achieved by do-it-yourself methods, was the driving force of Punk, in all of its manifestations. Style and fashion, in particular, led by style innovator Vivienne Westwood, became major vehicles for individuality and self-expression – the more exhibitionist, the better. Westwood's designs for Seditionaries, the Punk clothes shop she ran with Malcolm McLaren, created a new direction in style that saw clothing as a kind of subversion, in the process questioning power-symbolism, social conformity and gender stereotypes. Hence the Punk notion of 'appearance', constructed through clothing, body piercing, make-up and hairstyles, became an intense and exaggerated visual statement that expressed rebellion against social expectations across the board. Its 'unisex' elements, such as shaved heads, bondage trousers and heavy boots on both sexes, were particularly challenging to current media concepts of femininity and beauty, and remained influential for years to come.

Another of Punk's main modes of expression was 'self-publishing', usually carried out in the production of street magazines or 'fanzines'. Fanzines appeared in their hundreds from 1976 onwards. Although they were related above all to music, they were produced on a wide range of subjects, and were very much part of the ethic that anyone with a photocopier and some adhesive tape could publish. Although Punk had ended in Britain by the early 1980s, it thrived throughout the decade in America and Europe, causing an explosion of 'zines' and independent publishing on every imaginable subject, and fanzines have ever since remained a crucial means of communication for many cultural and political movements. In Britain, the emphasis on street fashion, urban creativity and do-it-yourself publishing led to the 1980s' preoccupation with streetstyle and youth-related formats, expressed through magazines such as *i-D* and *The Face*, both launched in 1980. *i-D* retained the influence of Punk and its fanzine culture through 'instant design' methods and an arbitrary cluttered layout, while *The Face* was seen as heralding a post-Punk era of young wealth.

Punk's contribution to feminism was substantial; not so much in what Punk had to offer feminism (it was often considered a very boys-orientated movement), but more for what feminism took from Punk. A new generation of young women made flagrant and very feminist use of Punk modes of self-expression and subversion, particularly borrowing its amateur methods and graphic vocabulary.

The graphic collages made by Manchester artist 'Linder' (created from 1977 to 1979) are a fine example of feminist statements made within a Punk context. Her rebellion against the stereotyped roles laid out by women's magazines expressed itself in meticulously-cut collages, which were used as the focal point of publicity for the Buzzcocks' single 'Orgasm Addict'. Their appearance on street posters and fanzines supplied British Punk with some of its most arresting graphic icons. A little later on, girls too would employ self-publishing methods to produce magazines such as *Shocking Pink*.

Punk's strong ethic of individualism had even more to offer women in terms of empowerment and a new image. Vivienne Westwood's subversive design vision created

I'm Joe Average
My family means more to me than anything else . . .

. . . that's why I share the responsibility for housework and caring for the kids.

a role for fashion and style as self-expression and attitude, offering women a new means of communication. Punk music also played an important part, with the women who performed in Punk bands breaking down the extremely limited female stereotypes in traditional rock music. Playing in all-female bands or fronting otherwise male groups, they assumed an unprecedented importance. Patti Smith, Deborah Harry from Blondie, Chrissie Hynde from The Pretenders, Poly Styrene from X-Ray Spex, The Slits, The Raincoats, and Siouxsie Sioux and the Banshees were all, in their way, influential on both sides of the Atlantic, and left a legacy that would be a powerful model for female artists and bands in the 1990s, and in particular for the Riot Grrrl movement. Through the combined contributions of Westwood, Harry *et al* in fashion, music and performance, Punk produced an alternative image of woman as tough, streetwise, uncompromising, non-conformist, exhibitionist, with attitude, defining sex and power on her own terms. A new generation therefore embraced a subversive attitude, image and street style, joining women of all ages in targeting the media, and waging a battle that raged throughout the decade – and that continues still.

Womanpower, girlpower, mediapower

By challenging the power lines of the media and its stereotyped roles, women found their own power: girlpower, womanpower, motherpower, sisterpower and so on. In Britain girlpower was prominent at the start of the decade through the work of such feminist or community poster groups as the well-known See Red poster collective, and 'Some Girls'. In the latter project, Carola Adams and Leah Thorn researched the 'risks in being young and being female' for the National Association of Youth Clubs. Their investigations and close contact with young women's groups generated an extremely popular and controversial series of posters which was published by the NAYC. (Interestingly, their attempts to produce an honest representation of their findings resulted in the withdrawal of co-sponsorship by a government department, obviously expecting a much 'sweeter' image to have emerged.)[1]

Another prime example of girlpower was the magazine *Shocking Pink*. Started in the early 1980s, it combined the fanzine tradition of do-it-yourself publishing with social critique and a hard feminist stance. Aimed at young women/girls aged ten upwards, it was produced by a collective aged sixteen to twenty-five, and was particularly keen to give space to young lesbians. With their own witty and irreverent delivery, they launched scathing attacks on the media and particularly on what they called the 'propaganda' of popular girls' magazines such as *Jackie* and *My Guy*. ('The average age of a *Jackie* reader is 12. She is told 22 times in each issue to buy more make-up'.)[2] Streetwise, sharp-tongued, and with a drop-dead attitude to any authority figures that got in the way, *Shocking Pink* also offered discussion and information on a broad range of subjects, from contraception to politics, and gave its audience an unrestricted sounding-board of its own.

On a broader scale, women everywhere began to challenge the oppressive representations of women that pervaded the dominant cultural milieu. In Britain, in the USA

1 Postcard showing a tights and stockings billboard ad amended by the guerrilla graffitists known as 'Angry Women', photo by Wendy Holloway, Britain, 1981.
2–4 Badges relating to violence against women, Britain, late 1970s.
5 Poster protesting war and rape, by artist Deej Fabyc of Jillposters, Australia, 1983.

The rapid rise and demise of the New Man:
6 'I'm Joe Average', poster produced for the Office of the Status of Women, Dept of Home Affairs and Environment, by the Australian Government Publishing Service, 1982.
7 'Some Men Will Do Anything', poster by Carol Porter of Red Planet posters, Australia, 1993.
8 Postcard by Biff (Chris Garratt and Mick Kidd), Britain, c1982.

POSTERS DESIGNED AND PRINTED AT MELBOURNE UNIVERSITY SCREENPRINTING CENTRE

Bloody Good Graffix

UNION BLD'G
PH: 341-5618 ask for the screenprint workshop

and in Australia, protests against sexism in advertising took the form of graffiti sprayed onto walls and billboards – or amended billboards (re-worked to express alternative messages) – by anonymous activists, such as the group simply known as 'Angry Women'. Jill Posener's photographs of graffitied billboards in Britain and Australia were widely reproduced in books, magazines and postcards, and became symbolic of the grassroots resistance of women against the public images that dominated their lives. In addition, stickers stating 'This Degrades Women' adorned sexist book covers, ads and posters; and feminist groups such as *Spare Rib* magazine encouraged actions and marches. Individual graphic artists, such as Julia Church in Australia, retaliated by producing posters that responded sharply to sexist advertising. The particularly vivid example by Church on page 114 was a riposte to a series of television and billboard advertisements in 1985 for a brand of women's underpants entitled 'No Knickers'. The advertisement involved a Marilyn Monroe-styled woman singing 'I'm wearing No Knickers' (and lifting her skirt at the end of the song to prove it) as well as 3D billboards comprised of a fibreglass reconstruction of a woman's derrière wearing a fabric skirt that billowed in the wind, exposing No Knickers. The advertisements were met with a great deal of protest, and Church's posters were sold and exhibited in community centres, in the streets and in galleries.

For most of the decade, the media fanned the anti-feminist fire with a campaign of persistent ideological coercion. It missed no opportunity to pronounce feminism 'dead' and to speak of 'post-feminism'; it created a stereotype of ugly, aggressive women displaying 'loony behaviour' (reminiscent of the anti-feminist attacks of the early part of the century); and continually repeated that the word 'feminist' had become a term of 'ribald abuse' and mockery.[3] The media also attempted to create a new counter-stereotype for men: the soft, caring, un-macho, role-sharing New Man, happy to change nappies and do housework, who somehow vanished into thin air with the end of the decade. Far more successful at teaching people to think about roles and stereotypes, and to laugh in the face of prejudice and sexism, were the efforts of independent presses such as the excellent Biff postcards, who were expert at poking fun at both sexes.

Womanpower also continued to harness graphics and other media forms to create its messages and propaganda. The Older Feminists Network was formed in London in 1981, with a view to addressing the particular needs and experiences of 'older women' (a self-defined category), and acknowledging older women's strength and personal identity. They also addressed the media's demeaning portrayal of older women, both in terms of its inhibiting effect on the women themselves and the way in which it restricts society's expectations and evaluations of them. Their network has been represented by a lively newsletter dealing with matters concerning older women, which carries a 'zine'-like crazy-quilt of news, events, opinions, press-cuttings and creative work – both inspiring and enraging. Still going strong in the 1990s, it remains a fascinating read.

Community and feminist poster workshops kept their eye on reality and worked to express the authentic voice of unrepresented groups – lesbians, black women, older women, immigrant communities – while also keeping up with the local, national and international conflicts of the day, such as the British Miners' Strike of 1984–5.

WOMEN IN IRAN

1   Poster self-promotion for Bloody Good Graffix poster group, by Julia Church and Kathy Walters, Britain, 1983.
2   Poster by the Iranian Women's Solidarity Group, Britain, early 1980s.
3   'Victory to the Miners', poster protesting a violent incident recorded at a demonstration during the British Miners Strike of 1984–5. The woman shown was from the protest group Sheffield Women Against Pit Closures.
4   'One Small Step for a Woman', poster by Julia Church, Australia, 1985.

LEZ-BEANS

A Wild Female Lavender-Edged Breed of the Human Bean

Available in a wide variety of colors, shapes and sizes.

Where to Plant. The Lez-Bean is guaranteed to grow in virtually any locality in the world. They can be seen growing in wild bunches in both rural and urban settings. They'll seem to pop up everywhere in the most unsuspecting places once you begin to recognize and keep an eye out for this fruit-like plant.

Planting: Although they will survive in the most adverse conditions, Lez-Beans thrive when placed in close bunches and given plenty of freedom,

fresh air, and Sunshine.

Harvesting: Lez-Beans emerge at their own pace. Some Lez-Beans will be very fruitful at an early age, where others will sprout an equally nutritious bean much later. Note: Certain species of the Lez-Bean appear under the guise of the Non-Lez-Bean variety, also known as the Closet Variety Lez-Bean. This type does not seem to grow as well, a condition often caused by isolation. Place this stifled plant back into a wild bunch of Lez-Beans, and the Closet Variety will thrive once again.

© Jean Vallon, 1982

Community poster workshops catered for groups that didn't have a voice, while also recording the conflicts of the day.

5 'Lez-Beans: A Wild Female Lavender-Edged Breed of the Human Bean', poster with text by Jean Vallon, Britain, 1982.

6 'Old Age Isn't Calm' (poem by Sonia Saxon), poster by See Red Women's Poster Collective, 1978.

7 Poster condemning skin-bleaching agents, artist unknown, Britain, mid-1980s.

8 'Black Lesbians', poster designed and printed by Ingrid Pollard at the Lenthall Road Workshop, London, 1984.

Meanwhile in Australia, a second generation of women postermakers, greatly influenced by Punk and its modern culture imagery, produced a highly colourful brew of feminism and politics throughout the decade. Bloody Good Graffix, Jillposters (a women's collective who lifted their name from the dictum that 'Billposters will be prosecuted'), The Wimmin's Warehouse Screen Printing Collective, Harridan Screenprinters and other groups became part of a long line of individuals that comprised a women's poster tradition, and included such artists as Mandy Martin, Toni Robertson, Julia Church, Kathy Walters, Jan Fieldsend, Leonie Lane and Alison Alder. In addition to addressing 'women's issues', women postermakers were particularly visible throughout the 1980s in protests surrounding the cause of the Aboriginal peoples (exacerbated by the 1988 Australian Bicentennial) as well as in the campaign against nuclear testing in the Pacific.

Feminist magazines continued to thrive and multiply, strengthening their international network, while publishing houses, such as Virago and the Women's Press in Britain, achieved great success in the expanding commercial climate. They produced a substantial increase in the body of knowledge and information about women, as well as fostering the work of new women writers, and reprinting works from the feminist past. The buoyant commercial climate allowed new, smaller, more specialized presses to emerge, such as the Sheba Press in Britain, which specialized in publishing writings by black women, lesbians and working-class women; and Barbara Smith and Audre Lorde's renowned Kitchen Table: Women of Color Press in the USA. (Unfortunately, once the recessionary climate of the 1990s took hold, many of the new small presses slipped away; those that remain do so in constant struggle.) The focus at this time on the sexism prevalent in language led to the publication of guidelines and dictionaries to promote non-sexist language, which gradually made an impact on the education system, in business and in the media.

In addition to the work being done by feminist publishers, the attempt to redress history and build on the foundations of 'women's culture' kept women's institutions, college courses, researchers and artists/designers busy excavating the past, communicating their findings through books, conferences, calendars, exhibitions and environmental projects. Notable examples from around the world include Sheila Levrant de Bretteville's Los Angeles concrete-wall tribute to Biddy Mason, the nineteenth-century slave, midwife and philanthropist, and Japan's only feminist calendar series, 'Sisters! The First Feminists in Japan'. Researched and published by Workshop for Women Jo-Jo, this project has introduced twelve different pioneering women from Japan's past (and present) every year since 1988.

The USA: street politics, art activism and guerrilla graphics

A similar taste for social critique was present in the USA throughout the 1980s, albeit in a very different form. Although the USA's involvement in Central America, its deployment of missiles in Europe and its commercial links with apartheid regimes had, together with other international issues, caused grave protest both at home and abroad, as the decade progressed, tensions over 'home issues' would threaten to cause far greater disruption.

Feminist graphics also changed character over the course of the 1980s, becoming angrier and more direct. Back in the 1970s feminism inspired activism and a mood of multi-disciplinary collaboration. This began a tradition of public art such as mural painting and site projects, as well as performance art and public 'rituals'. Women's activist groups, including The Feminist Art Workers (1976), The Waitresses (1977), Sisters of Survival (1981) in California, and No More Nice Girls (c1980) in New York, all continued into the 1980s, foreshadowing later groups such as Guerrilla Girls and WAC.

The late 1970s also saw art activists, such as Jenny Holzer and Barbara Kruger, take to the urban environment, producing apparently disembodied critical statements on billboards and other street formats, and leaving, like the Cheshire Cat's smile, only the shock of their inexplicable presence. One of Holzer's best known projects at that time was a group of enigmatic, poetic messages, numbering around three hundred in all, entitled 'Truisms' (1978–87). Originally a street-poster campaign, 'Truisms' came to be presented in a variety of formats, from t-shirts and phone-booth labels to massive electronic signs in Times Square in New York or Piccadilly Circus in London.

Barbara Kruger was also prominent in the art activism of the 1980s. Her sharply-honed and highly distinctive montages of text and (often photographic) symbolic images posed questions about consumerism, sexuality and societal values, often with an energy and immediacy that called for action. Where Holzer's statements were powerful by virtue of their contemplative aura, Kruger's were like accurately thrown darts. 'Your Body is a Battleground', her poster created for the 1989 March on Washington for abortion rights, was one of the most powerful graphic design statements of that era. Referring to a whole range of disputes, for many women it encapsulated all their anger into one sharp graphic icon – and as a call to action it remains exhilaratingly provocative.

A highly energized spirit of vigilantism appeared in 1985 with the Guerrilla Girls, the feminist art activist group set on a mission of exposing sexual and racial discrimination in the New York art world. Their street-poster campaigns gained them instant notoriety and acclaim, for they attacked the business practices of galleries and museums through listing statistics and 'naming names': all conveyed with the sharp ironic humour that soon became their trademark. Perhaps even more impressive was their ability to turn their need for anonymity into a type of performance; no-one has ever learnt the identity of the Guerrilla Girls, since they have worn gorilla masks or suits for all their public appearances. This strategy was intended to safeguard members from the risk of retribution by individuals or institutions attacked and keep the spotlight on issues rather than personalities or careers. But it has also given them a certain quasi-mythic status in the cultural world, keeping an international audience of admirers 'guessing' for over a decade. They have, in fact, been rumoured to include some of the USA's top female artists, as well as curators and critics from within the art establishment itself.

Their real weapon, however, remains their graphic delivery, together with their brilliant use of media manipulation, copywriting and design strategy. Over the years this has expanded beyond typographic posters stuck up in the streets, to include magazine page-art, a newsletter entitled *Hot Flashes*, postcards of all sorts and a book of their 'confessions', and televised interviews and talks. Their subjects have more recently included homelessness, rape, the Gulf War, abortion rights and other major issues. Their book offers the most comprehensive collection of their poster work, including the

---

1

THE ADVANTAGES OF BEING A WOMAN ARTIST:

Working without the pressure of success.

Not having to be in shows with men.

Having an escape from the art world in your 4 free-lance jobs.

Knowing your career might pick up after you're eighty.

Being reassured that whatever kind of art you make
  it will be labeled feminine.

Not being stuck in a tenured teaching position.

Seeing your ideas live on in the work of others.

Having the opportunity to choose between career and motherhood.

Not having to choke on those big cigars or paint in Italian suits.

Having more time to work after your mate dumps you
  for someone younger.

Being included in revised versions of art history.

Not having to undergo the embarrassment of being called a genius.

Getting your picture in the art magazines wearing a gorilla suit.

Guerrilla Girls CONSCIENCE OF THE ART WORLD

---

1 *'The Advantages of being a Woman Artist', poster and postcard by the Guerrilla Girls, USA, 1988.*
2 *Cover of Newsweek magazine (8 June 1992), created by US artist Barbara Kruger.*

2

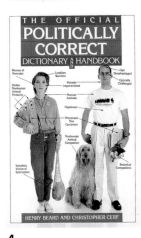

classic 'The Advantages of Being a Woman Artist' (page 122). It also contains examples of their wit, some visual, such as a photo of the Berlin cultural minister and a Guerrilla Girl eating bananas together, but most verbal. One, for example, is entitled 'Marilyn Monroe Announces Drastic NEA Cuts' in which the issue of art censorship is converted into a call for mass castration; another, entitled 'Biological Warfare', is a facetious joke about the fantasy of an 'Oestrogen Bomb': 'When it is dropped on an area of violent conflict, men will throw down their guns, hug each other, apologize, say it was 'all their fault' and then start to clean up the mess.' In this sarcastic yet humorous mode, the Guerrilla Girls have staged one of the most skilful social critiques of the conservative 1980s and 1990s.

As the decade moved on, professional art activists, graphic designers, street artists, and amateurs of all sorts, used photography, photocopying, stencils, stickers, and any other means to hand, in order to produce confrontational statements and 'demo-graphics' on a broadening range of issues affecting women. These included violence against women, government apathy towards the AIDS crisis (and women and HIV), homelessness and other matters. But one subject seemed itself to incite violence: the Pro-Life/Pro-Choice disputes.

Abortion was legalized nationally by the Supreme Court in 1973 via the landmark case of *Roe vs Wade*. The first bombing of an abortion clinic took place only five years later, in 1978. The 1980s then saw the rapid growth of an anti-abortion movement, including the establishment of major 'anti' organizations and lobbies, an escalation of violence against clinics, political sympathy from both Ronald Reagan and George Bush, and continual ground-level and state-level efforts to impose new restrictions. When, however, it seemed in 1989 that the Supreme Court was likely to repeal the rights granted in *Roe*, Pro-Choice forces retaliated. Once rolling, the resistance led to a major abortion rights march on Washington, followed by another in 1992, and suddenly abortion rights became a burning issue in upcoming election campaigns.

From a graphic point of view, the major anti-abortion groups generated far more visual propaganda in the 1980s than the Pro-Choice movement. They produced highly organized (and substantially funded) campaigns that spread their doctrine through a variety of techniques, including a 'clinical' approach whose statistics and medical quotations were all the more persuasive for their apparently 'scientific' authority. Or they employed hard-sell tactics, slapping slogans and logos on everything from bracelets and balloons to bumperstickers, unhelpfully polarizing the situation. Various organizations also made calculated use of the postal service, disseminating visual material that was not only forceful but at times highly sensationalist or frightening, as when buckets of foetus-like waste material were presented as the results of abortions.

Pro-Choice organizations were far less organized in terms of their graphic strategy, although they benefited greatly from isolated projects of personal conviction, such as Kruger's poster for the March on Washington. But the turn of the decade was a watershed for both the resistance movement and its graphics. Shocked into action, from then on Pro-Choice became one of the inflammatory issues taken up by many artists, activists and designers. In the 1990s it has spread onto every graphic format imaginable, from coffee cups to the websites of the Internet – in a show of comparable visual intensity. The foundations have been laid for a powerful (and at times necessarily brutal) visual imagery and symbolism – all of which can serve to confront Pro-life propaganda, keep the feminist arguments alive, and continually remind all women, including the generations to come, of the dangers of losing their hard-won freedoms.

5

Dear Sirs · man to man · manpower · craftsman
working men · the thinking man · the man in the street
fellow countrymen · the history of mankind
one-man show · man in his wisdom · statesman
forefathers · masterful · masterpiece · old masters
the brotherhood of man · Liberty Equality Fraternity
sons of free men · faith of our fathers · god the father
god the son · yours fraternally · amen **words fail me**

Words for a decade of redefinition:
3 The Handbook of Non-Sexist Writing by Casey Miller and Kate Swift which impacted on language use in both the public and private spheres, Britain, revised edition, 1981.
4 The Official Politically Correct Dictionary and Handbook, by Henry Beard and Christopher Cerf, saw the humourous side of a movement intending to bring social change by instigating changes in language and its use, USA, 1992.
5 Postcard published by The Women's Press in London, 1981.
6 Reworked billboard ad by guerrilla graffitists 'Saatchi & Someone' (original text in red box: 'United Colors of Benetton'), Britain, 1990–1.

6

lesbian mothers
are everywhere

Anarchy and unrest: the fairy tale ends

When the late 1970s heralded a new era of Conservative politics in Britain, revolutionary movements, including feminism and the peace movement, took to the streets or went underground, and struck back with a vengeance. The tension between the various forces brought a decade of social redefinition in the 1980s, with the dismantling of gender stereotypes, notions of 'beauty', sexuality, marriage and the family. The mainstream media hype of wedded bliss, typified in Britain by the wedding in 1981 of Lady Diana Spencer and Prince Charles, would be faced with a counter-movement of sharp-edged, smart-mouthed social analysis, wielded by activists and alternative media such as the radical girls' magazine *Shocking Pink*.

The Punk movement of the mid- to late 1970s played a key role in the visualizing of this alternative view of society, and also produced a brave, new image for women. Punk modes of individualism and urban creativity – such as playing in bands, do-it-yourself style and subversive fashion, street publishing and fanzines – all offered women new vehicles for self-expression. An alternative image was put forward of woman as tough, streetwise, uncompromising and with attitude, defining sex and power on her own terms.

1 **Vivienne Westwood, creator of subversive Punk clothing, wearing her 'Destroy' t-shirt. Taken from Terry Jones' Not Another Punk Book, Britain, 1978. Photo by Norma Moriceau.**
2 **Guerrilla graffiti as photographed and documented by Jill Posener, Britain, 1979.**
3 **'Love and Marriage', poster with encased wedding confetti, by Julia Church, Australia, 1986.**

4 **Badge created by Carole Spedding during the year of the royal wedding of Charles and Diana, and sold to help finance the feminist magazine Spare Rib, Britain, 1981.**
5 **Poster attributed to ISIS, Britain, mid-1980s.**
6 **Front and back cover of the spiky feminist girls' magazine Shocking Pink, issue 4, October–November 1988, Britain.**

Among the most memorable feminist statements to emerge from the Punk context in the late 1970s were the graphic collages of Manchester-based artist 'Linder' (Linda Sterling), a number of which formed the publicity for the Buzzcocks' single Orgasm Addict, and rapidly achieved the status of Punk icons. Her rebellion against the stereotypes and traditions of the time remains apparent throughout her series of collage-works, created by placing a pile of men's magazines (on cars, porn and so on) on one side of her desk, a pile of women's magazines (on fashion, the home, etc) on the other side, and then attempting to marry the two graphically. The collages also bear the influence of other recognized male/female traditions of that era and culture: a certain vintage of dingy porn which always paired nude female figures with gas cookers and other domestic appliances, as well as the ultimate importance attached to girls learning to cook; failure to put a meal on the table on time might earn the cook a slap from her husband.

Linder's overall series constructs a portrait of a world of restricted roles, possessive sexual expectations and demands, and closed doors: the reality behind the fairy tale now exposed and the beginnings of its sour rejection by a new generation of young women.

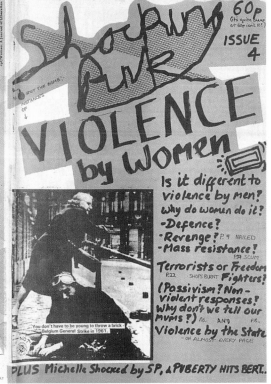

1

2

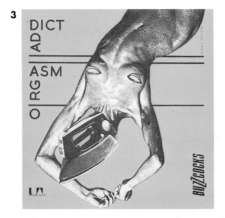

3

The meticulous cutting and craft of the artist Linder, shown in pho-tomontages created in the late 1970s:

1, 2 Linder's collages for The Secret Public, a one-off fanzine, Britain, late 1970s.

3 Cover sleeve of the record single 'Orgasm Addict' by the Buzzcocks, with type and design by Malcolm Garrett, using a photomontage by Linder, Britain, 1979. The pho-tomontage rapidly became a Punk icon.

4, 5 Satirical comments
on relationships, love
and romance by Linder,
Britain, late 1970s.

Romance

Girlpower:
the girls bite back

1, 2 Girlpower badges, Britain early 1980s.

3–11 'Some Girls', a series of nine posters resulting from a three-year research project. Researched by Carola Adams and Leah Thorn, and designed by Graham Peet and Johnnie Turpie, all in collaboration with Madeley Young Women's Group. Published by the National Association of Youth Clubs; and produced by the Some Girls printshop, Telford, Britain, 1981.

The fairy-tale image of sugar-sweet little girls came to an end in the 1980s. Girlpower took hold and unleashed its fury through irreverent projects such as the London-based girls' magazine *Shocking Pink*, which provided a feminist alternative to what they called the 'propaganda' of existing popular girls' magazines, invariably crammed full of tips on make-up and boyfriends. Originating in the early 1980s, *Shocking Pink* ran for only a few issues. It was later resurrected as the *Shocking Pink 2* collective in 1987, and produced one of the liveliest, young, radical feminist magazines around, lasting, despite being unfunded, until 1992 when it split to create a foundation for the grassroots feminist magazines *Bad Attitude* in London and *Subversive Sister* in Manchester.

Another popular visual manifestation of girlpower came through a series of posters created by the Some Girls project and published by the National Association of Youth Clubs (NAYC). Research and discussion with young women's groups on the difficulties of being young and female resulted in a gutsy, pictorial essay of hopes, hates and real-life experiences relating to issues such as contraception and stereotyping. Produced in poster, and later postcard, form, the series was widely appreciated at grassroots level, but apparently frightened off promises of government sponsorship at the time.

3

4

5

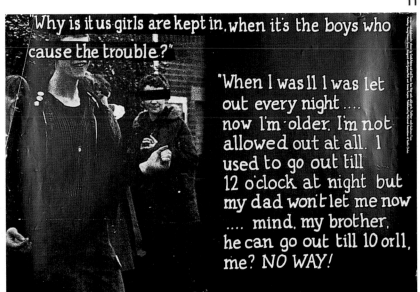

Womanpower vs mediapower

Throughout the 1980s, women found themselves continually in contention with media messages, and invariably did something about it, organizing and staging protests, and producing their own propaganda.

They challenged oppressive media representations of women in particular, and began to break through the stereotyping and cultural programming which such messages imposed, including notions that women were totally reliant on men, or that they were useless when past a certain age. In retaliation, artists, women's groups and alternative magazines everywhere produced positive statements, both visual and verbal, about women. Sexism in language and writing had become an issue, bringing an awareness of the power implications in language. Consequently, negative labels were reclaimed, such as 'dykes' and 'superbitch', and reinforcing statements were made, including 'Girls are powerful', 'Grandmas are great', and all were paraded on badges and t-shirts or printed as solidarity messages on postcards.

Womanpower also manifested itself in protests and in the creation of support networks. Women maintained a strong presence in the Peace Movement in Britain, as shown by the Women's Peace Camp at Greenham Common (yet another example of continual conflict with the press, see Chapter Five, pages 226–9). At the start of the decade in the USA, one woman in California, whose thirteen-year-old daughter had been killed by a hit-and-run drunk driver, decided to turn pain into positive action. She set up a group consisting of mothers who had lost children in drunk-driving crashes, called Mothers Against Drunk Driving (or MADD). It grew from one chapter established in 1980 to a grassroots network (in the 1990s) of over 500 chapters, state organizations and community action teams. It includes men, women, victims and non-victims, all determined to stop drunk driving and to support victims of drunk driving crashes. For over a decade they have run hotlines and support services for victims, staged candlelight vigils and memorials for those lost, lobbied for tougher laws in relation to drunk driving, kept a watchdog's eye on alcohol advertising, and have been responsible for numerous public awareness campaigns employing diverse media: radio and print public service announcements, posters, brochures, and direct mail. MADD is now one of the most widely recognized and influential public service organizations in America.

1940s PEGGY. MOTHER OF EIGHT.   Newmarch

WOMEN HOLD UP HALF THE SKY!

Newmarch 78

EVERY MOTHER is a WORKING MOTHER

NUCLEAR *families* WASTE *energy*

2   3   4

EVERY MOTHER IS A WORKING MOTHER

OGNI MADRE E' UNA LAVORATRICE
SVAKA MAJKA JE RADNA MAJKA
SER MADRE ES SER TRABAJADORA
ΚΑΘΕ ΜΗΤΕΡΑ ΕΡΓΑΖΕΤΕ

5

Celebrations and demonstrations of womanpower:
1   Poster with photo captioned '1940s. Peggy, mother of eight.', by Ann Newmarch, Australia, 1988.
2–4   Badges, Britain, mid-1980s.
5   Poster by Jan Fieldsend (Lucifoil Posters), printed at The Tin Sheds, University of Sydney, Australia, 1981.

6, 7   Logo and photo of a demonstration, from the US organization Mothers Against Drunk Driving or MADD, founded in 1980.
8   Postcard showing disabled women protesting against negative stereotyping in the (press) media, Britain, late 1980s. Photo by Brenda Prince.

6

7

Mothers Against Drunk Driving

8

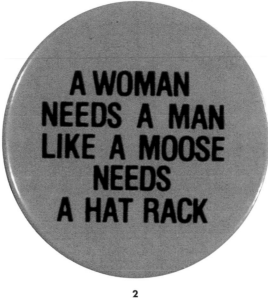

1

2

3

4

1–3 Badges showing variations on a popular feminist quote, Britain, mid-1980s.
4–6 Banners and newsletter from the London-based Older Feminists Network, founded in 1981. The long OFN banner (fig 4) was made in 1987 by Joan Woodward and others. Photos by Astra Blaug.

7 Logo for the National Black Women's Health Project founded in 1981, USA.
8 Poster announcing the Fourth International Feminist Bookfair, to be held in Barcelona in 1990. Designed by Pilar Villuendas and Josep Ramon Gomez.
9–13 Badges celebrating woman-power, Britain, late 1980s.
14 'My Message to the Women of Our Nation... Tough!', poster designed and printed during Margaret Thatcher's first term of office by See Red Women's Poster Collective, Britain, 1979.

5

6

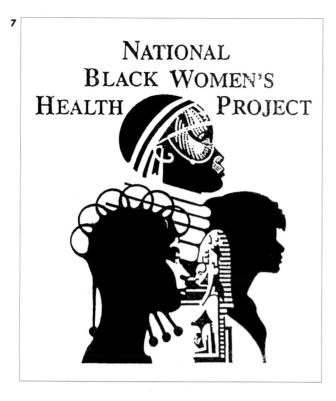

7

National Black Women's Health Project

IV International Feminist Bookfair

Barcelona, 19th-23rd June 1990 at Drassanes

IV FIRA INTERNACIONAL DEL LLIBRE FEMINISTA • IV FERIA INTERNACIONAL DEL LIBRO FEMINISTA • IV FOIRE INTERNATIONALE DU LIVRE FEMINISTE

INFORMATION: TELS. 487 13 93 / 487 28 54. FAX (34-3) 215 52 73

8

A WOMAN'S PLACE IS EVERYWHERE

9

SOME LEADERS ARE BORN WOMEN

10

WOMEN AGAINST APARTHEID

11

SUPER BITCH

12

AMAZON

13

MY MESSAGE TO THE WOMEN OF OUR NATION..

14

Feminist publishing in Britain

Boosted by an expansive economic climate, feminist publishing houses achieved real commercial power in the 1980s. Feminism may have proved to be too radical and unmarketable in the 1970s, but by the late 1980s the mood had changed dramatically and the outlook was positive. Britain led the field with the strength of feminist houses such as Virago and the Women's Press, whose greatest achievement collectively was to move feminist books out of radical bookshops and into mainstream outlets, thereby attaining a broader recognition and demand for women's writings than ever before.

Virago Press, the first feminist press to be registered in Britain (in 1973), started out reprinting forgotten works by women of past generations, such as Vera Brittain and Sylvia Pankhurst, as well as encouraging new work by modern writers. Virago grew from an initial list of eleven books to produce up to a hundred books a year, determined to be read by women of all ages and by a wider audience too – not just by feminists. They maintained a strong brand image throughout the decade, starting off with a distinctive masthead, Eve's green apple, as their logo, and their caustic name. (Virago, originally meaning 'an heroic woman', has in modern times come to be defined as a shrewish, bullying woman; and the Press enjoyed the shock value that the name carried.)

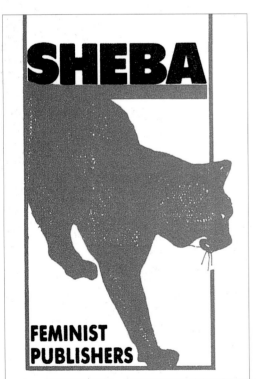

The Women's Press was set up in 1978 and ten years later was producing fifty to sixty new books a year. In addition to broadening the platform for women's writing, it was particularly respected for printing new authors or 'rising stars'. A sense of brashness, vitality and risk-taking was therefore an intrinsic part of its strong and intentionally rough-edged corporate identity, created and executed throughout its history by art director Suzanne Perkins. Key elements included the use of Day-Glo pink or rhodamine red as symbolic of rebellion; a sense of humour beautifully expressed in the original steam iron logo drawn by illustrator Donna Muir; a functional, economical work-a-day feel from the use of Gill Sans typeface and the brash use of basic or process colours; and a strong and highly individual look for book jackets, derived from the frequent use of new, unknown artists and illustrators. The Women's Press was therefore also known for giving artistic 'rising stars' their first print job, and had a loyal following in art colleges and other cultural establishments to prove it. In a variety of ways, the Women's Press was responsible for making feminist publishing a bright and brassy affair.

Other smaller (in some cases more specialized) presses maintained an international profile during this period, such as Attic Press in Ireland, Sybylla Press in Australia, Sheba Press in Britain (focusing on the writings of black women and lesbians), and the renowned Kitchen Table: Women of Color Press in the USA. But sadly, once the global economic bubble burst, many of these smaller presses slipped away or have remained under constant financial constraint in the recessionary climate of the 1990s.

6

Live authors...live issues

The Women's Press Ltd, 34 Great Sutton Street, London EC1V 0DX Tel: 01-251 3007

1   Symbol for Virago Press, Britain, late 1980s.
2   Poster celebrating Virago's twentieth anniversary (1973–93), Britain, 1993.
3   Logo for Sheba feminist publishers, Britain, late 1980s.
4   Logo for the Attic Press in Dublin, Ireland, late 1980s.

5, 6   Imprint graphic and promotional poster for The Women's Press in London, late 1980s. Drawing of the iron symbol by Donna Muir; art direction for all aspects of the graphic identity by Suzanne Perkins.

Celebrating women: recognition and herstory

1

The 1980s reinforced what the 1970s had started, building on the foundations of 'women's culture' and furthering a view of history from a woman's perspective. The ghosts of Women's Past kept revealing new names and faces, while feminist publishers, women's institutions, new college courses on Women's Studies, researchers, artists and designers everywhere added to the body of information by and about women. The results of their explorations inspired books, conferences, exhibitions, environmental projects, and all manner of graphic material.

A few notable examples from around the world are shown here. Sheila Levrant de Bretteville's poured concrete-wall (8 feet high by 82 feet long) entitled 'Biddy Mason: Time and Place', was a tribute to a black woman who had been a midwife throughout her period of slavery, and later a philanthropist in nineteenth-century Los Angeles. Completed in 1990, the wall was erected on Mason's original homestead site. It holds limestone photographs of Mason, her documents (freedom papers, the deed to the land, early maps of Los Angeles), and slate panels describing her life and the city's history, all embedded in the

2

Forty-four settlers from Mexico establish the pueblo of Los Angeles— twenty-six have African ancestors, 1781.

1–4 'Biddy Mason: Time and Place', a poured concrete wall (8ft high x 82ft long, also with slate, granite and painted steel), created by Sheila Levrant de Bretteville as a tribute to one of Los Angeles' historic black women. USA, 1990.

4

She owns land.

3

5–16 *Pages from 'The First Feminists in Japan' calendar series produced by Workshop for Women Jo-Jo in Japan (taken from the years 1989, 1991, 1995 and 1996):*

5 *April 1989: Toyotake Rosho (1874–1930). Reciter of ballad dramas.*
6 *September 1991: Yamashiro Tomoe (1912–). Writer.*
7 *June 1995: Kimura Komako (1887–1980). Actress, dancer and mystic.*
8 *January 1996: Kusunose Kita (1836–1920). Suffragist.*
9 *December 1989: Hasegawa Teru (1912–1947). Anti-war activist and Esperantist.*
10 *November 1991: Sasamoto Tsuneko. First female news photographer.*
11 *August 1995: Kagawa Aya (1899–). Researcher, nutritionist and educator.*
12 *August 1996: Ishigaki Ayako (1903–). Peace activist and writer.*
13 *July 1989: Kuroda Chika (1884–1968). Chemist.*
14 *October 1991: Nozoki Yae (1916–). Pioneer aviator.*
15 *July 1995: Yamazawa Eiko (1899–). Photographer.*
16 *February 1996: Midorikawa Katako (1872–1962). Suffragist. (Names are listed with the last name first according to Japanese practice.)*

concrete. Thus the wall not only addresses women's historical concerns, but also includes broader issues of civic history and community.

The Amsterdam-based studio Wild Plakken, renowned for its graphic work for the Dutch anti-apartheid movement, has also focused on women's issues. It has produced extraordinary posters expressing women's history, and on the theme of women against apartheid (see Chapter Five, pages 212–3). The portable exhibition shown on page 139 was originated and executed in 1981 by Wild Plakken, showing eighty years of women's history (1898–1978) with an emphasis on the daily lives of ordinary women. Divided into three 'sections' of political struggle – House, Work and the Street – the exhibition was devised to be small, compact and easily erected: it folded up to fit into the boot of a car.

The 1980s saw renewed interest in political needlework and banners for use in a modern context. Banners played a prominent role in Greenham Common peace protests; and the 1989 exhibition of political needlework entitled 'The Subversive Stitch' borrowed its title from an influential book written earlier in the decade. Rozsika Parker's *The Subversive Stitch* (1984) was a historical study of the political role of embroidery – its place in shaping the ideals and constraints of 'femininity', as well as its use as a tool of resistance. Mention must also be made of Lisa Tickner's book *The Spectacle of Women: Imagery of the Suffrage Campaign 1907–14* (1987), the scholarly, definitive survey and cataloguing of all manner of graphics and visual spectacle relating to the British women's suffrage movement of the early part of this century, thorough in its description of the surrounding historical and political events.

Calendars became another way of delivering newly-researched 'herstories'. This included the start (in 1988) of Japan's only feminist calendar series, 'Sisters! The First Feminists in Japan', produced by Workshop for Women Jo-Jo. Each calendar has since introduced twelve more pioneering women from Japan's past and present, including suffragists, writers, scientists and social activists, as well as an early aviator, nuclear physicist, magician and others. The 1996 calendar marks fifty years of women's suffrage (achieved in 1946) by celebrating women who waged a protracted struggle, dating as far back as the activist Kusunose Kita in 1878. Early calls for women's civil rights were unfortunately quashed in 1890 by the Meiji government's issue of laws prohibiting women from political participation, imposing male superiority and a 'good wife, wise mother' model. Nevertheless, women's rights activism had been born, and Jo-Jo's calendar shows the long line of women who continued to fight back until the vote was finally achieved.

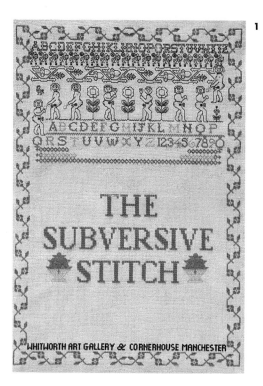

1 Invitation to 'The Subversive Stitch', an exhibition of political needlework, Britain, 1989.
2 Cover of the book The Spectacle of Women, Lisa Tickner's extensive survey of British suffrage imagery, published in Britain in 1987. (The banner illustrated on the cover was designed by women students at Cambridge University in 1912: see Foreword, page 6.)
3–6 Poster (fig 3) and three panels (figs 4, 5, 6) from a portable exhibition on eighty years of women's history in Holland (1898–1978), designed by Wild Plakken design group, Holland, 1981.
The exhibition title appears diagonally on the poster. It roughly translates 'As if you were throwing a bucket full of water', but is more a Dutch expression for having a large amount of something thrown at you, or (in this case) having a great deal to tell. There were three major themes, all shown on the panels here: Home, Work and the Street. (The writing on the women's bodies shown in the Street panel translates as 'Our Bodies Are Our Own'.) The exhibition was designed to be transported in the back of a car and set up within twenty minutes, and could be borrowed for a week or so, or for organizing quick events. Its value and popularity shows in the fact that it travelled and was used for nearly ten years. The exhibition was conceived by Lies Ros; researched by Lia Gorter, Lida Kerssies and Lies Ros; and text written by Neeltje Hennink. It was designed by Frank Beekers, Lies Ros and Rob Schröder – the members of Wild Plakken at that time. Photos by Pieter Boersma.

TENTOONSTELLING
Tachtig jaar vrouwenleven van alledag

3

WERK
Inleiding

11

Tachtig jaar geleden werd de positie van vrouwen op de arbeidsmarkt sterk bepaald door haar maatschappelijke status. Ze was echtgenote, moeder of dochter. De alleenstaande werkende vrouw was een nog een onbekend fenomeen. Hun lonen werden uitsluitend als aanvulling gezien van het gezinsinkomen. Hierdoor verdienden vrouwen vaak de helft of een derde minder dan mannen. Hun inkomsten waren noodzakelijk omdat een arbeiderssalaris alleen onvoldoende was voor de voeding en kleding van het gezin. Vrouwen deden het minste, zwaarste en slechtstbetaalde werk. Als ze in de huisindustrie werkten was hun positie nog slechter omdat thuis de uitbuiting door het isolement nog eens kon worden versterkt. De socialistische arbeidersbeweging heeft gejijverd voor allerlei beschermende maatregelen voor werkende vrouwen. Voor vrouwen uit de betere kringen lag de situatie anders. Zij wilden graag werken, maar mochten dat niet omdat het 'onfatsoenlijk' gevonden werd. Ze verschaften zich bijvoorbeeld toegang tot de middelbare school en de universiteit. En ze hielden zich bezig met – even onfatsoenlijk gevonden – 'liefdewerk'; hulp aan armen en zieken. Alhoewel de strijd van deze beide stromingen verschillend was, is ze voor beide zwaar geweest. De beroepen die vrouwen uitoefenden lagen in het verlengde van de huishoudelijke taak. Vrouwen waren dienstbode, naaister of verpleegster. Niet zelden oefenden vrouwen een beroep uit naast hun huishouden, waardoor ze twee banen hadden. Pas toen er sprake was van een economische bloeiperiode werden de meeste belemmeringen voor werkende vrouwen opgeheven en werden de arbeidsomstandigheden verbeterd.

Toch blijven er duidelijke verschillen bestaan tussen de arbeidspositie van mannen en vrouwen. Dat wordt het duidelijkst tijdens de economische depressie. Vrouwen worden dan het eerst ontslagen. Ze vormen een reserve-arbeidsleger. Aparte vrouwengroepen in vakbonden houden zich tegenwoordig bezig met de bijzondere positie van vrouwen op de arbeidsmarkt.

De bijzondere positie van vrouwen op de arbeidsmarkt als arbeidsreserve maakte in de jaren zeventig allerlei acties noodzakelijk.
Bij Optilon (rits-sluitingen) in Emmen vond een van de eerste, geslaagde stakingen plaats voor gelijk loon voor mannen en vrouwen. De Optilon-vrouwen werden gesteund door de vakbonden en de vrouwenbeweging (1972). Twee jaar later werd de wet op gelijk loon aangenomen.

De arbeidsomstandigheden van arbeidsters in de aardewerkfabrieken van Regout in Maastricht waren ronduit bar. Vrouwen deden het minste en slechtstbetaalde werk.

4

HUIS
1898-1980
Voorbehoedmiddelen en abortus

5

GROOTE OPENBARE VERGADERING op Maandag 20 Maart • 8 uur.
Spreker: Dr. RUTGERS van DEN HAAG
Onderwerp: Het Nieuw Malthusianisme en de Zedelijkheids-Wetten

9

Rond de eeuwwisseling waren vrouwen vaak ieder jaar zwanger. Het was slopend voor hun gezondheid die door de armoede toch al niet best was. De Nieuw-Malthusiaanse Bond, opgericht in 1881, was de eerste die informatie over het voorkomen van zwangerschap verstrekte. Coïtus interruptus, een sponsje in de vagina of een irrigator waarmee je de vagina spoelen kon waren de door de Bond aanbevolen, maar niet helemaal veilige, methoden. Het meest betrouwbaar waren het nog erg dure kondoom en het pessarium. Het laatste middel werd door de Amsterdamse arts Aletta Jacobs uit Engeland geïmporteerd. De weerstand ertegen was enorm. Vooral vreemd genoeg onder artsen, die meenden te weten dat je van een pessarium kanker krijgen kon en dat je er melancholisch van werd. Daarnaast was de kerk aktief om vrouwen op hun voortplantingsplicht te wijzen. Maar wanhopige vrouwen, zwanger van hun zoveelste kind, zochten hun eigen weg en belandden maar al te vaak bij illegale aborteurs. Het gerommel met breinaalden en zeepsop had regelmatig desastreuze gevolgen. Om de gevolgen tegen te gaan werd in 1911 in de Tweede Kamer het ook nu nog beruchte artikel 251 bis aangenomen, waarin abortus als een misdrijf tegen de zeden werd gezien. Het was een verscherping van de abortuswet van 1886 waarin abortus al eerder verboden werd. Abortus werd strafbaar, evenals het verhandelen of propageren van voorbehoedmiddelen. Het aantal abortussen nam hierna alleen nog maar toe. Intussen kwam er een duidelijke reaktie van de kerk. In 1918 werd de katholieke bond voor grote gezinnen opgericht. Deze bond heeft de moederdag uitgevonden. De Nieuw-Malthusiaanse Bond, de enige die voorbehoedmiddelen bleef verkopen, groeide ondanks de weerstand. In 1939 telde het meer dan 30.000 leden. Door de oorlog en de nadruk op het gezinsleven in de tijd daarna, verminderde de belangstelling voor geboortebeperking. In 1953 werd Dr. Storm, voorzitter van de NVSH – de naoorlogse voortzetting van de Nieuw-Malthusiaanse Bond – veroordeeld wegens het uitvoeren van abortussen. In de jaren zestig was de ontwikkeling niet meer tegen te houden. In 1965 had de NVSH een record aantal leden, 200.000, dat daarna daalde door de enorme populariteit van een nieuw voorbehoedmiddel, de pil. Toen in 1967 het verbod op de verkoop van voorbehoedmiddelen opgeheven werd, bleef de NVSH alleen nog noodzakelijk voor het laten aanmeten van een pessarium. (Als gevolg daarvan richtte de bond zich op zaken als relatieproblemen, pedofilie en homoseksualiteit.)

Abortus bleef strafbaar. De diskussie over legalisering laaide op. De afgelopen tien jaar is de strijd voor een legale, abortus die door het ziekenfonds wordt vergoed waarbij de vrouw beslist het belangrijkste onderwerp geweest in akties van vrouwen. Als het pessarium, het kondoom, de spiraal, het schildje of de pil faalden, als vrouwen te weinig kennis van voorbehoedmiddelen tóch zwanger werden, dan moest er een mogelijkheid zijn om de ongewenste zwangerschap te breken. Daarvoor werden er vanaf 1969 Stimezoklinieken geopend, daarvoor werd in 1974 de kliniek Bloemenhove bezet en de aktiegroep 'Wij vrouwen eisen' opgericht. Talloze abortusdemonstraties zijn erop gevolgd. Artikel 251 bis staat nog steeds in het Wetboek van Strafrecht.

139

STRAAT
Inleiding

18

Aan het eind van de vorige eeuw hadden vrouwen geen recht van spreken. Figuurlijk gesproken. Voor alles wat ze deden hadden ze toestemming nodig van hun vader of echtgenoot. Ze hadden geen politieke rechten en hadden dus ook geen stemrecht; ze hadden geen toegang tot het voortgezet onderwijs; vrouwen uit de betere kringen mochten niet werken en arbeidsters die moesten werken kregen de helft van het mannenloon omdat ze vrouw waren. Vrouwen uit de betere kringen die getrouwd waren, werden zo gedwongen tot ledigheid. Ze kwamen daartegen in opstand. Er ontstond de Vrouwenbeweging. Ze probeerden het eerst kiesrecht te krijgen. Het heeft tot 1919 geduurd voordat dat erdoor was. Daarna kon dus goed begonnen worden met de strijd voor gelijkwaardigheid van mannen en vrouwen. De strijd gaat door tot op de dag van vandaag. Zoals het kiesrecht het belangrijkste onderwerp was van de 'eerste feministische golf', zo is de strijd voor abortus het 'belangrijkste' onderwerp van de 'tweede feministische golf'. De strijd die door de meeste vrouwen wordt ondersteund.

Parallel aan de 'eigen akties', hebben vrouwen zich sinds het begin van deze eeuw ook massaal ingezet voor de vrede en voor een menswaardig bestaan. Dat leidde tot vredesmarsen en anti-fascistische akties. Bij al deze akties blijkt hoe belangrijk een organisatie, een vereniging of een komitee is. Het is echter wel duidelijk dat het belang daarvan in de loop der tijd verschuift. De vrouwenbeweging is op dit moment veel breder en heeft een veel diepgaander effekt op de maatschappij dan we hier kunnen laten zien.

Utrecht, 14 maart 1970. Duizendeen leuze op een vergadering van vrouwenaktiegroepen in de leus 'Baas in eigen buik'.

BAAS EIGEN

Baas EIGEN

6

Taking to the streets:
art activism in the USA

The 1980s also became a decade of social critique in the USA, particularly developed through urban expression and self-publishing. Art activists such as Jenny Holzer and Barbara Kruger expanded social comment into the environment, using formats such as massive electronic signs, installations, billboards, stickers, t-shirts or street posters. Holzer defined a new form of urban/visual poetry with her 'Truisms' (1978–87), while Kruger used her editorial design instincts to produce incisive critiques of modern culture through photomontages of text and image, as if forcing modern magazine culture to ask provocative (if not profound) questions. City streets were also home to the posters and demonstrations of the Guerrilla Girls, the anonymous feminist art activist group born in 1985 and charged with the mission of exposing sexual and racial discrimination in the New York art establishment. Their posters attacked the business operations of museums and galleries through the listing of statistics or 'naming of names', all conveyed with the ironic humour that has made them famous. It was their anonymity however that established them as a modern legend – they have worn gorilla masks or full gorilla suits for all public appearances, keeping an international audience of admirers baffled, but attentive, for over a decade.

1

2

3

5

1   'Mixed Messages' by Jenny Holzer: Spectacolor Board (repeating 18 messages) at Piccadilly Circus, London, 1989.
2   Street poster from Jenny Holzer's series of 'Truisms', New York City, 1978.
3   T-shirt worn by graffiti artist Lady Pink, from Jenny Holzer's series of 'Truisms', New York City, 1983.
4   'Men Don't Protect You Anymore', sign message from the 'Survival' series by Jenny Holzer, USA, 1983.
5   'We Don't Need Another Hero', painted billboard (installed in London), created by US artist Barbara Kruger, 1986–7.
6   Cover of Hot Flashes, nos 2 and 3 (double issue), 1994, the newsletter of the Guerrilla Girls.
7, 8   Street posters by the Guerrilla Girls, New York City, 1985 and 1989.

6

7

HOW MANY WOMEN HAD ONE-PERSON EXHIBITIONS AT NYC MUSEUMS LAST YEAR?

Guggenheim	**0**
Metropolitan	**0**
Modern	**1**
Whitney	**0**

GUERRILLA GIRLS
532 LAGUARDIA PL. #237
NEW YORK, N.Y. 10012

8

WHEN RACISM & SEXISM ARE NO LONGER FASHIONABLE, WHAT WILL YOUR ART COLLECTION BE WORTH?

The art market won't bestow mega-buck prices on the work of a few white males forever. For the 17.7 million you just spent on a single Jasper Johns painting, you could have bought at least one work by all of these women and artists of color:

Bernice Abbott · Anni Albers · Sofonisba Anguisolla · Diane Arbus · Vanessa Bell · Isabel Bishop · Rosa Bonheur · Elizabeth Bougereau · Margaret Bourke-White · Romaine Brooks · Julia Margaret Cameron · Emily Carr · Rosalba Carriera · Mary Cassatt · Constance Marie Charpentier · Imogen Cunningham · Sonia Delaunay · Elaine de Kooning · Lavinia Fontana · Meta Warrick Fuller · Artemisia Gentileschi · Marguérite Gérard · Natalia Goncharova · Kate Greenaway · Barbara Hepworth · Eva Hesse · Hannah Hoch · Anna Huntingdon · May Howard Jackson · Frida Kahlo · Angelica Kauffmann · Hilma af Klint · Kathe Kollwitz · Lee Krasner · Dorothea Lange · Marie Laurencin · Edmonia Lewis · Judith Leyster · Barbara Longhi · Dora Maar · Lee Miller · Lisette Model · Paula Modersohn-Becker · Tina Modotti · Berthe Morisot · Grandma Moses · Gabriele Münter · Alice Neel · Louise Nevelson · Georgia O'Keeffe · Meret Oppenheim · Sarah Peale · Ljubova Popova · Olga Rosanova · Nellie Mae Rowe · Rachel Ruysch · Kay Sage · Augusta Savage · Vavara Stepanova · Florine Stettheimer · Sophie Taeuber-Arp · Alma Thomas · Marietta Robusti Tintoretto · Suzanne Valadon · Remedios Varo · Elizabeth Vigée Le Brun · Laura Wheeling Waring

Information courtesy of Christie's, Sotheby's, Mayer's International Auction Records and Leonard's Annual Price Index of Auctions.

Please send $ and comments to:
Box 237, 496 LaGuardia Pl., NY 10012 **GUERRILLA GIRLS** CONSCIENCE OF THE ART WORLD

Taking to the streets: art activism in the USA

The issue of violence against women was also focused on the streets in the 1980s. New York art activist Ilona Granet created and erected street signs in lower Manhattan (known as the Emily Post series of 1985–8, named after America's best known authority on good manners). The signs were a protest against street behaviour threatening to women (cat-calls, whistles and suggestive comments) and made their point with wit and a sense of humour. Their underlying message, however, was deadly serious; such everyday bouts of intimidation could be viewed as symptomatic of potentially greater abuse.

The recognition of violence and assault in its many forms – rape, domestic violence, sexual harassment in the streets or at work, and so on – produced a surge of public service art and graphics such as publicity for rape help-lines and crisis services. It also generated intense protest art, including Sue Coe's harrowing illustration of a widely reported incident in New Bedford, Massachusetts, entitled *Woman Walks into a Bar – is Raped by Four Men on the Pool Table while Twenty Watch* (1983). It was one of a number of powerful pictorial protests against rape – created by Coe – which, in their brutal rendition, remained in the mind to disturb the viewer for weeks, months, even years afterwards.

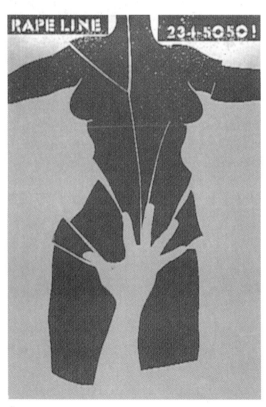

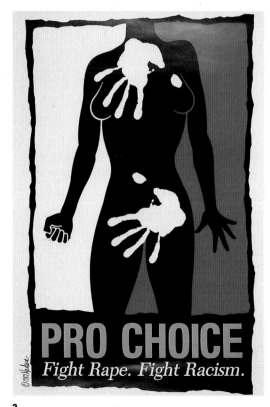

4

1 Feminist street sign (approx 2ft x 2ft) from the 'Emily Post series' by New York artist Ilona Granet, aiming to curb sexist street behaviour (cat-calls, whistles and so on) and bring back 'good manners'. The series of signs were posted in selected streets in lower Manhattan, 1986.

2 Poster for a rape help-line by Lanny Sommese, USA, 1986.
3 Pro-Choice poster commenting on a number of violations committed against women by both institutions and individuals, by Rob Cheung, USA, 1989.

4 Woman Walks Into Bar – Is Raped by Four Men on the Pool Table While Twenty Watch, illustrator Sue Coe's powerful pictorial indictment of rape, which marked a widely-reported incident in New Bedford, Massachusetts. USA, 1983.

Barbara Kruger

Your body

March on Washington
Sunday, April 9, 1989

is a

Support Legal Abortion
Birth Control
and Women's Rights

battleground

On April 26 the Supreme Court will hear a case which the Bush Administration hopes will overturn the Roe vs. Wade decision, which established basic abortion rights. Join thousands of women and men in Washington D.C. on April 9. We will show that the majority of Americans support a woman's right to choose.

In Washington: Assemble at the Ellipse between the Washington Monument and the White House at 10 am; Rally at the Capitol at 1:30 pm

The graphic culture of Pro-Life and Pro-Choice

2

The Pro-Life and Pro-Choice forces that built up over the decade in the USA developed their own distinctive forms of graphic culture. The rapidly-growing organizations of the anti-abortion movement produced substantially-funded campaigns of propaganda, using hard-sell tactics that slapped Pro-Life slogans on everything from balloons to bumperstickers, and imagery that grew more sensational as hard-sell translated into violent tactics and terrorism in the 1990s (often aimed at abortion clinics).

The Pro-Choice movement initially benefited from isolated projects of great conviction, such as Barbara Kruger's majestic poster 'Your body is a battleground', a call-to-arms on behalf of the 1989 march on Washington for abortion rights. But further threats to abortion rights in the early 1990s brought fresh strength to the resistance movement, both politically and graphically. A new visual language of resistance emerged, and art and design activists laid the foundations for an expressive movement of great intensity, employing both new and old graphic symbols and references. There have, for example, been references to the 'Gag Rule', which prohibited federally-aided family planning clinics from offering abortion counselling or referrals (a policy issued by the Reagan administration in 1988, and upheld in the Bush administration in 1991). Old symbols and references have also survived over the years and remain in use – for all cultures have their representations for backstreet abortion. In Britain, the reference has always been to knitting needles and disinfectant; in the USA it has traditionally been the coat hanger – a symbol that has been applied with renewed vigour in the new mood of resistance.

3

1 *'Your Body is a Battleground', poster by Barbara Kruger for the 1989 Pro-Choice March on Washington, calling for support for birth control and basic abortion rights for women. The image was also later used to promote women's rights issues in other countries.*
2, 3 *Balloons and bumperstickers from the Pro-Life movement, USA, 1992 (a Presidential election year).*

GAG ME

WITH A

COAT HANGER

1

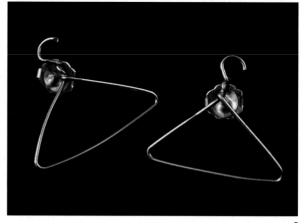

2

Our Bodies, Our Lives, Our Right to Decide

Abortion without Apology–
We Won't Go Back!

3

The coat-hanger remains a potent symbol for abortion, particularly in the USA:
1   Poster by US artist Robbie Conal, condemning Chief Justice William Rehnquist – one of five Supreme Court members who upheld the 'Gag Rule' in 1991.

2   Pro-Choice earrings, sold by NOW (the National Organization for Women), USA, 1995.
3   Pro-Choice poster by T Forman, Fireworks Graphics Collective, USA, 1989.
4   'Dr Back Street Bush Develops a Case of Fetal Attraction', illustration by Sue Coe, USA, 1992.

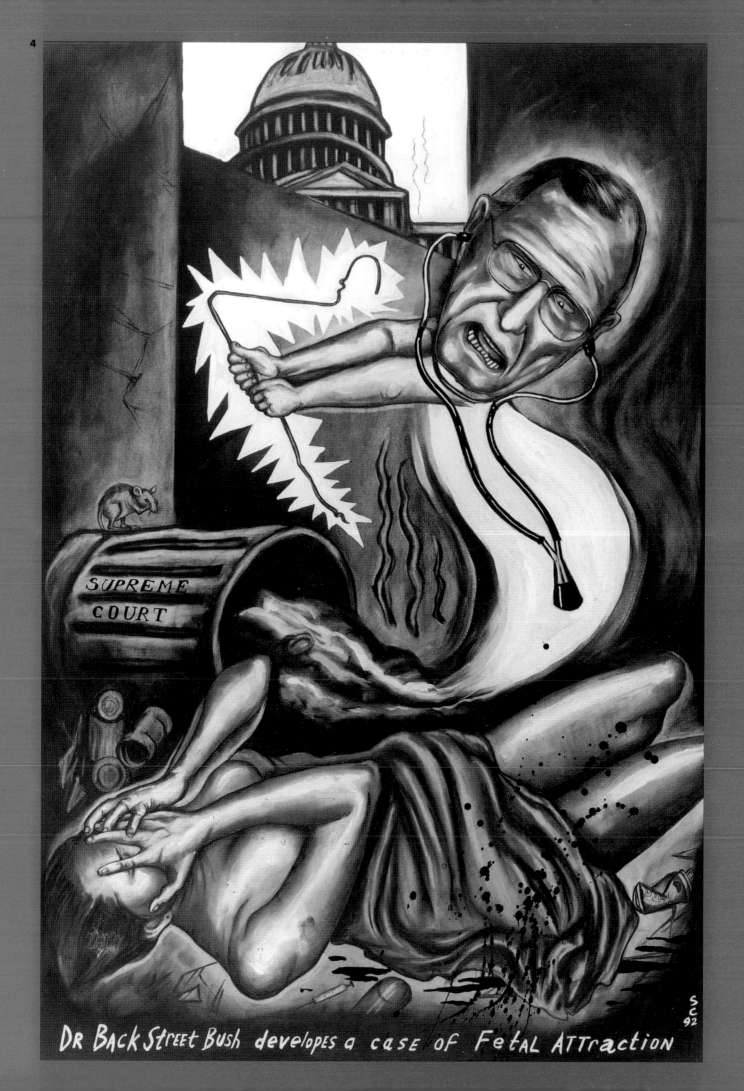

DR BACK STREET BUSH developes a case of FETAL ATTRACTION

Fighting Back and Looking to the Future (1990s)

From the very start, the 1990s proved to be about issues relating to power: confrontations with power, having power, even romancing power. 'Being in control' became, for many women, as much a matter of finding ways of exercising control over their own lives as of fighting back against controls imposed on them or defending their achievements. Visibility and empowerment became new words for the same goal: self-determination, and nothing less.

The 1990s have been about breaking down the security of gender barriers and the exploration of new roles and new identities – crossdressing, androgyny, role reversal, non-gender, transgender, and even gender-switching on the Internet. Various women have become icons of power: Madonna's obsessions with power, and the supermodels' use of their power in the media for political purposes are two clear examples. The power of media misogyny and the religious Right in the USA provoked a resistance movement that found artists such as Barbara Kruger and activist groups such as SisterSerpents expressing themselves in tougher, more explicit terms than ever before.

Yet it has become increasingly important to understand the opponent: Naomi Wolf's book *The Beauty Myth* (1990) indicated how the image of female beauty has become a 'political weapon', a form of social control, stymying the advancement of women and their rights. This issue formed part of the analysis in Susan Faludi's *Backlash* (1991), whose study of the growth of anti-feminism over the 1980s soon provoked a wave of fury and activism. So, to a great extent the 1990s have also been about being angry and taking action: having something to say, and saying it through fanzines, queerzines, electronic zines, music, e-mail, faxes or other forms of communications technology – through the underground, as Riot Grrrls have done, or through the use of mainstream media and direct action by, for example, the Women's Action Coalition (WAC) or the Lesbian Avengers.

Now, drawing close to the new millennium, the 1990s have become a platform from which the Beyond can be glimpsed: a vision of the transformations and connections offered by the new technologies, or the potential of the

Gender-bending, grrrlpower, androgyny and 'connecting' as preoccupations of the 1990s:
1 Body graffiti (here printed on women's underpants) in the 'Half-Dressed City Gent' outfit designed by Vivienne Westwood, Spring 1990 collection, Britain. (Photo by Robyn Beach.)
2 Sketch cartoon advertising the zine Screambox, by Justina. Taken from the ad pages of Real Life magazine (no 21/22, 1991), CalArts Press, USA.
3 'Equal Equal', sticker by Claire Corey, USA, 1995.
4, 5 A selection of fanzines and comics from West Coast USA (fig 4) and London (fig 5), 1993–5.

EQUAL
EQUAL

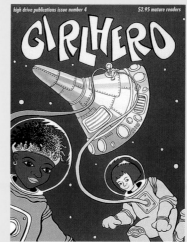

Internet as another medium in which women can 'find a voice'. The emerging digital technologies may offer a world in which women are free from patriarchal oppression, and may provide a new arena in which we can transform ourselves. Or they may lead to a nightmarish scenario of corporate exploitation and social division. But whatever the future may hold, it is obvious that women must become involved with the technologies now – if they are to be fully active in their development and use throughout the next century.

Being in control:
power images and power plays

Being in control, in the early 1990s, meant creating a power image, often through sexual confrontation. As in the Punk movement of earlier decades, music provided women with a useful starting point. Madonna, the pop superstar, created the quintessential, sex-based power-image for the 1980s and 1990s, packaging her sexuality through music, graphics (print) and film. At times, the 'image' threatened to overshadow all; after multiple changes and guises, notions of self-empowerment slid into self-obsession. Nevertheless, Madonna provided a powerful new role-model for women, and carved out new ground for strong women in the music industry. Some even argue her status as a feminist icon.

The American youth culture known as Grunge produced such inspirational rock stars as Courtney Love and her band Hole, L7, and Babes in Toyland – all of whom created a defiant form of self-expression through sexual confrontation, aggression and hard-driving energy. The reversal of gender roles, crossdressing and androgyny became an important part of their self-defined attitude. Sexual confrontation was also the hallmark of the Riot Grrrl movement. Fed up with the male domination of the Punk music scene and the music media, Riot Grrrls grew out of young women creating their own underground music culture, communicating through meetings, women-only gigs, letter-writing and (importantly) fanzines or Riotzines. Originating in America in 1991 and spreading to Britain soon after, the Riot Grrrl movement was fuelled by anger, frustration and a passion for feminism inspired by Faludi's *Backlash*. One of the ways in which Riot Grrrls showed their defiance of sexism was by writing words like 'slut' in black marker pens on their stomachs or bare arms, confrontationally reclaiming abusive words.

On both sides of the Atlantic, the subversive appropriation of language, gestures and images became an important part of young women's resistance to sexism, and the calling card of a new young generation of up-front feminism. Sexual confrontation consequently moved into the arena of fashion. Young British designer and feminist Karen Savage has used modern Girls-orientated fashion, and particularly 'club babe' t-shirts, as a format through which to question attitudes and centuries-old stereotypes. Her placement of word combinations such as virgin/whore and baby/bitch on the front and back of dresses, t-shirts, etc, transforms the clothing and its wearer into a defiant piece of walking concrete-poetry. The gestures of sexual directness and defiance printed on her t-shirts have almost become a trademark for a generation, typified by the vicious but stylish two-fingered 'up yours' symbol (page 150). Hence another stereotype has been overturned: fashion and glamour, traditionally about 'the beauty myth' and male control and possession over women, have mutinied – women now have the power to say 'up yours'.

Being in control has therefore also meant being visible. Lesbians found power and control through the Lesbian Avengers, the direct action group founded in 1992 in New York City, who have focused on strategies and issues vital to lesbian visibility and survival. With retribution on their minds and a kick-ass attitude, their call to action came through the brassy slogan 'We Recruit', a logo of a bomb with a lit fuse, ready to blow,

4

5

and a manifesto that says it all – shouting at fever pitch, in the brilliant typography of Carrie Moyer, who also designed the logo.

Another generation of satire and social critique (carrying on from Barbara Kruger, Gran Fury, the Guerrilla Girls *et al*) was embodied by Dyke Action Machine! (DAM!), the lesbian graphics project. Evolving from the activist organization Queer Nation, DAM! was founded in 1991 by Carrie Moyer, painter and graphic designer, and Sue Schaffner, photographer. DAM! produces public art/poster campaigns, pasted up around the city, which spoof general advertising by inserting lesbian images into a currently recognizable commercial ad. The result is a sharp critique of the crass and restrictive values often promoted through mainstream marketing, a critique which also provides recognition and visibility for lesbian culture.

Last, but most certainly not least, being in control in the 1990s has meant resistance to the increasing erosion of women's rights over ten years of conservative politics. Nowhere was this more evident, at the start of the new decade, than in the USA.

1

Fighting back: women's activism in the USA

Labelled by some the third wave, America's new era of feminism and activism was triggered by a number of developments: the threat in 1989 that the Supreme Court might overturn the abortion rights enshrined in *Roe vs Wade*; the acknowledgement of the counterattack on feminism, which found its most prominent expression in 1991 in Faludi's *Backlash*; as well as the intense media coverage in the autumn of 1991 of a number of cases highlighting society's increasing tolerance of violence against women. Anita Hill contested the nomination of Clarence Thomas to the Supreme Court, on grounds of sexual harassment; William Kennedy Smith was accused and acquitted of rape; the boxer Mike Tyson was accused and convicted of rape. All put sexual violence into media focus as never before. Out of this climate of outrage and media attention grew a number of activist groups – all committed to resistance, and often resorting to harsh graphic statements, to combat the equally harsh tactics of the political and religious right wing.

Women's Action Coalition, or WAC, founded in January 1992, was one of the most visible of these groups, directly linking its strategies with the power of the media. Its original membership was composed mainly of artists and designers, although it remained open to all women, and it committed itself to direct action on a wide range of issues relating to women's rights, particularly abortion rights, rape and other forms of violence against women. Its commitment to the visual power of design and the media was implied by its manifesto, which ends 'We will exercise our full creative power to launch a visible and remarkable resistance. WAC IS WATCHING, WE WILL TAKE ACTION.' Hence, strategies for confronting and, at the same time, using the media – and for motivation and identity through the use of graphics – were at the core of WAC. Their first action was a demonstration against the acquittals in the St John's rape trial where Marlene McCarty's famous all-seeing eye logo 'WAC is Watching' was introduced along with the WAC symbol of the blue dot, appropriated from the televising of criminal trials where it protects identity. Their drum corps, which also featured strongly from the start, was a shrewd device for leading chants at WAC actions. It attracted attention, directed the energy vented at protests, and kept the police and other threatening bodies in line. All such devices were designed to make effective use of the media, who were often invited to the protests. Portable blue dots, for example, were carried to

2

flash or display text messages and graphics easily picked up by television cameras during interviews and on-site broadcasts. Much of the eye-catching work used in early demonstrations was created by designers Bethany Johns and Marlene McCarty.

WAC excelled at running a high-profile, multi-media protest strategy, making use of all the resources of current communications technology – photocopy and fax machines, computers (desktop publishing and e-mail), video cameras, telephones and answering machines. It put itself forward through the use of print formats – posters, advertisements, flyers/handouts; body and fashion graphics – t-shirts, baseball caps, buttons, temporary tattoos; performance and sound, using drum rhythms, chants, costumes, banners; plus letter, fax and phone 'zaps'. For the following two years, WAC staged direct actions at large-scale events like the national Pro-Choice rally in 1992 in Washington DC and the Republican Convention in summer 1992 in Houston, Texas. But it also took action over countless other situations where it saw injustice or crimes against women, particularly in established legal and governmental practice. They were especially sharp at making those in positions of power accountable, confronting politicians, judges and others through the media. While the Guerrilla Girls insisted on naming names, WAC, in its line of 'demographics', paraded portraits of 'heroes' such as kd lang, and 'public enemies' such as George Bush. WAC was also well known for its skill at working the media, developing relationships with reporters and producers that led to its members appearing in newspapers, on magazine covers and on television. At the same time, it attempted to challenge media stereotypes of women activists, but without compromising or softening its message.

Information gathering was essential to WAC, both in its graphic and media campaign work. Its publication *WAC Stats* is evidence of its commitment to getting the research right: on issues relating to women it is, quite simply, a compilation of facts and figures, plainly designed in sans serif type (see page 158). Although most of the material it contains is gloomy, reading it is a strangely empowering experience, for identifying the issues is the first step to taking action. To this extent, the book is a good indicator of the emotional temper of the times.

The growth of WAC, originally based in New York, was phenomenal: in the first year (1992) weekly meetings numbered up to 500 in attendance; overall membership peaked at 2,000 in the autumn, and its base expanded to nearly thirty cities in the USA, as well as to Canada and France. WAC reached the level of a volunteer corporation with an elaborate network of members, supporters and media contacts, making it highly effective at enacting change. After two years in operation, with many successful actions under its belt, a Republican presidential line broken, and many new women candidates elected to office with its support, its members dispersed and moved on.[1]

During this period of intense activity, WAC collaborated with other activist groups, notably the Guerrilla Girls – still going strong and encompassing broader issues such as abortion rights, the Gulf War and homelessness – as well as the widely

Rebels of the new decade:
1 Being in control with a t-shirt from the 'Sex Symbol–Sex Target' collection by fashion designer Karen Savage (seen here wearing the t-shirt), Britain, 1994.
2 'Spliff' postcard, drawing by Morton, produced by Raven Images, USA, 1995.
3 Body graffiti shown on Kathleen Hanna, singer of Punk band Bikini Kill and one of the first contributors to the US Riot Grrrl movement of 1991. Photo by Linda Rosier, USA, 1994.

4 Poster for a fantasy film of dyke revenge by Dyke Action Machine! (Carrie Moyer and Sue Schaffner), USA, 1994.
5 Logo for the New York direct action group the Lesbian Avengers; designed by Carrie Moyer, USA, 1992.

5

known group, WHAM. Women's Health Action and Mobilization (f 1989) devoted itself to direct action in demanding and defending women's health issues. They were perhaps best known for supplying escorts to abortion clinics to accompany women past Pro-Choice harassers, countering the actions of groups such as Operation Rescue, as well as for targeting the sexist bias of organized medicine and pointing to the need for a focus on breast cancer. WHAM has generated posters, stickers, stencils, buttons, t-shirts, postcards and other forms of guerrilla graphics that thrive at street level, but has also set up discussions, strategies and information sources through e-mail and its own Web site – all motivated by the slogan 'Women's Health Care is Political!'

SisterSerpents, a collective of Mary Ellen Croteau and other anonymous feminist artists, represents yet another type of graphic critique which targets male oppression, and the deep embedding of misogyny in the media, business, religious institutions and, indeed, throughout society. Originating in Chicago in 1989 and spreading to other American cities, SisterSerpents have produced a large number of skilfully constructed poster-collages, usually pasted on walls in the street, which are disturbingly effective at confronting the propagation of sexism in all its forms – in little boys' games, wartime pin-ups, and a wide assortment of other 'harmless' social practices.

A veritable catalogue of stickers with suitably poisonous phrases, rubber stamps, manifestos and collective exhibitions have added to the weight of the SisterSerpents' statements. Most significantly, they have been responsible for delivering a new form of graphic rage. Their visual language can be extremely humorous, but it is also, above all,

1

deeply confrontational and at times even violent (making a point of 'going too far') – in direct retaliation against the real violence women suffer. Hence a recipe for stopping a rapist is presented in a poster showing a well-known television chef, beaming from behind a surreal banquet of food, and brandishing a kitchen knife – with male genitalia propped on the end. 'Go for the groin, gals!', the poster quips (page 160). In a direct response to anti-abortion groups who use images of the foetus (producing ghoulish propaganda

A new wave of US women's rights activism energized the 1990s:
1 Installation by US artist Barbara Kruger, USA, 1991.
2 Poster by Guerrilla Girls satirizing the well-known American politician Newt Gingrich, USA, 1995.
3 Sticker and badge produced by Women's Health Action and Mobilization (WHAM!), the New York-based reproductive rights and women's health group, USA, 1995.

2

WHO IS THIS SLIMY CREATURE?

Raised by a single mom, but wants to put other fatherless children in orphanages.

Smoked pot in college, but seeks harsher penalties for drug use.

Dodged the draft, but plans to increase military spending.

Rants about government corruption, but agreed to a $4.5 million book advance/bribe from a company under investigation by Congress.

Divorced wife number one while she was in the hospital with cancer and is a deadbeat dad, but supports "traditional family values."

IT'S NEWT!

A PUBLIC SERVICE MESSAGE FROM GUERRILLA GIRLS

3

BREAST CANCER
WHAM!
WOMEN'S HEALTH ACTION AND MOBILIZATION
212/713-5966
AN EPIDEMIC

WOMEN'S HEALTH
WHAM!
ACTION & MOBILIZATION

4

4 'Bend Over I'll Drive', an installation of paintings (heat transfer on canvas) in which the artist inserts her own language into popular slogans, and thus subverts two male-orientated forms of communication: bumperstickers and paintings (it is therefore an obvious poke at the male art world). Created by Marlene McCarty, USA, 1990.

5, 6 Also included in the installation (fig 4) were two specially-printed bumperstickers, 'Bend Over I'll Drive' and 'Pray for RU486'. (RU486: a drug used for non-surgical termination of pregnancy, available in some countries but forbidden in the USA.) Examples of both bumperstickers could be taken away by visitors, and are shown here displayed on cars.

imagery of 'foetuses' or abortion remains, and sticking foetus logos on bracelets and balloons), SisterSerpents have reclaimed the foetus and turned it to their own purposes, exposing its oppressive manipulation by the Right. One of their most controversial posters shows a foetus under the title 'For all you folks who consider a fetus (sic) more valuable than a woman', followed by a list of suggestions such as 'Have a fetus cook for you, Have a fetus affair, Jerk off to photos of naked fetuses', and others, including 'Fuck a Fetus'. Although humour serves to lighten the touch and strengthen the comment, such tactics have inevitably generated intense anger. Nevertheless, SisterSerpents have undertaken a brutal mission, attempting to reclaim an intimate symbol which has now come to signify the terrorization and ultimate oppression of women; only brutal tactics will do.

In addition to these feminist activist groups, individual voices have made valuable contributions to the visual language of resistance. Barbara Kruger (exerting the greatest influence since the 1970s) tackled issues of violence; Peggy Diggs took on domestic violence (see Chapter Five, page 204); Sue Coe grappled with the horrors of rape as well as creating an icon to Anita Hill's ordeal; Marlene McCarty made explorations into the American psyche and its prejudices; Mary Beth Edelson (creator of the feminized 'Last Supper' poster of the 1970s) produced a metaphor for power and self-determination in the image of a gun pointing out from the bedsheets, and so a place of vulnerability becomes symbolic of strength and retaliation (page 165).

Other groups, not necessarily feminist activists, lent understanding and vital imagery to the resistance. The art activist collective Gran Fury, responsible for producing some of the most challenging public imagery relating to AIDS awareness in the 1980s, aimed a number of their posters directly at women – as a group whose vulnerability is not widely acknowledged, in need of care, protection and information relating to the HIV virus and to AIDS. Women and HIV was also the subject of a widely acclaimed interactive installation, created in 1993 by the collective Class Action, as part of the exhibition 'Aiding Awareness: Women's Stories' in New Haven, Connecticut. The project included testimonies from women – in the various roles of health-care provider, patient, mother, sister, daughter, wife or lover – whose lives had been affected by the virus. Significantly, New Haven had one of the highest incidences in the USA of AIDS-related illness among women and children.

Class Action itself began as a collective of graphic designers and artists coming from Yale School of Art in the early 1990s, and has worked since then to create awareness of social issues through pro-active, largely self-authored, design. They have dealt with such issues as reproductive rights and domestic violence and have also taken on board the thankless task of being 'agitators' within the design community itself – pointing to such issues as the woefully small number of women speakers at design conferences and investigating oppressive representations of the female form in conference material and in general (see pages 172–3).

Finally, The Clothesline Project, started in 1990 as a lasting reminder of the violence perpetrated against women, consists of thirty-one hand-painted t-shirts hung on a clothesline, each one representing a woman or child who has experienced violence or abuse. Beginning with one line of thirty-one shirts, the project developed into a national network; by 1995 there were 250 clotheslines and 35,000 shirts. It is one of the most courageous and educational visual symbols of the 1990s (see Chapter Five, page 205); an extraordinary and overwhelming call to end violence against women.

1, 2 Posters by SisterSerpents, the Chicago art activist group that uses art to combat misogyny, USA, 1990 (fig 1) and 1989 (fig 2).
3 The provocative 'Fuck a Fetus' poster, by SisterSerpents, USA, 1989.

4 'Aiding Awareness', an interactive installation based on the personal testimonies of women (in New Haven, Connecticut) affected by AIDS, created by the art/design collective Class Action, USA, 1993. (Project team: Debra Drodvillo, Pamela Hovland, Marta Huzar, Mark Maltais, Brad McCallum, Louise Scovell, Tom Starr.)

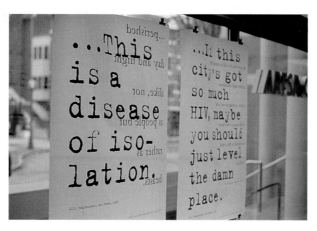

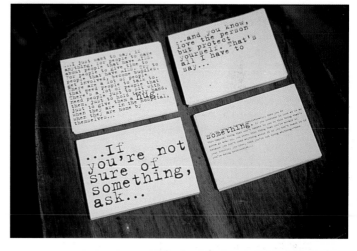

The feminization of new technology

Women have been programmed – socially, educationally and culturally – to stay away from computer technology. Computers have been a male domain: first developed on a large scale by the military, they were usually operated by men in white coats (either technicians or scientists, and of course science was a male domain). In visual terms, they produced imagery that was hard-edged, cryptic and male: dot-pattern outlines of Mickey Mouse (or even pin-ups) or squarish nerd-like repeat-patterns.

The advent of microprocessors in the 1970s and the increased availability of personal computers in the 1980s didn't help matters much – the computers became smaller, the culture remained the same. Women had only one role to play, if anything – and that was to be draped over a console in a bikini in order to sell the horrid little box. Cyberpunk, a movement in science-fiction writing that started in the early 1980s, also didn't help. It conjured up images of cyberspace and other visions of the technological future, traversed by hyper, young Punk-males, and created a popular culture in which men run the computers, jack-in and take drugs, while women are reduced to fetishized objects of desire. Needless to say, it all runs on high-voltage violence. The rise of computer video games propagated this image of a fantasy, shoot-em-up, boys computer culture, which reinforced stylized roles for women as ravishing beauties or princesses to be rescued, making computers even more alienating and repulsive to women.

Thankfully, this situation began to disintegrate in the 1990s. A female-driven cyberculture emerged, encouraged from 1985 on by scientific historian Donna Haraway's theories relating to the non-gendered cyborg – the fusion of organism and machine – as having potential for women's liberation.[2] For if gender is rendered obsolete, then women's oppression as experienced under patriarchy is not possible: hence equality becomes achievable. Soon many other female techno-theorists, science-fiction writers and digital artists proved men's God-given technological affinities (and their lack in women) to be a myth. Cyberfeminism, initially a media-hype term coined to describe a small group of theorists, has now become a term by which many female digital artists and designers define themselves, who wish to claim the technology for their own.

Another change, highly significant for visual designers, has made computer technology less alienatingly male. It has to do largely with developments in software and the interface (the means by which we interact with the machine). In previous decades, interaction with a computer was defined by programming languages and software based on linear structures and organizational hierarchies. In essence, the male vision of (corporate) cultural organization – centralized power, hierarchical systems and codes of control – was transplanted straight onto computers. But now, other structures have been developed and have come into play. The lateral organizational structures of webs and networks (found in hypertext, the World Wide Web and the global network of the Internet) are all more akin to the female or feminist vision of democratization and diversity that was first articulated in the 1970s, when women rejected male hierarchies and 'ladders', finding that they could think and live more easily in lateral movements. These developments were combined with a new emphasis on a visual interface, and although we are still often lumbered with lists and menus, things can only get better.

Donna J. Haraway

As more women become involved with the new technologies, more creative possibilities seem to open up. But the accompanying dangers are very serious. Every techno-feminist knows that social divisions may only be confirmed and exacerbated by future cyber-developments. The real question looming in the distance is 'who will have access to or possession of the technology?', and it is not only women who may be disempowered. The potential for introducing centralized power structures on the vastness of the Internet is great; the potential for a small minority owning and controlling the new currency of information is equally great. So the message of the moment is that women must not hesitate. They must claim the technology for their own while the debate and the development is happening – get it, use it, explore it and transform it – or risk being excluded forevermore, subject to the same old male-orientated representations and constructs.

At the moment, women, virtual sisters, cyberfeminists, techno-babes, spiderwomen and cybergirls seem to be transforming the shape of the future. Women are using digital technology for research, education and empowerment: for connecting across continents as never before and, as in times past, sharing experience and information. They are also beginning to explore its great potential for breaking down divisions of distance or wealth, as development agencies continue to plant monitors in the most interesting and unusual places. This is particularly true in certain parts of Africa, for example, which have 'jumped' a generation of technology, missing out faxes and going straight on to e-mail and the Internet (see Chapter Five).

Women are also exploring the new technologies creatively. Although any proper discussion would fill an entire book, it is worth mentioning just a few highlights on this front. Christine Tamblyn's interactive CD-ROM, 'She Loves It, She Loves It Not' is a primer on the subject of women and technology. It provides an enjoyable and informative compilation of reasons, examples and references relating to the exclusion of women from technology, which is shown to be a facet of male domination over women. The message is enhanced by the creative use of the multi-media facility. The rigid finesse of the usual male-orientated graphic style of on-screen design is exchanged for a fluid experience of movement, sound and animated navigational tools that excite the user to interact with a body of researched facts, literary references, television ads, films and anecdotes.

VNS Matrix, a group of four Australian women artists, offer a new tack on cuntpower for the next century. They formed in 1991 with a mission, in part: 'to hijack cowboy toys and remap cyberspace'. Their interactive computer-simulation, entitled 'All New Gen' (1992) employs the constructs and mentality of boys-own computer games, but subverts the gender stereotypes. Hence, All New Gen and her band of renegade DNA Sluts (Patina de Panties, Dentata and the Princess of Slime) go on a journey to sabotage Big Daddy Mainframe, tangling along the way with various technomutants such as Circuit Boy (a techno bimbo and Big Daddy's sidekick), whom they castrate cyber-style at a convenient point. It is a wild and wonderfully orgasmic vision, which also subverts the notions of winning or losing, and even scoring. For the rules keep changing: ultimately 'the linear is redundant on the All New Gen Net, and the polymorphous and the perverse rule'.

The notion of connectivity fits in comfortably with the space-age futuristic mentality of the World Wide Web and the Internet. If we can't have space stations and be interplanetary, at least we can be cyber-social as Web sites begin to crop up everywhere, almost café-style. It is now possible to drop in and pay a visit to The Girlie Network, the interactive Web site for

1

Simians, Cyborgs, and Women
The Reinvention of Nature

4

NET CHICK
A Smart-Girl Guide to the Wired World

CARLA SINCLAIR

3

1 Until recently the 'boys' culture' of the computing world generated advertising and products that were full of sex and violence. Although not quite so upfront in presentation anymore, the promotion of boys' cyberculture still lives on. Britain, 1992.
2 Cover of scientific historian Donna J Haraway's book Simians, Cyborgs and Women (1991), containing 'A Cyborg Manifesto' and other writings that saw the beginning of a new female-driven cyber-

culture in the mid-1980s.
3 Virtual artist and designer Diane Gromala at work, USA, 1994/5. See pages 157, 186–7 for her explorations in the realm of virtual reality.
4 Getting the girls involved: cover of Net Chick, subtitled A Smart-Girl Guide to the Wired World, a guide to some of the wild minds and activities to be found on the Internet. Written by Carla Sinclair, USA, 1996.

5 Image taken from the popular Web site of the cyberfeminist zine Geekgirl, first created by Rosie Cross in Australia, 1995.
6 Poster publicizing 'Infiltrate', the art exhibition of the computer game simulation 'All New Gen', created by cyberfeminist art group VNS Matrix, Australia, 1992.

a fantasy television station created by New York's Dyke Action Machine! or to explore the lively forums of electronic zines such as *Geekgirl*, created by Rosie Cross in Australia.

The future promises excursions into new dimensions and other worlds, possibilities suggested in the experimental work in virtual reality conducted by Diane Gromala, US visual artist and designer. Her project 'Dancing with the Virtual Dervish: Virtual Bodies' (1994), created with dancer Yacov Sharir, combines a physical dance performance (a real experience of one dancer performing for an audience), with a journey through virtual environments – experienced by one person (an audience member or the dancer himself) using a head-mounted display and dataglove. The journey is simultaneously viewed by the entire audience by means of large video projections.

In the VR environment, the dancer/HMD user enters and journeys through an enormous body – Gromala's – passing through a skeleton frame wrapped with letterforms and text, and entering organs that operate like chambers, and open up into further chambers. A virtual representation of the dancer is also contained within the virtual body, manifested as a series of video-grabs, texture-mapped onto a planar surface. The dancer therefore exists simultaneously in two worlds – as a representation in the virtual environment, and as a performer in the physical space – and can, in essence, dance with himself. The project offers extraordinary performance possibilities, and exists in other iterations, where both audience and dancer don the equipment at various points. (A fuller description and illustrations of the project follow on pages 185–187.)

The experience of both dancer and interactors in the body, immersed within the virtual world of graphic and typographic imagery, offers clues to what may lie ahead in multidisciplinary experimentation. It also represents the ultimate non-linear experience: the reconfiguration of the outer and the inner. This introduces a fascinating prospect for women and their future cyber-explorations. For the private and public dimensions that have defined (and limited) women's experience have, in these experimental terms, ceased to exist. Outer and inner have merged. For the future of women's graphic expression, whether visual or textual, the implications are exhilarating. Forget about designing the page – become the page.

5

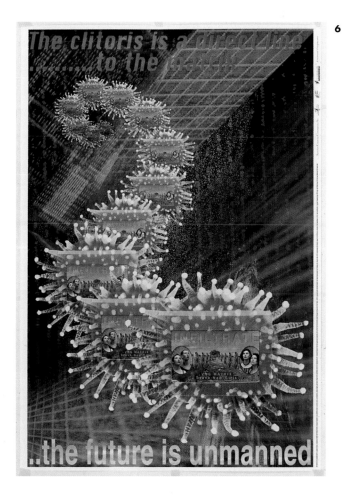

6

Fighting back: women's activism in the 1990s

The 1990s in the USA brought a new spirit of resistance to the erosion of women's rights experienced throughout a decade of conservative politics. Well-known art and design activists, such as Barbara Kruger, the Guerrilla Girls and Marlene McCarty, maintained high visibility, while new groups also began to emerge.

The New York-based Women's Action Coalition (1992–4) was one of the most prominent of the new activist groups, and committed itself to direct action on a variety of issues, particularly abortion rights and violence against women. One of its unique features was a direct engagement with the visual power of design and the media. It consequently ran a high-profile multi-media protest strategy, involving current communications technology (fax machines, computers, video cameras and telephone networks) as well as 'working the media' – by utilizing both press and broadcast coverage to strategic advantage. It also employed a wide range of more traditional media formats to great effect, such as demo-graphics (placards and signs), t-shirts and baseball caps, advertisements and flyers. The famous WAC blue dot symbol was appropriated from the blue dot used to protect identities in televised trials; while designer Marlene McCarty was responsible for their powerful logo of a watchful, all-seeing eye. She also collaborated with Bethany Johns to create much of the graphic work used in early WAC demonstrations.

1 Inside spread and cover from WAC Stats: The Facts About Women, published by the Women's Action Coalition (WAC), USA, 1992. The cover bears the WAC logo of the eye, by Marlene McCarty.
2 '1992 Election Year Coffee Cup' (Buffalo China, edition of 1992) designed by Marlene McCarty and published by Permanent Press, with all proceeds contributed to WAC. 1992 was the year George Bush was running for re-election, and the cup is a protest comment on his upholding of the 'Gag Rule': regulations that forbade family planning clinics from discussing, recommending or even mentioning abortion.

Hence the phrase 'Bush makes me Gag'. An added play on words lies in the fact that 'bush' is American slang for a woman's pubic area; at the bottom of the cup it says 'I'm into you now'.
3 'Keep Your Rosaries Out of Our Ovaries', a WAC poster depicting Cardinal John O'Connor of New York, designed by Marlene McCarty and Bethany Johns, USA, 1992.

RAPE

In the U.S. it is estimated that a woman is raped every 1.3 minutes.[1]

One out of every three women will be the victim of sexual assault during her lifetime.[2]

75% of rape victims know their attacker.[1,5]

71% of rapes are planned beforehand.[2,3]

It is estimated that 85% of rapes are never reported to the police, and that less than 5% of the rapists go to jail.[1,2,3]

67% of convicted rapists are repeat offenders.[2]

The majority of rape cases occur during childhood and adolescence. 61% of all rapes occurred when the victim was 17 years old or less; 29% of all rapes occurred when the victim was less than 11 years old. 6% occurred when the victim was older than 29.[1]

In one survey 51% of college men said they would rape if they were certain they could get away with it.[4]

The United States rape rate is four times that of Germany, 13 times as much as England, 20 times as much as Japan.[5]

Reported rape survivors have been as old as 96 years and as young as 3 months.[2]

68% of rapes occur at night from 6 p.m. to 6 a.m.[2]

More rapes take place in the summer than in any other time of the year.[2]

More than 1 in every 7 women who have ever been married have been raped in marriage.[8]

Marital rape is legal is two states: North Carolina and Oklahoma.

40

In a *Ms.* Magazine survey from 1988, 42% of the rape victims told no one about their assault.[9]

One out of eight Hollywood movies depicts a rape theme. By the age of 18, the average youth has watched 250,000 acts of violence and 40,000 attempted murders on TV.[4,5]

In a national survey more than 70% of rape victims said they were concerned about their families discovering that they were raped, 65% said they were worried they might be blamed for being raped.[1]

According to 1989 Justice Department statistics, in more than 75% of rapes the rapist and rape survivor belong to the same race.[5]

Rape victims are nine times more likely than non-victims to have attempted suicide.[9]

In a study of teenagers' attitudes, 42% of females and 51% of males feel it is OK to force sex if "she gets him excited".[6]

41% of the raped women expected to be raped again.[10]

41% of rape victims in one study were virgins.[10]

21-30% of college women report violence from their dating partner.[10]

1

WAC STATS

WAC IS WATCHING

WOMEN TAKE ACTION

THE FACTS ABOUT WOMEN

2

KEEP YOUR ROSARIES

OUT OF OUR OVARIES

3

The Chicago art activist group SisterSerpents also made great disturbances at this time. An anonymous group, with the exception of their spokeswoman Mary Ellen Croteau, it directed its venom at the many levels of sexism in society, creating a confrontational visual language that stopped at nothing to make a point. Many symbols of sexism were explored and targeted – including little boys' games, army pin-ups and more – alongside a manifesto that promised to 'disturb and inspire' and weaponry involving stickers, rubber stamps, posters and exhibitions of work that aimed to shock. The group's most famous and controversial battle has been to reclaim the foetus symbol from the religious right wing, producing extremely provocative imagery, such as their 'Fuck a Fetus' poster (page 154), all created as part of a strategy of 'idea warfare', waged against a system that allows for the brutalization of women.

1 Poster recommending treatment for a rapist via the cooking equipment of a well-known television chef, USA, c1992.
2 The manifesto of the US art activist group SisterSerpents, founded in 1989.
3 A collection of photo-collaged posters by SisterSerpents, USA, 1994/5.

1

Julia's simple method for stopping a rapist

GO FOR THE GROIN, GALS!

SISTERSERPENT NOT NEA FUNDED

2

SisterSerpents proclaims an end to women's acceptance of their own oppression!

SisterSerpents is fierce and uncompromising, refusing to plead, or gently persuade. We recognize and confront the misogyny that exists deep within society. We will sever our connection with men who do not care to recognize our oppression because we realize that this is a survival mechanism.

Our struggle hopes to bring the demise of the system which allows for our brutalization. Our hostility is now in the streets, at public meetings and events, and in the media. We are guerrillas in the war against sexism.

We involve ourselves with idea warfare, instead of the physical and emotional violence which has for so long been used upon us.

We bare our ideological fangs for the purpose of shocking and frightening those who have never bothered to understand. Concerns about judgement or keeping up appearances are totally irrelevant.

Our actions are warnings to our oppressors, that we are a force that will not be ignored. But more importantly, our actions are encouragement for women, to rid ourselves of the shackles on our brains, to release our splendid imaginations, and discover our own voice and needs in the process. We do not want paternalistic interference.

Our work is done anonymously. We identify ourselves as SisterSerpents, but our individual names are constantly changing. Anonymity does not imply a low profile. We are present anywhere and everywhere(so watch what you say and do, our numbers are growing).

SisterSerpents has no modesty. We will bombard the world with words and images that will disturb and inspire, and we claim our right to this very public speech even if no one dares respond.

Our art is merely and marvelously our weapon.

3

Tribune photo by Nanceé E. Lewis

VAGina ENvY

SisterSerpents '94

which baby benefited from operation rescue's post-natal health program?

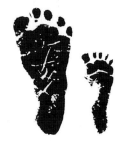

neither.

SISTERSERPENTS

MADWOMAN '93

Maybe you don't need another diet. Maybe what you need is a faster metabolism.

Aerobic exercise.
The best way to lose weight and stay that way.

If your last diet didn't work, there's probably a good reason.
When you cut less, your body automatically adjusts its metabolism to a lower level making you tired, grumpy and hungry.

The best way to raise your metabolism while you diet is through regular aerobic exercise.

NordicTrack is the most effective way to get the aerobic exercise you need.

NordicTrack burns more calories in less time than any other type of indoor exercise machine. Up to 1,100 calories per hour, according to fitness experts.

You'll look forward to stepping on the scales.

Exercising on NordicTrack reduces your fat, increases your muscle and raises your metabolism, making it easier to stay in shape. And easier to face those weigh-ins.

SISTERSERPENTS

SENSE THE CONFIDENCE. THE WARMTH. THE *POWER.*

SENSE THE MAN.

(MAN IS NOT SO SIMPLE, AFTER ALL.)

TIPS FOR MEN #27: STAY INDOORS AFTER 6pm

SisterSerpents '91

Amid scandals, pope tells priests to remain celibate

SISTERSERPENTS

GET ANGRY... PISS ON PATRIARCHY

SISTERSERPENTS

But men are oppressed too!

SISTERSERPENTS

Every American boy should own at least one of these during his lifetime.

SISTERSERPENTS

"The media would have you believe that it's always madness, never misogyny. But when was the last time a *woman* cut a *man* into little pieces?"

–Jackie Stevens

Fighting back: targeting stereotypes and language

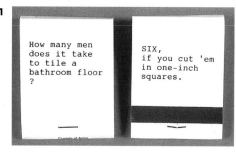

Another aspect of the new retaliatory spirit of the 1990s saw artists and designers everywhere targeting all forms of stereotyping and language use and abuse. This exploratory process applied a magnifier to the everyday 'little' irritations that women constantly endured, to reveal that they in fact harboured very big cultural nasties, suddenly grotesquely spotlighted for all to see.

Examples of such revelations include Claudette Dunkley's postcard-comment on the racial stereotyping that renders all black women as Tina Turner. Fashion designer Karen Savage parodies the harsh duality, imposed on women throughout the centuries, of being labelled virgins or whores, as well as conjuring up further associative pairings such as love and hate, or sex and violence. Marlene McCarty's enamel choker (with a chain too short to be worn without choking, literally) reminds us of the painful, if not suffocating, quality of such abusive labels. Her matchbooks, however, point to the ordinary, everyday objects of sexist ephemera – produced in many cultures – which make abusive, crass jokes about women or use offensive imagery. In keeping with this spirit, she makes them do a flip turn: this time the nasty little jokes are on men – the nude models lean forward suggestively and spout cuntpower, while another matchbook jeers at men and jokes about cementing them all to the floor.

1, 2 'Friends of Anita', matchbooks to be given out at US newsstands (where it is quite common to receive free matchbooks carrying phrases such as 'Call 1-900-HOT-CHIX'); by Laura Cottingham and Marlene McCarty, USA, 1992.

3 'Choker' (silver filled with enamel), by Marlene McCarty, USA, 1993. Notice the chain is too short to actually wear.

4 'Just Like Tina Turner', postcard with drawing by Claudette Dunkley, Britain, 1995.

5 The duality of stereotyping to which women are subjected is shown here in t-shirts designed by Karen Savage, Britain, 1992.

5

Fighting back: the graphic symbolism of 'no'

As debates about rape continued to intensify in the early 1990s, the use of graphic symbols became ever-more forceful and began to express the power tensions and threats to which women felt constantly subjected. All the images on this spread can be viewed as interpretations of the word 'No', both to rape and to all violence and threats – and they illustrate an escalation from self-defence to potential aggression. The first image is a loud, defiant verbal 'No' (loudness and strength are conveyed by the highly magnified detail, implying closeness or shouting). This moves on to a sturdy, raised hand making a STOP sign. The next step exudes the power of a gun – here self-defence turns to empowerment. A woman is pointing a gun from the bedsheets, to intimidate, ward off threats or keep danger away from that most vulnerable of places. Finally, the gun is given an almost spiritual posture, and a worry is disclosed: can we get hooked? Within only four images, a connected line of emotion has been traced, starting from an assertive 'No', to the worry and confusion that arises when self-defence becomes part of an aggressive action – the woman herself firing the gun.

1, 3 Portable 'blue dots' carried in Women's Action Coalition (WAC) demonstrations to flash protest messages in front of TV cameras (see also page 150). Normally blue on one side, they flipped around to show graphics and text on the other. Made from the cardboard rounds of pizza or cheesecake boxes, with popsicle-stick handles. USA, 1992. Fig 3 photograph by Donna Binder.

2 Advertisement placed in the student newspaper by WAC, during the 1992 rape trial of students at St John's University in Queens, New York.

4 Full-size pillowcase and bedsheet set entitled 'Get It?: Bedsheets', screenprinted with a photograph of actress Gena Rowlands in the film 'Gloria'. By Mary Beth Edelson, USA, 1992.

5 Front cover of Ms. magazine, May/June 1994, discussing issues surrounding women and guns, USA.

5

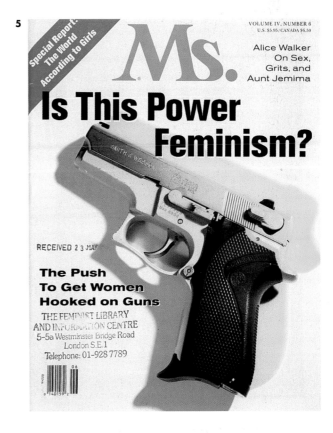

Women and AIDS awareness: the influential graphics of Gran Fury

The most confrontational and illuminating posters produced during the 1980s on AIDS awareness were a product of the New York-based collective Gran Fury. Originally part of the AIDS activist coalition ACT UP, in 1988 it established itself as an autonomous collective 'dedicated to exploiting the power of art to end the AIDS crisis' while still remaining responsible for much of ACT UP's guerrilla graphics.

The combined forces of ACT UP and Gran Fury excelled at targeting different audiences in need of AIDS awareness and prevention, including women. Gran Fury's poster 'Sexism rears its unprotected head', for example, first appeared in conjunction with direct actions organized by ACT UP's Women's Committee as part of the nationwide 'Nine Days of Protest' against AIDS in Spring 1988. ACT UP was attempting to get straight men to take responsibility for protecting their female partners, as they were convinced most men still did not use condoms, and 'official' advice on safe sex was usually aimed at women.[3] As time went on, Gran Fury continued to tackle the problems of women and HIV and AIDS in other formats, including its well known bus shelter poster 'Women don't get AIDS: they just die from it', and its installation billboards at the Venice Biennale in 1991.

All in all, Gran Fury's graphic strategy of appropriating imagery and styles from recognizable works of fine art and commercial advertising (while delivering a confrontational verbal message) created a new genre of activist art. But it also broke ground in the boldness of the gay imagery it used. The 'Kissing Doesn't Kill' poster (1989) carried by San Francisco, and later New York City buses, imitated the look of a United Colors of Benetton advertising campaign, but delivered a twist in the lively line-up of couples shown kissing: boy + girl, boy + boy, girl + girl. It achieved an international standing through creative magazines and other cultural grapevines, and opened the way for further inspiring images of same-sex couples in love (or in sex) from groups such as Dyke Action Machine! in New York and Big Active in London. So in addition to its life-saving mission relating to AIDS awareness, Gran Fury also began to break down invisible barriers relating to public imagery, and gay and lesbian culture was on the threshold of becoming more visible graphically than ever before.

1 Illuminated bus shelter poster addressing AIDS awareness for women, by Gran Fury, USA, 1991. Sponsored by the Museum of Contemporary Art, Los Angeles and the Public Art Fund, New York.

2 'Kissing Doesn't Kill', bus advert which ran in San Francisco and New York, by Gran Fury, USA, 1989.

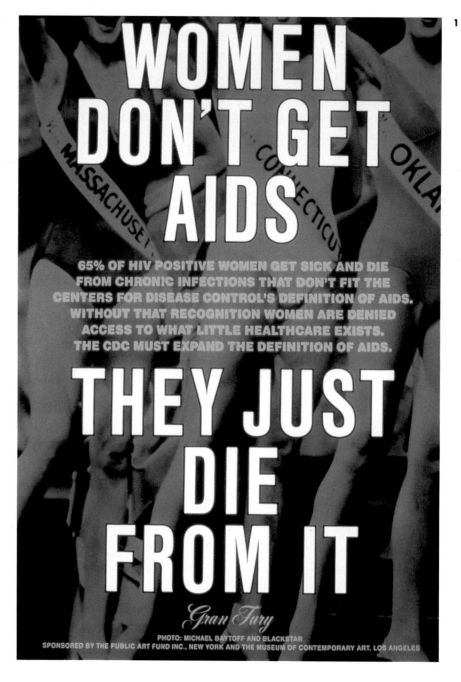

1

WOMEN DON'T GET AIDS

65% OF HIV POSITIVE WOMEN GET SICK AND DIE FROM CHRONIC INFECTIONS THAT DON'T FIT THE CENTERS FOR DISEASE CONTROL'S DEFINITION OF AIDS. WITHOUT THAT RECOGNITION WOMEN ARE DENIED ACCESS TO WHAT LITTLE HEALTHCARE EXISTS. THE CDC MUST EXPAND THE DEFINITION OF AIDS.

THEY JUST DIE FROM IT

Gran Fury

PHOTO: MICHAEL BAYTOFF AND BLACKSTAR
SPONSORED BY THE PUBLIC ART FUND INC., NEW YORK AND THE MUSEUM OF CONTEMPORARY ART, LOS ANGELES

KISSING DOESN'T KILL: GREED AND INDIFFERENCE DO.

CORPORATE GREED, GOVERNMENT INACTION, AND PUBLIC INDIFFERENCE MAKE AIDS A POLITICAL CRISIS.

3

SEXISM REARS ITS UNPROTECTED HEAD
MEN USE CONDOMS OR BEAT IT **AIDS KILLS WOMEN**

The Catholic Church has long taught men and women to loathe their bodies and to fear their sexual natures. This particular vision of good and evil continues to bring suffering and even death. By holding medicine hostage to Catholic morality and withholding information which allows people to protect themselves and each other from acquiring the Human Immunodeficiency Virus, the Church seeks

"The truth is not in condoms or clean needles. These are lies ... good morality is good medicine."
John Cardinal O'Connor, First Vatican Conference on AIDS, 1989

to punish all who do not share in its peculiar version of human experience and makes clear its preference for living saints and dead sinners. It is immoral to practice bad medicine. It is bad medicine to deny people information that can help end the AIDS crisis. Condoms and clean needles save lives as surely as the earth revolves around the sun. AIDS is caused by a virus and a virus has no morals.

4

SEXISM REARS ITS UNPROTECTED HEAD

MEN: Use Condoms Or Beat It.

AIDS KILLS WOMEN

SPRING AIDS ACTION '88: Nine days of nationwide AIDS related actions & protests.

3 'The Pope and the Penis', installation billboards devised by Gran Fury for the Venice Biennale in 1991, which criticized the Catholic Church's position on AIDS. They were suppressed by both the Biennale officials and the Italian customs, until press interest and exposure caused them to be exhibited and the issues they represented to be discussed widely.
4 Poster created for the 'Nine Days of Protest' (against AIDS) in Spring 1988, by Gran Fury, USA.
5 Safe sex poster (from a series of six) designed by Big Active for the Terrence Higgins Trust, Britain, 1992.

5

Lesbian culture strikes back

Lesbian power thrived as a result of the direct actions of the members of the New York group, Lesbian Avengers. The group was founded in 1992 in order to focus on strategies and issues vital to lesbian visibility and survival. Their direct actions not only echoed through New York streets, but resounded around the world. They marched with flaming torches, pestered politicians, stormed editorial offices, held around-the-clock vigils, ceremonially ate fire and staged many other vigorous activities – fuelled by what they called 'ready-to-blow-up' anger. All such actions were crucial to their mission of demanding respect for lesbians, as well as attempting to teach lesbians how to organize and think politically. Their manifesto and logo, designed by the painter and graphic designer Carrie Moyer, encapsulated the explosive energy that has made them a legend.

Lesbian culture also achieved visibility through the graphic wit and social critique of Dyke Action Machine! (DAM!), the lesbian graphics project established in 1991 by Carrie Moyer and the photographer Sue Schaffner. DAM!'s poster campaigns criticized the prejudiced attitudes and programming of mainstream advertising by inserting lesbian images into currently recognizable advertising campaigns. (The results were then displayed around the city, preferably next to the original advertisements.) Their spoofs of GAP (1991) and *Family Circle* advertisements (1992) not only subverted the postures and styling normally reserved for heterosexual fantasy in magazines, but also began to subvert established visual profiles of society as a whole, as a new view of lesbian reality struggled to emerge.

Within a couple of years it did emerge (not to say explode) with Dyke TV and other forums, bringing DAM!'s more recent projects into a power league of their own. Their 1994 poster for a fantasy film of violence-wielding dyke revenge (page 151) carries a subtext of real emotion expressed by a social group who refuse to be victimized any longer. Their Web site, presently an interactive promotion for a fantasy television station called 'The Girlie Network', shows how the lesbian 'visual experience' may, in the future, expand and indeed illuminate cyberspace.

1

1 Party ticket for the Lesbian Avengers, USA, early 1990s.
2 Poster announcing meetings of the Lesbian Avengers, and which pastiches a Constructivist poster (see page 66), by Carrie Moyer, USA, early 1990s.
3 The Dyke Manifesto by the Lesbian Avengers, designed by Carrie Moyer, USA, 1993.

2

DYKE MANIFESTO

CALLING ALL LESBIANS!
WAKE UP!

IT'S TIME TO GET OUT OF THE BEDS, OUT OF THE BARS AND INTO THE STREETS.
IT'S TIME TO SEIZE THE POWER OF DYKE LOVE, DYKE VISION, DYKE ANGER, DYKE INTELLIGENCE, DYKE STRATEGY.
IT'S TIME TO ORGANIZE AND INCITE. IT'S TIME TO GET TOGETHER AND FIGHT.
WE'RE INVISIBLE, SISTERS, AND IT'S NOT SAFE—NOT IN OUR HOMES, NOT IN THE STREETS, NOT ON THE JOB, NOT IN THE COURTS.
WHERE ARE THE <u>OUT</u> LESBIAN LEADERS? IT'S TIME FOR A FIERCE LESBIAN MOVEMENT AND THAT'S <u>YOU</u>: THE ROLE MODEL, THE VISION, THE DESIRE.

WE NEED YOU.

BECAUSE: WE'RE NOT WAITING FOR THE RAPTURE. WE ARE THE APOCALYPSE. *We'll be your dream and their nightmare.*

LESBIAN POWER

LESBIAN AVENGERS BELIEVE IN CREATIVE ACTIVISM: LOUD, BOLD, SEXY, SILLY, FIERCE, TASTY AND DRAMATIC. ARREST OPTIONAL.
THINK DEMONSTRATIONS ARE A GOOD TIME AND A GREAT PLACE TO CRUISE WOMEN.
LESBIAN AVENGERS DON'T HAVE PATIENCE FOR POLITE POLITICS. ARE BORED WITH THE BOYS.
THINK OF STINK BOMBS AS ALL-SEASON ACCESSORIES. DON'T HAVE A POSITION ON FUR.
LESBIAN AVENGERS BELIEVE CONFRONTATION FOSTERS GROWTH AND STRONG BONES.
BELIEVE IN RECRUITMENT. NOT BY THE ARMY; NOT OF STRAIGHT WOMEN. DON'T MIND HANDCUFFS AT ALL.
LESBIAN AVENGERS DO BELIEVE HOMOPHOBIA IS A FORM OF MISOGYNY.
LESBIAN AVENGERS ARE NOT CONTENT WITH GHETTOES: WE WANT YOUR HOUSE, YOUR JOB, YOUR FREQUENT FLYER MILES.
WE'LL SELL YOUR JEWELRY TO SUBSIDIZE OUR MOVEMENT.
LESBIAN AVENGERS DON'T BELIEVE IN THE FEMINIZATION OF POVERTY. WE DEMAND UNIVERSAL HEALTH INSURANCE AND HOUSING.
WE DEMAND FOOD AND SHELTER FOR ALL HOMELESS LESBIANS.
LESBIAN AVENGERS ARE THE 13th STEP. LESBIAN AVENGERS THINK GIRL GANGS ARE THE WAVE OF THE FUTURE.

LESBIAN SEX

BELIEVE IN TRANSCENDENCE IN ALL STATES, INCLUDING COLORADO AND OREGON.
THINK SEX IS A DAILY LIBATION. GOOD ENERGY FOR ACTIONS.
LESBIAN AVENGERS CRAVE, ENJOY, EXPLORE, SUFFER FROM NEW IDEAS ABOUT RELATIONSHIPS:
SLUMBER PARTIES. POLYGAMY (WHY GET MARRIED ONLY ONCE?). PERSONAL ADS. AFFINITY GROUPS.
ARE OLD FASHIONED: PINE, LONG, WHINE, STAY IN BAD RELATIONSHIPS.
GET MARRIED BUT DON'T WANT TO DOMESTICATE OUR PARTNERS.
LESBIAN AVENGERS LIKE THE SONG "MORE MADONNA, LESS JESUS"
USE LIVE ACTION WORDS: *lick, waltz, eat, fuck, kiss, play, bite, give it up.*
LESBIAN AVENGERS LIKE JINGLES: SUBVERSION IS OUR PERVERSION.

LESBIAN ACTIVISM

LESBIAN AVENGERS SCHEME AND SCREAM.
THINK ACTIONS MUST BE LOCAL, REGIONAL, NATIONAL, GLOBAL, COSMIC.
LESBIAN AVENGERS THINK CLOSETED LESBIANS, QUEER BOYS AND SYMPATHETIC STRAIGHTS SHOULD SEND US MONEY.
BELIEVE DIRECT ACTION IS A KICK IN THE FACE.
LESBIAN AVENGERS PLAN TO TARGET HOMOPHOBES OF EVERY STRIPE AND INFILTRATE THE CHRISTIAN RIGHT.
LESBIAN AVENGERS ENJOY LITIGATION. *Class action suits fit us very well.*

TOP 10 AVENGER QUALITIES
(IN DESCENDING ORDER)

10. COMPASSION
9. LEADERSHIP
8. NO BIG EGO
7. INFORMED
6. FEARLESSNESS
5. RIGHTEOUS ANGER
4. FIGHTING SPIRIT
3. PRO SEX
2. GOOD DANCER
1. ACCESS TO RESOURCES (XEROX MACHINES)

THE LESBIAN AVENGERS. WE RECRUIT.

Serious Sapphists.
MARIA, writer/poet and JILL, Pink Panther.
Photographed by GIRL RAY.

INTENSE.

DAM!

Anti-violence whistle as blown by
SAMANTHA, Pink Panther.
Photographed by
GIRL RAY.

SHARP.

DAM!

QUEER FUTURE
DYKE FASHION
QUEER PLANET
DYKE ACTION

DAM!
DYKE ACTION MACHINE!

Lesbian-wear as modeled by
SARAH, dyke academic and
KRIS, hip dyke activist.
Photographed by GIRL RAY.

SMOOCH.

DAM!

JAN, singer/songwriter,
CARYN, feminist poet and
DYKEDONNA, lesbian diva.
Photographed by
GIRL RAY.

FEMALE BONDING.

DAM!

Gee whiz tradition has been showing up in the most **lesbian** places

Dyke Action Machine

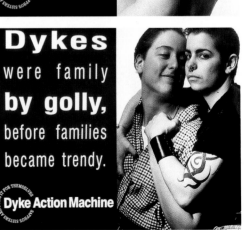

Dykes were family **by golly,** before families became trendy.

Dyke Action Machine

1 The GAP Celebrity Campaign, by Dyke Action Machine! (Carrie Moyer and Sue Schaffner), USA, 1991.
2 Family Circle/Family Values Campaign, presenting the 'family' tradition in lesbian culture, by Dyke Action Machine!, USA, 1992.

all girls...all the DAM! time

3 Images from DAM!'s Web site – an interactive promotion for a fantasy lesbian TV station entitled 'The Girlie Network'. Created by Dyke Action Machine! (Carrie Moyer and Sue Schaffner), USA, 1996.

SPECIAL INSERT
The Girlie Network
Hottest
Hits

"The best part about our show is getting to feel up Lilly every week."

LUCIANA & LILLY
Up-Close and In Your Face

	9:00	9:30	10:00	10:30	11:00	11:30	12:00
	East Village 10009	MONDAY NITE SOFTBALL LIVE from Park Slope Sappho Sluggers vs. Lipstick Lezzies				Leave Us the Beaver	Late Night with the Lesbian Avengers
	My Ex's Ex	Domestic Partners with Children	Season Premiere! OB-GYN		FRESH MEAT: A Special Eyewitness Report on America's Schools		Snip Squad
	Living with Queen Latifah	Luciana & Lilly	DON'T BUY HET: Dyke Trade Embargo? A TOWN MEETING		HOT Right-Wingers	The 90% Solution	Meet the Lesbian Nation
	Chelsea's Girlfriends	Unrepentant Sinner	The Girlie Network Movie of the Week: STRAIGHT TO HELL			Castratin' Bitches: GO GIRL!	Peg!
	Marriage Butt	Martina	America's Stupidest Straights	Clueless	Bring Us Your Children	The Activist Files	Live From the Clit Club

THE GiRLie NeTWORK FALL LINE-UP

OB-GYN

Season Premiere!
Tuesday
10 pm

Going to the doctor never felt like this...

Take Our Straights puh-leeze!

Peg Tackles the Het Invasion of Our Neighborhoods

Peg!
Thursdays at Midnite

The politics of the body: 1990s style

1 Official programme of the 44th International Design Conference in Aspen, USA, 1994.
2 Preliminary collages for the Conference Leaflet Subversion by Louise Scovell.
3 The Aspen Design Conference Leaflet Subversion, by design collective Class Action. Project team: Debra Drodvillo, Mark Maltais, Louise Scovell, USA, 1994. The leaflet is shown here unfolding to poster size.

The 1990s have witnessed the ongoing battle against oppressive representations of women in the media, as well as new examples of women using their bodies to create their own power-messages for political causes.

An important discussion was instigated by the collective of graphic designers and artists known as Class Action, who took issue with the representation of a female form used as the logo for the 1994 International Design Conference in Aspen, Colorado, on the theme of Design and Human Bodies. They produced a pamphlet using reconfigurations of the conference's logo of a female body, as a way of explaining how the original rendition was open to multiple interpretations, ranging from a helpless resistance to violation, to a show of life force (a position for birth). The pamphlet was distributed at the conference and used to encourage debate via workshop discussion, and later it generated even more discussion through the design press. It therefore produced a much-needed call to all designers and those commissioning design to look more critically at the image-making process, while also delivering a strong reminder of the need to be responsible and sensitive to the various communities being addressed.

1

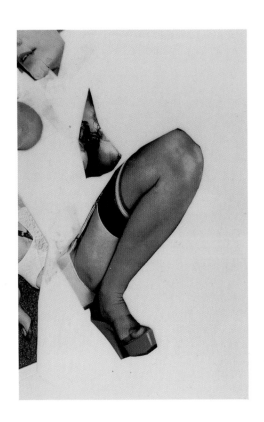

2

3

Human Bodies

Interpretation of

Human Bodies

Representation of

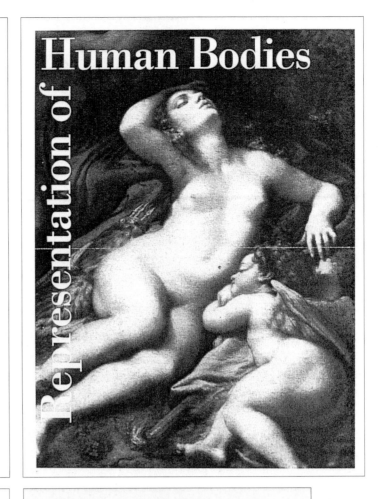

Human Bodies

Consumption of

This is an image
of a woman...

naked
on her back
legs spread
contorted
passive
available
resisting
willing
afraid
in control
a mother
a whore
a decoration
a symbol.

She has no identity.
She is an identity.
She is the logo for
this conference.

Class Action produced this commentary
to initiate discussion at IDCA 1994 about
the representation of human bodies.

The politics of the body: 1990s style

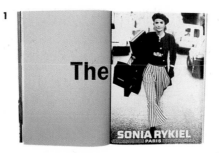

At about the same time as the Class Action protest (pages 172–3), various attempts were made to use women's bodies in the media for purposes of empowerment. Among the best and most direct were Demi Moore's challenging nude pose on the cover of *Vanity Fair* during her pregnancy, as well as Nike's attempts to show their understanding of a woman's relationship with her own body, in a campaign of sensitive 'insights' into women. In Britain, however, the attempt to create a highly confident advertising image of a modern power-woman in a Wonderbra, projecting her sexuality on her own terms, misfired due to the 'boys' humour' innuendos of the copywriting. The Wonderbra advertisement provoked mixed reactions: some read it as the modern, self-defined woman, ready to walk over any man; some reclaimed it and aimed her sexual advances at women; some produced spoofs that turned the boys' humour into a castration threat. In the end, difficulties tend to arise when attempting to use women's bodies to make empowering statements through commercial advertising channels more traditionally known for abusing them. The focus on posturing and appearances overwhelms any deeper meaning or message.

More direct statements inevitably come from a grassroots level. Power and body politics were central to the May 1992 Class Action campaign for Pro-Choice entitled 'The Ruling Body': a phrase intended to challenge the events of the time (when the overruling of *Roe vs Wade* by the Supreme Court was a real threat), as well as declaring women's will to take back control of their own bodies. 'The Ruling Body' campaign involved a billboard, as well as plans to place the headline in the centrefold of *Playboy* magazine (a design that almost went to press, but was withdrawn at the last minute). The headline was also placed on a t-shirt and achieved great popularity at a major Pro-Choice rally in Washington DC that summer. The words not only deliver the intended Pro-Choice message, particularly when worn, but also have broader associations for the ordinary woman in the street, who remains a source of political power and decision-making, and is therefore a force to be reckoned with.

1 Two items from the Pro-Choice campaign entitled 'The Ruling Body': a t-shirt, and a proposed design (see text) intended to replace the centerfold in an issue of Playboy magazine. (The title 'The Ruling Body' was a play on words protesting against the possible 'overruling' of Roe vs Wade in 1992.) The campaign was created by the art–design collective Class Action, USA, 1992. Project team: Rodney Abbot, Debra Drodvillo, Lisa Mangano, Louise Scovell and Lisa Shoglow.
2 'Hello Boys', Wonderbra billboard advertisement, by London ad agency TBWA, 1994, also shown alongside 'Hello Girls', a spoof of the Wonderbra ad, produced by agency Euro RSCG for client Kaliber beer, 1994.
3 Guerrilla graffiti marking the Wonderbra ad on a hoarding on Vauxhall Bridge, London. Photograph and graffiti by Laurence Jaugey-Paget, 1994.
4 Yet another spoof on the Wonderbra ad that incorporates the newsworthy Lorena Bobbitt (famous for castrating her husband with a kitchen knife, after alleging years of sexual abuse). Taken from the back cover of Bad Attitude magazine, issue 7, February–April, 1995, London.

3

4

The politics of the body: 1990s style

Finally, women with high profiles in the media and enormous commercial 'pull', particularly supermodels, began to use their media power to make political messages, providing additional provocation by using their bodies to make their point.

In 1985, Lynx, the anti-fur trade campaign based in Britain, produced their ground-breaking 'forty dumb animals' poster and cinema advertisement, showing a model dragging a bloody fur coat down a catwalk. It helped to create a stigma against wearing fur that almost brought down an industry, while also strengthening an animal rights movement which has been growing internationally ever since. Ten years later, in 1995, world-renowned fashion models stepped forward (rather than allowing themselves to be simply targeted as fur users) to join forces with animal rights organization PETA and produced their own series of statements against wearing fur. (PETA, or People for the Ethical Treatment of Animals, remains one of the most influential bodies in the international animal rights movement.) A number of high-profile celebrities, including actress Kim Basinger, singer Melissa Etheridge and Ronald Reagan's daughter Patti Davis, also joined the series in order to make a radical statement.

"I'd rather go naked than wear fur."
—Christy Turlington

1 History-making billboard and poster for Lynx anti-fur campaign by Yellowhammer (art direction by Jeremy Pemberton; photo by David Bailey). Originally commissioned by Greenpeace in 1985.
2 Lynx cinema ad by Yellowhammer, 1985.
3, 4, 5 Poster campaign by PETA (People for the Ethical Treatment of Animals), featuring supermodels and celebrities (fig 5 shows Ronald Reagan's daughter, Patti Davis), USA, 1995.
6 Anti-fur badge by PETA, USA, 1995.

4

5

6

Body and soul: self-image, eating and health

In 1978, Susie Orbach's pioneering book *Fat is a Feminist Issue* tackled the relationship between a woman's self-image and eating problems such as compulsive eating, bulimia and anorexia. Over ten years later, Naomi Wolf's *The Beauty Myth* (1990) pointed to the use of images of female beauty as a means of controlling women. 'Beauty' is understood as an artificial value judgement, intended to keep women in their place by instilling them with self-hatred, fear of ageing and a host of other worries. Despite both warnings, the myth of the 'ideal woman' lived on; the magazine models kept getting thinner, and the stereotypes and attitudes propagated by the media (such as thin is good, fat is bad) have continued to affect the health and happiness of many women. Although today's women may be more educated about eating disorders, their self-image and self-esteem still remain under constant assault – an issue taken up by the graphic protests shown here.

British designer Sarah Brown's expressive artist's book on the subject of eating disorders takes the reader on a nightmarish journey through social pressures – media, peer group, family – verbal associations and distorted imagery, ending with a real-life case study. A shattered mirror on the cover not only connects the reader to the scenes with which s/he will be confronted, but also reminds the reader that the issue to hand potentially exists in everyone, as if to say 'this could be you, or someone you love'. The extremely colourful and disturbingly effective posters by Carol Porter in Australia, and the activist group SisterSerpents in the USA confirm, moreover, that beauty pressures and myths – and the damage they do – have an international reach.

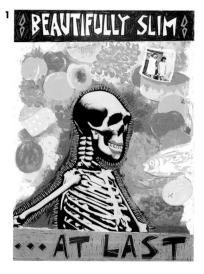

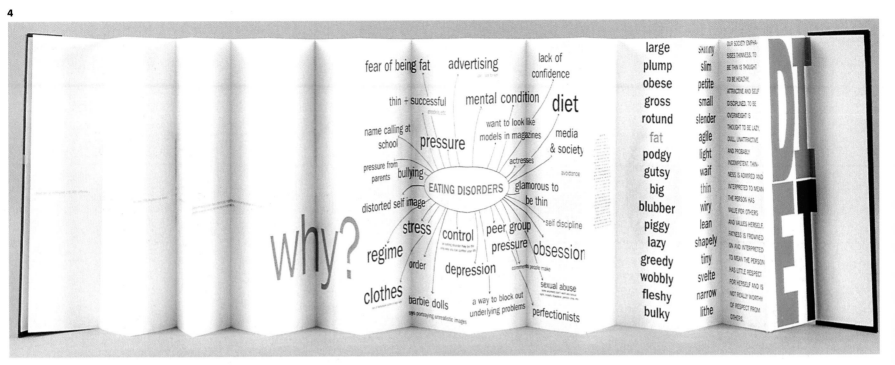

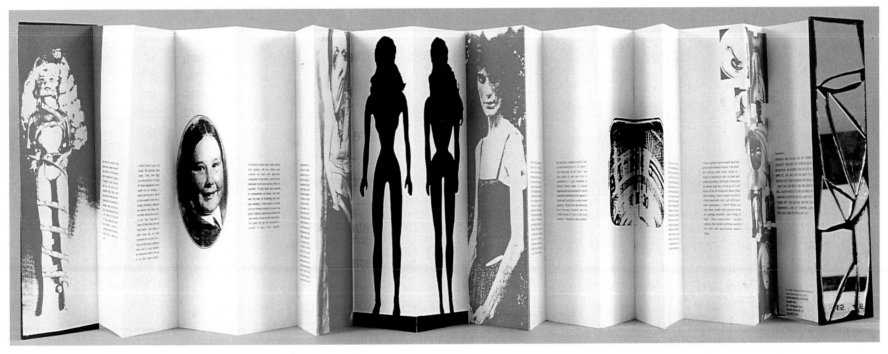

1 'Beautifully Slim... At Last', poster by Carol Porter of Red Planet Posters, Australia, 1992.
2 'Made to Measure', poster on a Cinderella theme by Carol Porter of Red Planet Posters, Australia, 1992.
3 'Superslims', poster by SisterSerpents, USA, 1993.
4 Artist's book on eating disorders, by Sarah Brown, Britain, 1995.

The new graphic heroines

As new power images emerged for women in music, fashion and the media, so too did tough, new graphic heroines, in some cases bearing characteristics such as man-hating and/or bloodlust, as well as humour.

Tank Girl first appeared in late 1988 as a cartoon strip created by artist Jamie Hewlett and writer Alan Martin, in the London-based *Deadline* magazine. Combining vestiges of Punk, New Age traveller and other forms of underground culture, Tank Girl soon became the superheroine of the 1990s – a spunky, foul-mouthed, chain-smoking, violent female in combat gear. She spends her time cruising around the Australian outback in a tank having strange adventures and fantasies, and is prone to killing-sprees. Adored by her fans for her 'no-shit' attitude and lawless behaviour, she also has had a heavy influence on the British fashion and style industries, generating a look that relies heavily on tattoos, shaved heads, combat trousers and Doc Marten boots. She has been hailed as a feminist icon in America, and although at times she can still seem to be a product of a distinctly male fantasy, she remains a confirmed power symbol for young women in Britain, as well as a cult heroine on the Internet.

SHE, on the other hand, is a heroine of American credit-card culture: post-1960s revolution; post-Punk; and definitely in tune with thirtysomethings. SHE originated as a comic strip in *Mirabella* fashion magazine in 1993 (created by Marisa Acocella, based in the heart of the New York advertising world), and in 1994 her autobiography appeared in book form entitled *Just who the hell is SHE, anyway?*. SHE's attraction doesn't centre around extraordinary adventures, but is very much about enjoying a sharply-honed, wise-cracking view of modern, middle-class American culture. For example, SHE naturally pours insults on the cultural institution of Barbie and her 'sky-high butt', while at least crediting her for introducing middle America to the concept of 'man as accessory', in the form of Ken.[4]

The heroine to end all heroines appeared in the USA in 1991 with the life adventures of 'Hothead Paisan, the Homicidal Lesbian Terrorist' who gets her kicks from beating the hell out of men (if not killing them stone dead). Created by Diane DiMassa and produced by Giant Ass Publishing as a quarterly comic book, Hothead is far more than a mindless man-hating cliché. She personifies a combination of angers, injustices and rebellions against the narrowness of modern society. Hothead's violence is an outlet for all her fans and readers: a vengeance-seeking fantasy for all lesbians to savour. The incredible humour of her struggles stems from DiMassa's well-observed rendering of social behaviour and attitudes (hilarious confrontations with thugs in the street, for example). Add heartbreaks, love and soul-searching to the combination and it amounts to a very soulful read.

1

2

3

1 Cover of i-D magazine, May 1995. Tank Girl cartoon by Jamie Hewlett.
2 Tank Girl 2, by Jamie Hewlett and writer Alan Martin, published in both USA and Britain in 1995.
3 Tank Girl shown in a typical stance.

4 Logo for Giant Ass Publishing, producers of Hothead Paisan in comic book form, USA, 1995.
5, 6 Two images that illustrate the explosive attitude of 'Hothead Paisan, the Homicidal Lesbian Terrorist' created by Diane DiMassa, USA, 1993 and 1995.
7, 8 Cover and inside page from the book depicting the life and times of 'SHE', entitled Just who the hell is SHE, anyway? by Marisa Acocella, USA, 1994.

New technology takeover: finding a voice in the twenty-first century

After decades of exclusion from the male world of computer technology, women have engaged with the new digital technologies of the 1990s in exciting, experimental ways; the (digital) future will certainly be female, and also a lot of fun. Women are using the new technologies for research, education and empowerment around the globe, forming digital networks to replace the snail-mail feminist networks of old. They are also using them for creative exploration, and a few projects are shown here which hint at creative pathways for the future.

The CD-ROM 'She Loves It, She Loves It Not: Women and Technology' (1993) created by Christine Tamblyn, Marjorie Franklin and Paul Tompkins, provides a good starting point for anyone wishing to examine the relationships between women and technology. This is an enjoyable journey through an informative compilation of facts, anecdotes and references. Each page or screen takes the form of an interactive collage that can include: texts explaining the causes and effects of women's exclusion from technology; sounds, such as the pounding of typewriters and washing machines; memos from the great abyss of cyberspace; anecdotal, handwritten letters to the user (accessed through click-on envelopes that wobble suggestively); and Quicktime movie clips of advertisements and films. The free-ranging artistic styling of the screens, as well as the continual movement of animated buttons, and a churning, grating background sound, not only bring the screens to life but also show how stagnant much on-screen design can be when restricted by a hard-edged, modernist grid mentality. In the new world of digital technology, breaking the rules is essential.

Using the computer and its keyboard as the basis for a number of metaphors, the Women's Design and Research Unit (WD+RU) in London produced the typeface-design project Pussy Galore as a means of exploring the propaganda about women embedded in both visual and verbal language. Created for *FUSE* magazine (issue 12) in 1995, it was devised as a 'conceptual typeface' – the keyboarding of a word yields, not letterforms, but a string of ideological 'icons', appearing in the form of word-clusters or pictogrammes. Use of the various shift levels reveals additional layers of icons with themes, such as bad

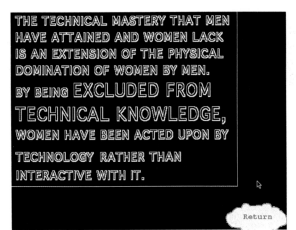

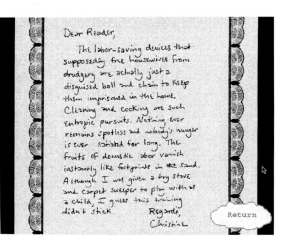

1 Screen images from Christine Tamblyn's CD-ROM She Loves It, She Loves It Not: Women and Technology, a studied and entertaining primer for those wishing to explore the subject, USA, 1993.
2 Poster describing Pussy Galore, the conceptual screen-based 'typeface' which uses strings of icons to explore propaganda about women. Created for FUSE magazine (issue 12) by the Women's Design and Research Unit (WD+RU), London, 1995.

pussy galore

The Women's Design + Research Unit (WD+RU) has been established to recognize and encourage women working internationally in the field of visual graphics including graphic design, typography and multi-media.

Empowerment
Stereotypes
Choices
Bad Language

*
"We wore girdles on our bodies, and girdles on our minds."

con Women's voices have been restricted for too long fine

*
Hidden Heroines who have made important contributions to the areas of art, design and film appear as surprise elements – the start of a growing database.

*
Women and technology are equal parts of the future and, for women, technology is the vehicle for their liberation.

abused
dog
gash
mother tucker
nympho
pussy
real slag
whore

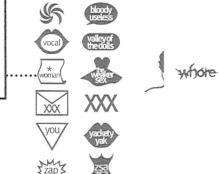

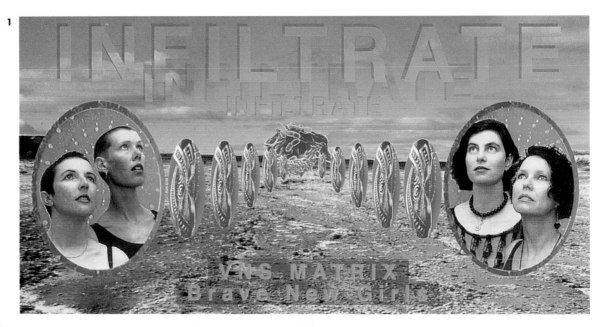

language or stereotypes; while asterisks act as a cue to open up textual quotes or animated image sequences. Designed as a real-time system, Pussy Galore remains, above all, an experimental tool for raising awareness and self-expression, as users are encouraged to reconstruct the existing icons (or design their own) and thus build their own linguistic experience.

The cyberspace that hangs over and around Australia has yielded interesting movements in cyberfeminist art and experimentation. The four artists known as VNS Matrix have created a vision of twenty-first century cuntpower in their interactive computer-simulation All New Gen (1992), which takes on the constructs and mentality of boys' computer games, but subverts the gender stereotypes. Hence the heroine, All New Gen, and her band of renegade DNA Sluts go on a journey to destroy Big Daddy Mainframe, and along the way have to tangle with various technomutants such as Circuit Boy (a techno bimbo who undergoes cyber-castration: when his penis is unscrewed, it 'morphs' into a cellular phone). The screens shown here give the gist of the many dangers and ecstasies to be experienced throughout their quest; while in broader terms, VNS Matrix pursue their own aim to 'remap cyberspace'.

In this same spirit of adventure, Australian radio producer, writer and videomaker Rosie Cross founded the first cyberfeminist zine in 1995. *Geekgirl* aims to be a friendly, fashionable and accessible read for women who work and play in cyberspace, and for grrrls who may not yet be connected to what Rosie X calls 'a tool of butt-kicking empowerment'. Hence the Geekgirl motto is 'Grrrls need Modems'. T-shirts and wild computer covers add to the fun, and the zine itself exists in both hard copy and digital formats – an aid to those who may be in need of a slow introduction to info-tech. Any hesitancy will not last long, however, for the most impressive thing about *Geekgirl* is the fast and furious, fun-seeking energy which it generates, all heavily contagious. A true vehicle for 'the online woman warrior', *Geekgirl* also produces Australia's most popular webzine site.

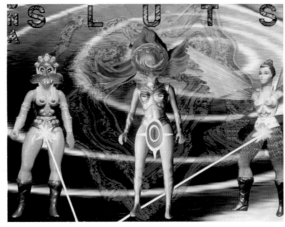
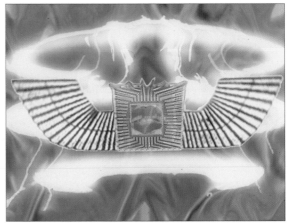

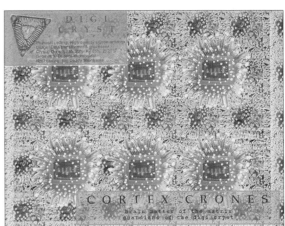

Lastly, the potential for future excursions into other worlds is shown in US artist/designer Diane Gromala's project 'Dancing with the Virtual Dervish: Virtual Bodies', created with dancer Yacov Sharir and performed in 1994. It combines one dancer's physical performance with a journey through virtual environments, experienced through an HMD (head-mounted display) and a dataglove. As an experimental performance, it exists in a number of iterations involving audience members and one dancer: sometimes the dancer wears the VR equipment while creating a performance, sometimes a member of the audience wears it while the dancer performs – although in both cases the VR 'journey' can be seen by large video projections in real time.

Donning the HMD and dataglove locates the dancer/HMD user within a virtual environment – a body of monumental proportions, with a virtual representation of the dancer contained within it. The body, which has slowly moving parts to represent constant decay and transition, consists of a rib cage, spine, pelvis, heart, liver and kidneys: all texture-mapped with x-ray and MRI images of Gromala's own body, and wrapped with letterforms and text. The dancer/HMD user enters and travels through this enormous body. The organs act as 'portals', which the dancer/HMD user can enter in order to experience another environment – and, if entering an enclosed chamber, the dancer/HMD user can in fact keep on moving through increasingly larger chambers. Each organ represents one of the traditional dervish's seven veils (in character, text, structure, etc); the heart refers to 'desire', the liver to 'avarice and parsimony', and so on. The virtual representation of the dancer is manifested as a series of video-grabs, texture-mapped onto a planar surface. Thus in the course of the journey, the (real) dancer can dance with his (virtual) self, and at some future stage of development his virtual self may even be able to interact with or respond to him.

The dancer/HMD user therefore exists simultaneously in two worlds, the physical and the virtual, which interact during the performance. When the dancer/HMD user is wearing the VR gear, he can only experience the virtual environment. The audience, however, can experience his physical 'dance', limited by the wires of the electronic gear and the tracking sensors, as well as viewing his journey through the virtual body – seeing what he sees via the large video projections, in real time. Other performance iterations also exist, where both audience and dancer don the equipment at various points.

As one of the first VR projects to fully integrate dance as a primary component, 'Dancing with the Virtual Dervish' offers extraordinary performance possibilities, as well as transgressing the symbolic construct of outer and inner experience, revealing new dimensions and new territories for women's future cyber-explorations.

1 Images (both screen and print) from 'Infiltrate', an art installation/exhibition, 1995, of the interactive computer-simulation 'All New Gen' (created 1992), which parodies a boys-oriented computer game but subverts the gender stereotypes. The stills shown (top to bottom, left to right) are: 'Infiltrate', 'DNA Sluts', 'Silicon Angel', 'Fractal Mountains of Bliss', 'Cortex Crones' and 'Oracle Snatch'. Created by the cyberfeminist art group VNS Matrix, Australia. VNS Matrix (f 1991) consists of Francesca da Rimini, Josephine Starrs, Julianne Pierce and Virginia Barratt.
2 Cover of issue 4 of Geekgirl, the first cyberfeminist zine created in 1995 by Rosie Cross in Australia. It exists in both hard copy and digital formats, and also has a highly popular Web site.
3 Geekgirl sticker, Australia, 1995.
4 Image from the Geekgirl Web site, Australia, 1995.

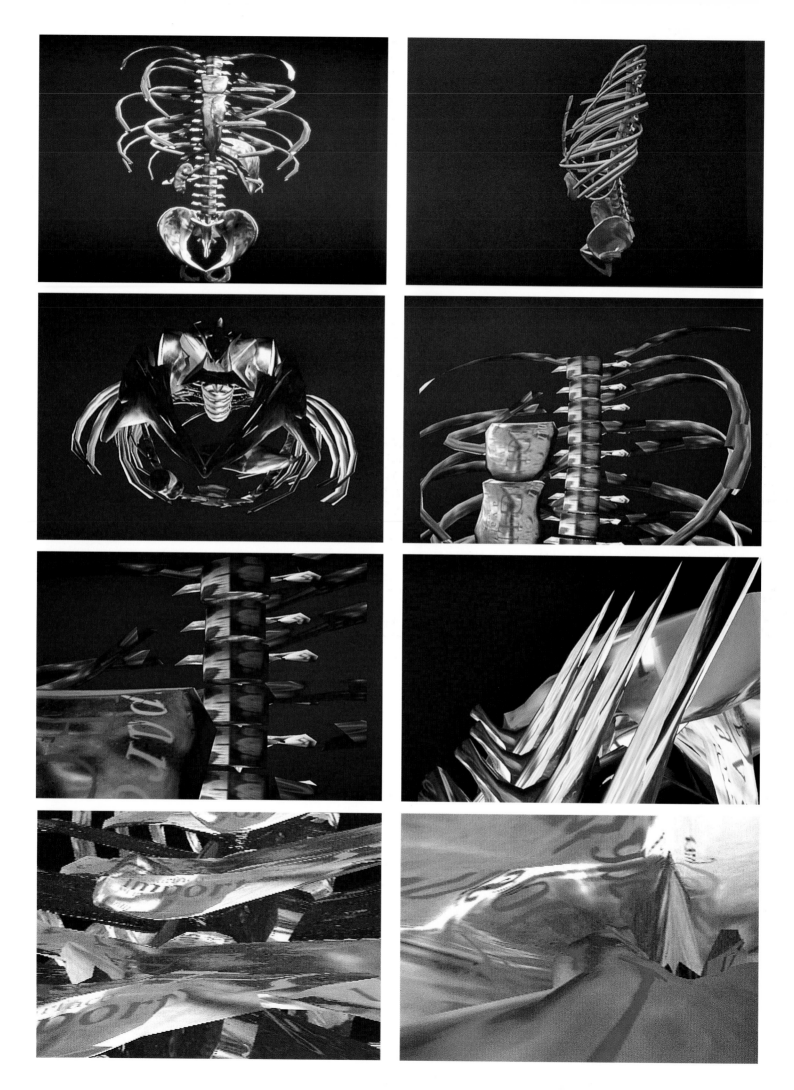

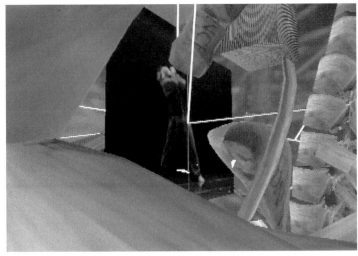

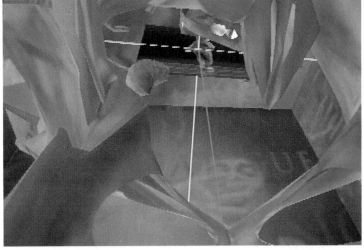

HYPOCRISY

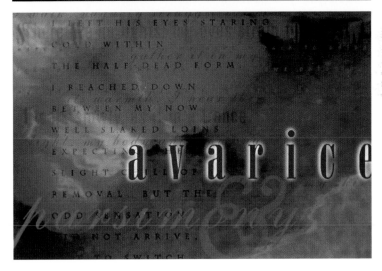

avarice

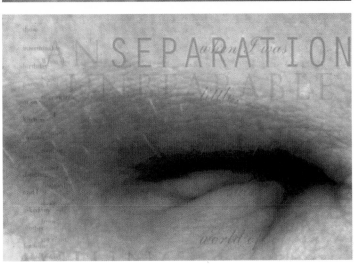

Images from the project Dancing with the Virtual Dervish : Virtual Bodies, which combines a physical dance performance with a journey (by that same dancer) through a virtual body that includes a skeleton frame wrapped with letterforms and text, and organs that act as portals into chambers or other environments. (A very small part of the dancer's journey is shown here.) Created by US visual artist and designer Diane Gromala (with dancer and choreographer Yacov Sharir) at the Banff Center for the Arts in Canada, and performed in 1994. See also the explanation on pages 157 and 185.

The International Women's Movement

Women Organize and Take Action

Throughout this century, the various waves of feminism – liberation movements, activist groups and individual struggles – have all been stepping stones on the pathway to international freedom and rights. As we approach the start of a new millennium, the prospect of global feminism looms large: a movement has now been established which reaches from grass-roots to an international level, calling for the empowerment of women worldwide.

The seeds for a worldwide women's movement were sown in the 1970s, with the second wave of feminism. International feminist networks were established through magazines and newsletters anxious to extend their reach, such as *Women's International Network News* (f 1975); or through communications services attempting to connect women's organizations around the world, such as Isis International (f 1974, Geneva and Rome) and the International Women's Tribune Centre (f 1976, New York City); or, of course, through the efforts of the lifeblood of the movement: the individuals, small groups and collectives themselves.

The movement gained impetus when the United Nations designated 1975 as the International Year of the Woman, and then launched the UN Decade for Women (1975–85) with a major conference in Mexico City. Two further conferences resulted from this move, focusing on the problems of women worldwide: one in Copenhagen in 1980, and a final conference to end the UN Decade in Nairobi in 1985. (A fourth UN Conference for Women would follow in Beijing in 1995.) Reaching as far ahead as the end of the century, these conferences laid down strategies for action to help organizations promote an end to discrimination against women. In addition, their offshoot reports and investigations, and new organizations such as the International Tribune Centre, played a vital role for the movement at grass-roots level. With their tremendous precision and scope in searching out information and publishing new statistics, they began gradually to construct a clearer and more accurate picture of women and their status in the world: their problems, their workload, and how they lived their lives under the burden of the traditions and customs imposed on them. Some of the statistics were revelations: 'Women constitute half the world's population, perform nearly two-thirds of its work hours, receive one-tenth of the world's income and own less than one-hundredth of the world's property.'[1] This was the statement that launched the 1980s as the decade that would consolidate an international movement.

A 1985 world report stated: 'Women living in rural areas produce half the world's food. In Africa, they do three-quarters of the agricultural work; in Asia, they are half of the agricultural labour force.'[2] From another source: 'Women are the sole bread-winners in one-fourth to one-third of the families in the world.'[3] The statistics also showed harrowing realities of violence against women and a lack of education, nutrition and health care. The UN reports were only the beginning; other important surveys and anthologies also appeared, including Robin Morgan's landmark international feminist anthology *Sisterhood is Global* (1984), as well as the New Internationalist's compilation of information on the state of the world's women at the end of the UN Decade for Women, entitled *Women: A World Report* (1985).

The build-up of this global picture in itself brought a strength and commitment to change, and an acknowledgement of a

1

Women
constitute half the world's
population,
perform nearly two-thirds
of its work hours,
receive one-tenth of the world's income
and own less than one-hundredth
of the world's property.

United Nations Report, 1980

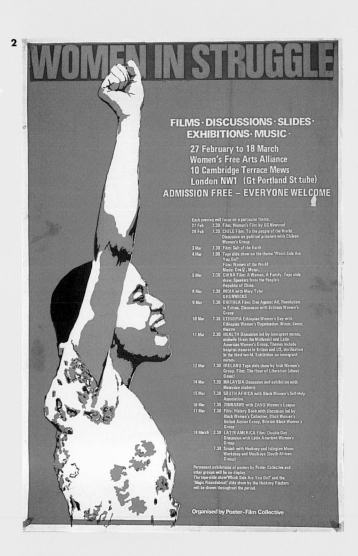

2

WOMEN IN STRUGGLE

FILMS · DISCUSSIONS · SLIDES ·
EXHIBITIONS · MUSIC ·

27 February to 18 March
Women's Free Arts Alliance
10 Cambridge Terrace Mews
London NW1 (Gt Portland St tube)
ADMISSION FREE – EVERYONE WELCOME

Organised by Poster-Film Collective

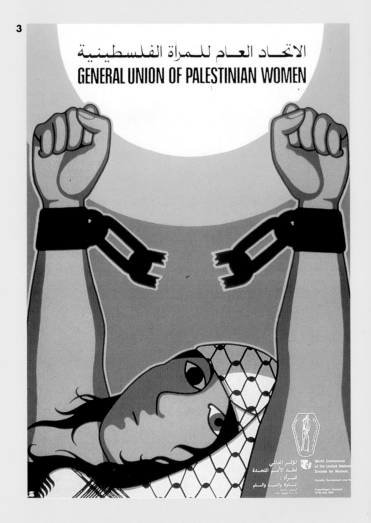

3

الاتحاد العام للمرأة الفلسطينية
GENERAL UNION OF PALESTINIAN WOMEN

4

shared agenda of problems and issues. Communication and education therefore became the key, and have remained so ever since. Now, in the 1990s, women's education is finally being viewed as a means of educating communities and ensuring their cultural, social and economic survival in many parts of the world.

The worldwide movement for women's rights will take us into the next century. It will continue to grow and to gain impetus, with the help of new communications technology; it will continue, against all odds, to challenge the traditions of male domination and oppression. For it is based on an unshakeable belief in women as a force for change. The old liberation motto is still heard around the globe: 'Women have the power to change the world.'

A long line of struggle

While the UN reports and other information surveys achieved an increasingly focused 'official' perspective on how women were living their lives around the world, a more intimate picture was built up over the decades, mainly visually. This occurred through the 'unofficial' or independent channels of posters, magazines and other visual media, all of which reflected the political struggles, national liberation movements, large-scale social problems and everyday personal dilemmas affecting women everywhere.

Certain issues have been integral to the international women's movement: matters to which all women can relate, or at least feel solidarity, even if they appear in different forms from culture to culture. This chapter is not intended to cover all of them; it can merely hint at some of the struggles and achievements that have generated interesting graphic developments.

There is, for example, the struggle against war, militarism, and the testing of nuclear weapons. Women have, throughout the century, aligned themselves with the international peace movement, and have made their protests highly visible. The Women's Peace Camp at Greenham Common in Britain in the 1980s and 1990s, which is still in existence, has been the subject of many visual documentaries, and is in itself a highly 'decorated' environment, as shown on pages 226–9. The colourful posters and billboards of Australian artists such as Pam Debenham, protested throughout the 1980s against nuclear testing in the Pacific (page 230), only to see its return yet again in the 1990s.

There is the struggle against the extreme right-wing political forces of fundamentalism and conservatism, which pose a threat to women everywhere. Both attempt to retract the gains women have made and to uphold traditions of subservience and male rule, by removing women from the public sphere and denying them control over their own future, in terms of education, health and their own reproductive processes. Both tend to do so through the use, and abuse, of the instruments of organized religion or cultural tradition. Fear and sensationalism are ever present in their propaganda material. An insight into conservatism and 'the undeclared war against women' in the 1980s was provided by Susan Faludi's *Backlash* (1991), while a perspective on the global manifestations of fundamentalism, and the implications for women now and in the future, has been laid out in Jan Goodwin's highly readable *Price of Honour: Muslim Women Lift the Veil of Silence on the Islamic World* (1994).

Struggles persist against a wide range of cultural and religious 'traditions' or 'customs' which are injurious to women, such as female genital mutilation, dowry murders, 'crimes of honour', early marriage, early childbearing, or female infanticide, most of which emanate from cultural traditions that value men over women, or that view

1 Postcard published by The Women's Press in London, bearing one of the most famous quotations to emerge from the UN (and other) reports of the early 1980s.
2 'Women in Struggle', poster for three weeks of evening events organized by the Poster Film Collective (who also created the poster) and focusing on themes from different countries, Britain, 1978.
3 Poster for the General Union of Palestinian Women, designed by Palestinian artist Jihad Mansour for the World Conference of the United Nations Decade for Women, 1980.

4 Graphic illustration attributed to Afroza, Bangladesh (of SIMORGH screen printing collective of Pakistan), taken from the magazine Women's World, December 1989.
5 Inside page of Sauti Ya Siti, the magazine of the Tanzania Media Women's Association (TAMWA), November 1992 special issue on Violence Against Women. Illustration by Micky Redhood.

5

SAUTI YA SITI
A TANZANIAN WOMEN'S MAGAZINE

A SPECIAL ISSUE
On Violence Against Women

CONTENTS:
1. Editorial.
   Women's Rights are Human Rights.
2. Violence Against Women is a Violation of Human Rights.
3. Human Rights Conference in the Hague.
4. Levina Mukasa Remembered.
5. Working Women and Marriage Stability.
6. Violence Against the Aged: Old Women & Witch Hunts.
7. Crimes Against Women.
8. The Saga of Mfadhaiko.
9. How Common is Sexual Harassment in Tanzania.
10. Gender Sensitisation Seminar.
11. My Faithful Campaign Against Assault.
12. Two Decades of Punch.
13. Woman's Crisis Centre in Magomeni Mapipa.
14. Domestic Violence.
15. Discrimination, Culture & Aids.
16. Zanzibar Legal Services Centre.
17. Another Form of Violence.

EDITOR:
Leila Sheikh Hashim

EDITORIAL TEAM:
Fatma Alloo
Edda Sanga
Chemi Che Mponda
Pili Mtambalike
Ananilea Nkya

TRANSLATOR: Christopher Magola

COVER ILLUSTRATIONS BY:
Micky Redhood

DESIGNED BY: Khuzema F. Mussaji

PRINTED BY:
Tanzania Printing Services Ltd.

THANKS TO:
Shabnam Sheriff
Jennifer Kissila

This Special Issue has been produced with funding from
SWEDISH INTERNATIONAL
DEVELOPMENT AGENCY
(SIDA)

women as low status or, even worse, as expendable. Help groups and organizations which are trying to prevent further tragedy by re-educating communities produce visual material which prompts oppressed women to a new self-awareness and resistance.

Bad health conditions, lack of food or proper nutrition, lack of reproductive health care and family planning, the threat of HIV or AIDS, and the inadequacy of education on these and many related subjects, all continue to be problems for women around the world, remaining subjects of a prolific amount of graphic informational material and media projects. Although development agencies and other organizations noted changes in perceptions and attitudes throughout the 1980s, a struggle still remains for women's labour to be acknowledged and valued, so that they may acquire necessary skills, be paid fairly and equally, and be protected from exploitation and sexual harassment. Their prominence in strike action and industrial disputes around the world shows their ability to make such demands, both for themselves and for others.

There is, moreover, the struggle against violence against women, which seems to be endemic to all cultures, both rich and poor. Visual campaigns are included here from a number of countries, in order to counter any assumptions or illusions that violence against women is the problem solely of poverty, or of the developing world. The strategies used in campaigns relating to domestic violence are particularly ingenious in their efforts to filter through society and convey their message as effectively as possible in order to reach an 'invisible' audience. The environmental strategy of the Zero Tolerance campaign of Edinburgh, Scotland and the informational milk cartons created by artist Peggy Diggs in the USA both represent provocative approaches to a problem that continues to stay behind closed doors or undercover (pages 204, 206–7).

Women are strengthened by the power of the media in confronting this daunting range of struggles. They are using communications media as a tool for change: to educate communities, convey health information, and combat gender oppression; to explore new ways of raising the status of women and halting violence, and to find new ways of empowering women by offering them a voice.

An example of the imaginative use of communications media for these purposes can be seen in the work of the Tanzania Media Women's Association (TAMWA) and their 'visuals of empowerment'. Interestingly, TAMWA grew out of concerns for women's lack of voice in the media. In 1979, a number of women journalists formed a group to protest the

Over the years, women worldwide have struggled for many freedoms, including freedom from political oppression:

1 'Women Fight for Freedom', poster in support of women in the struggle, with a quote by Dora Tamana of South Africa. Issued by the African National Congress (ANC) on its 75th anniversary in 1987.

2 Poster calling for support for the SWAPO Women's Council (SWAPO: South West African People's Organization), designed by Wild Plakken design studio, Holland, 1982.

Two surveys that helped to construct a global view of women's lives:

3 Robin Morgan's Sisterhood is Global: The International Women's Movement Anthology (1984).

4 Women in the World: an International Atlas (1986), by Joni Seager and Ann Olson, an extraordinary attempt to provide a global geographical mapping of women's experience, ranging from agricultural work and abortion issues to cosmetic surgery.

unrealistic portrayal of women in the mass media. They created a series of programmes on a real issue: schoolgirl pregnancies. The programmes were aired and were highly successful, generating a great deal of feedback. But efforts to create another series on violence against women were blocked, bringing home the reality that Tanzanian women had no real media forum of their own. Nevertheless, the same women grouped together ten years later, this time helped by the fact that the 1980s had brought an upsurge in the feminist movement in Tanzania. Thus TAMWA was formed in 1987, dedicated to 'capturing the voices of women' who are not normally heard. It sees a distinct role for media women to play in uplifting the status of women, and in using the media as a mobilizing force.

TAMWA promotes the concerns of women through the development and use of contemporary mass media as well as more traditional media including dance and drama, and, in addition, provides a forum for media women, exchanging ideas, skills and resources. Its activities are wide-ranging and prolific. Research provides the basis for all it does, and is carried out on a broad range of topics: from school pregnancies mentioned above and violence against women, to issues of women's literacy, women's legal rights, and representations of women in the media. A Health Unit works on improving the provisions for women's health; an Environment Unit deals with issues of sanitation and industrial waste; the Cultural Unit documents women's history and explores the use of cultural forums, such as dance, drama, music and fashion, to mobilize women on development issues; and a Children's Unit deals with issues of child labour, child abuse and so on, while even doing research into the role of children's playsongs in perpetuating gender roles.

Units exist for radio, publishing, publicity and TAMWA's magazine *Sauti Ya Siti*, all of which act as tools for development and education. TAMWA also runs a Women's Crisis Centre for victims of assault and abuse, in direct response to one of their campaigns that focused on a student suicide caused by sexual harassment.

As the only publishing house in Tanzania run by women, TAMWA creates booklets, pamphlets and papers on many issues relating to women, and also publishes children's books. *Sauti Ya Siti*, launched in 1988 and produced in both English and Swahili, is probably their most 'visible' product. This lively magazine acts as a forum in which views and opinions can be aired, while it also carries essential information, functioning as an educational tool, and providing an outlet for women who want to write about their lives and aspirations. It therefore acts as a vehicle for the positive portrayal of women, undermining negative conceptions of them as sex objects or beasts of burden. TAMWA hits hard at many stereotypes and forms networks through which to distribute its information and programmes at an international level, in order to provide a more realistic picture of Africa itself, and challenge the existing stereotypes that are consumed by the West. So although TAMWA sees itself as being concerned with grass-roots activities, it maintains connections (and ambitions) with a broader global community of women's networks.

Finally, there is the ongoing struggle for

The struggle for freedom from old traditions and customs:

5 'Beware!', a poster relating to female genital mutilation, published by Forward, Britain, early 1990s.

6 Trans, moving downwards: 'Female Genital Mutilation', 'It's a Recurring Nightmare'. Poster published (in Somali) by Forward, Britain, early 1990s. Forward is a London-based organization formed in 1983 to promote good health amongst African women and their children both in the UK and Africa. Its main concern is reproductive health, with a special focus on 'harmful cultural practices' such as female genital mutilation. These posters were displayed in Forward offices and distributed to communities in Africa.

1

freedom from political or military oppression. There have been many instances over the past few decades, recorded through the feminist network as well as in the mainstream media, where women have played important roles in national liberation struggles; in resistance to oppression (for example human rights violations) from military dictatorships; and in ensuring community survival, identity and resistance during periods of war or prolonged occupation. In Nicaragua's revolution in the early 1980s, women made up thirty per cent of the fighting force; they were shown marching, laughing and carrying guns and babies, on posters and newsletters that have become well known throughout the world (see page 198).[4] In the prolonged cultural and educational disruption during the Palestinian–Israeli conflict in the 1980s, the mass-based (feminist) Palestinian women's movement was responsible, through its popular women's committees, for keeping daily life going by providing medical attention, support to families, nurseries, and education for children, despite school closures. In Chile, and in other Latin American countries, women stepped forward courageously to protest the 'disappearances', torture and imprisonment inflicted on their loved ones. Those in exile formed women's groups (such as the Chilean women's group Avanza in London) and worked hard to provide solidarity and financial support for those still at home or in prison. The many posters they produced through community presses brought great attention and support for their cause.

The role that women played in a number of the national liberation struggles of Africa during the 1970s and 1980s generated highly inspirational images that were circulated worldwide through poster networks, magazines and other forms of alternative media. These struggles often received courageous sup-

2

port from women's organizations founded on the principle that revolution has no meaning or success without the active participation of women, so that national liberation was seen as the road to emancipation for women. Robin Morgan, however, has made it clear in *Sisterhood is Global*, that in many such cases of national liberation around the world, things didn't necessarily happen that way – once liberation was achieved, women were often shifted to the bottom of the list of new political priorities.[5]

To name but a few of the struggles in which women freedom-fighters were highly visible: Eritrean women carried arms in the attempt to liberate their nation (from c 1970 to 1991); Mozambiquen women fought alongside men to achieve independence (1975), as did Angolan and Zimbabwean women; Namibian women fought in the armed struggle against the South African military occupation of their country, mainly organized under the SWAPO Women's Council, which began in 1970 and mustered tremendous international support throughout the 1980s. Images of women as guerrilla fighters were highly inspirational and emotionally moving for Western women, and did much to further both their knowledge and sense of solidarity with women struggling in other parts of the world.

Women and the democratic movement in South Africa

Freedom from political oppression was central to decades of struggle waged by the black South African population against the South African government and its system of apartheid. Women played a prominent role in the popular democratic movement, while building a 'culture of resistance' that kept black communities going by sustaining their political identity through an emphasis on awareness and education. In 1955 and 1956, women organized nationwide protests against the pass laws (the laws restricting the movement of Black Africans, particularly from rural to urban areas): the first involved 2,000 women in Durban and Cape Town, while in the second 20,000 women marched to the government buildings in Pretoria, all walking in groups of not more than three to get around the ban on processions that day. On their arrival they handed over petitions and stood in a silent protest for thirty minutes. As they dispersed they sang anthems of defiance, including the refrain that became a rallying cry for women's organizations, appearing on posters and other graphic material for years to come: 'Now you have touched the women you have struck a rock, you have dislodged a boulder, you will be crushed.'[6] The Pretoria march on 9 August 1956 marked what is now called Women's Day in South Africa.

In the following decades, women fought and protested alongside men, and suffered tremendous hardships in their fight against racial oppression. They were shot, detained without trial, imprisoned, tortured, banned, forced into exile and harassed in their everyday life. So were children and young people. In addition, women bore the responsibility of taking care of the families of those in jail, and through community groups provided support for detainees and prisoners. Leaders and heroines of the struggle began to emerge along the way, outspoken and instrumental in mobilizing women to join together in organizations such as the Federation of South African Women (FEDSAW), and the United Women's Organization, or playing an important part in developing the African National Congress. These included Dorothy Zihlangu, Dora Tamana, Albertina Sisulu, Lilian Ngoyi, Annie Silinga, and many others, including Winnie Mandela.

In the 1980s the South African government adopted policies of unstinting repression, bringing intense and widescale resistance from the popular democratic movement, culminating in the Defiance Campaign of 1989. Throughout the decade, graphic design played a vital role in the popular struggle. Resistance posters, as well as the highly popular t-shirts, banners, badges, stickers and other ready-made graphics, were used to publicize meetings, to promote support for organizations, to memorialize

The struggle for freedom from violence:
1   Logo for Project for Legal Action Against Sexual Assault, designed by Lin Tobias, Australia, 1995.
2   T-shirts and photographs from the Clothesline Project, the grass-roots movement that became a national network dedicated to exposing and ending violence against women, USA,1995. (See also page 205.)

3   'Crimes Against Women', a poster by Women's Action Forum in Lahore, Pakistan. The newspaper headings at the top are dated 1983–4, the black strip in the middle reads 'Do women have the same rights as men?', and the newspaper cuttings relate to cases of rape, wife-murdering, kidnapping and so on.

events or people, and to protest injustice and make demands. Each one provides a visual document of the determination of the people. They were produced in silkscreen workshops, by collectives and activists, often in secret and under the threat of detention, beatings or even death.

Women appear as a driving force in these vibrant, brightly coloured posters, as well as in the photographic documentation that filtered into the outside world through books, magazines and other forms of alternative, or independent, media. These documents of the struggle were often produced by humanitarian organizations, such as the International Defence and Aid Fund for Southern Africa (IDAF), or by women's groups such as the Black Sash or the SPEAK collective. Both produced magazines familiar to the international feminist network.

Community projects and alternative media also played a critical role throughout the decade in attempting to halt the political, social and cultural destruction of the apartheid regime. These destructive forces included forced removals, when the state uprooted black communities and forced families to relocate to designated areas; a migrant labour system which forced men to separate from their families in order to earn a living; the instability of living in a squatter environment, as well as years of disrupted or inadequate education, poor social conditions and political repression in all its forms, including the detention of men, women and children. The effect that all these circumstances had on children was addressed by the community project Molo Songololo.

Molo Songololo was founded in 1979 in Cape Town by a group of four women community workers. They organized activities for children which aimed to help them express the impact that the forces of apartheid had on their lives through writing and drawing, all as part of the UN International Year of the Child programme. The wealth of material produced became the start of *Molo Songololo* magazine for children, launched in 1980 around objectives that remain just as relevant today.

It encourages contact between children of all backgrounds, to break down barriers and help develop understanding between races and religions, and helps stimulate children to express their ideas and experiences. It tries to ensure that when children speak out, they are taken seriously. It promotes the needs of children – publicizing their hardships, working with children living in the street – and makes an ongoing call for community involvement. Furthermore, it calls for the creation of new, alternative, relevant and educational reading material. The word 'alternative' is important here: historically speaking, Molo Songololo has not been funded by government grants or official state institutions, but by outside Christian

The struggle for recognition of women's strength, value and work:
1 African commemorative cloth (roller printed fabric) celebrating the UN International Year of the Woman and incorporating the UN logo. Ivory Coast, 1975.
2 'The Hand That Rocks the Cradle Should Also Rock the Boat': a quote taken from the 1985 Nairobi conference at the end of the UN Decade for Women. Poster published by Oxfam, Britain, 1985.

3 Trans, moving downwards: 'Without women's votes, the Republic is not complete', (the slip of paper says 'vote'), 'For our country's advancement, you must advance'. Poster by the Women's Foundation (logo, bottom right); Pakistan, c1995.
4 Letterhead from the office stationery of Molo Songololo magazine for children, Cape Town, South Africa 1995. Since its launch in 1980, Molo Songololo has worked for the cause of

Children's Rights – the name, in Xhosa, means 'hello centipede'. See also page 219.
5 'Women's Work is Never Done', poster published by the Speak Collective of Durban, South Africa. Original drawing taken from Mukti (issue 4, Autumn 1985), a quarterly Asian Women's magazine based in London. Reproduced here from the international magazine Women in Action, issue 3, 1988.

عورتوں کے ووٹ کے بغیر جمہوریت ادھوری ہے

ووٹ ڈالیئے
اپنی ترقی کے لیے
آپ کی ترقی ملک کی ترقی ہے

or humanitarian sources. In every sense, it has existed outside the mainstream press, and continues to do so.

Molo Songololo aims to advocate and lobby for Children's Rights. To this end, it works for the development and awareness of their rights, and uniquely encourages interaction between children and politicians. Children's rights can, in this context, range from the right to good health care, to the right to a loving, caring family and a proper home; the right not to be held in prisons or police cells; or the right to free, equal, non-racist, non-sexist education. In 1992, Molo Songololo organized and hosted the National Children's Summit on the Rights of Children in South Africa. During its course, participating children drew up the Children's Charter of South Africa, which was presented to press and politicians and resulted in the extraordinary, if not unique, inclusion of a clause on Children's Rights in the constitution of the new South Africa. In addition to the magazine, Molo Songololo conducts workshops, exchange programmes, and other activities such as their Children's Film Festival. The first, held in 1993, screened films in cinemas, schools, libraries and community halls and made it possible for over 50,000 children to watch movies. For many, it was their first visit to a cinema, giving some welcome fun to a young generation that has been exposed to far too much violence.

The democratic elections of April 1994, which made Nelson Mandela State President, have brought great hopes for the new South Africa's future; but all acknowledge that there is still much work to be done. The group Mediaworks (formerly known as CAP: Community Arts Project, Cape Town) has dedicated itself to the long-term process of democratizing the media by establishing independent projects in marginalized (rural and peri-urban) communities. It also operates a Women's Project, which runs courses on gender awareness in relation to the media and operates a Media Watch Group. The group addresses issues of women's representation in the media and women's lack of access to channels of communication, and its members are willing to stage protests or picket mainstream newspapers in order to make their point (page 218). So the need for alternatives – and alternative media – is still very much there. For in trying to ensure a democratic future, all voices must be heard – and that includes women and, as Molo Songololo has demonstrated, children too.

WOMEN'S WORK

Women make up half the world

They work nearly two-thirds of the world's work hours

Yet they earn one-tenth of the world's income

IS NEVER DONE

6   *Trans, moving downwards: 'I'm doing an assessment', 'Status of Women Month in Israel – Na'amat 1991'. Poster (in Hebrew) produced by Na'amat: the Movement of Working Women and Volunteers in Israel, in order to encourage women to be involved in finance, know their rights, and demand equal treatment and equal opportunities. (There is a gap between the average salary of the Israeli working woman and that of a man.) The use of the late Prime Minister Golda Meir's image is significant: Israel's 10 shekel note carries her picture; she was also formerly the Chairperson of Na'amat.*

MOLO songololo

The global presence: signs and symbols of a worldwide movement

Much of the international women's movement was established in the 1970s, as women's groups, networks and organizations were set up all over the world. They connected via communications services such as Isis International and the International Women's Tribune Centre; through their own programmes of sharing and collaboration; and through the magazines, reports, journals and newsletters which they all generated and distributed far and wide. By the 1980s, the expanding movement was consolidated, and a new knowledge and vision began to emerge of how women lived their lives around the world.

The movement's ongoing stream of journals and magazines (see Chapter Two, pages 106–7) also carried a mass of popular graphics around the globe. Logos and symbols became important identifiers of women's groups, their concerns, or particular causes or revolutions along the way, and visually reflected the tremendous diversity contained within the global experience. Posters, diaries and other graphic paraphernalia were circulated and posted around the world, extending awareness of the extraordinary roles women played in various societies and cultures. For example, images of women as freedom fighters – and depictions of their involvement in wars, conflicts and national liberation movements – made a tremendous impact on women in the West. Such images were highly inspirational in their show of courage and strength, and provided a weighty counterbalance to the mass of frivolous, negative images of women churned out by the Western media throughout the 1970s and 1980s.

1 Poster announcing the World Conference in Nairobi to end the UN Decade for Women, designed by Liz Mestres, USA, 1985.
2 Badge carrying the symbol of the UN Decade for Women (1975–85).
3–14 Logos and symbols from selected women's groups, organisations and programmes around the world:
3 'A Woman's Right to Learn': a World University Service (UK) Women, Education and Development campaign, logo designed by Anthea Eames, Britain, 1980s.
4 Women's Action Forum, Pakistan, 1980s.

5 Women's Association/Dubai, United Arab Emirates (UAE), 1993.
6 Akshara, a feminist library and information centre in Bombay, India, 1990.
7 Womankind Worldwide, Britain, 1980s.
8 National Union of Students (NUS) Women's Campaign, Britain, 1990s.
9 The Palestinian Federation of Women's Action Committees (PFWAC), Jerusalem, 1991.
10 Tanzania Media Women's Association (TAMWA), Tanzania, 1990s.

11 Women, Ink., a project of the International Women's Tribune Centre, concerned with distributing resource materials on women and development, USA, 1995.
12 CIPAF: Centro de Investigacion Para la Accion Femenina – Centre of Investigation for Women's Action, Dominican Republic, 1980s.
13 Mudechi: Mujeres de Chile (Women of Chile), a national women's organization, Chile, 1980s.
14 'Women's Affairs': a research and training centre for Palestinian women (also the name of its journal), Nablus and Gaza, 1988.

3

4

5

akshara

6

WOMANKIND
WORLDWIDE

7

SUS WOMEN'S CAMPAIGN

8

9

TAMWA
CHAWAHATA

10

WOMEN, INK.

11

CIPAF

12

MUJERES DE CHILE
Mudechi
26 Dic. 1982

13

14

AMNLAE

1   Emblem/illustration for AMNLAE: the Luisa Amanda Espinoza Nicaraguan Women's Association, the first women's association of the Nicaraguan Revolution. (Its namesake Luisa Amanda Espinoza was the first woman fighter of the Sandinista National Liberation Front – FSLN – to be killed in battle in 1973, aged 21.) The association was founded in 1977, and became known as the AMNLAE in 1979, the year of the Sandinista Revolution and the overthrow of the Somoza dictatorship. With the beginning of a de-stabilizing Contra War in the 1980s, the AMNLAE became an instrumental force in the building and defending of the new Nicaragua.

2   Double-page spread with an illustration of an enamel plate showing a foetus holding a Palestinian flag. Taken from a 1991 diary produced by the Palestinian Federation of Women's Action Committees (PFWAC). The diary contains art works from their brass and enamel project, established at Essawiyeh in 1985 to encourage women to acquire skills traditionally considered to be solely a male domain since they required 'great effort and persistence'.

3   'Nicaragua Must Survive', anonymous poster published by AMNLAE, Nicaragua, c1985. Photo by Orlando Valenzuela.

NICARAGUA DEBE SOBREVIVIR
NICARAGUA MUST SURVIVE

AMNLAE

4 Solidarity badge for OMA: Organizacao da Mulher de Angola (Angolan Women's Organization), founded in 1963 during Angola's struggle for liberation, with women fighting alongside men throughout. Liberation was achieved in 1975, although guerrilla attempts to destabilize the country continued. The OMA worked to involve women in the development of the new country and, in the 1980s, in setting out women's rights in the new constitution.

5 Logo/rubber stamp from the Women and Children Under Apartheid Newsletter (issue no 1, 1987), issued by the ANC Women's Section, Lusaka, Zambia. (ANC: African National Congress)

6 'Namibia Women's Day – 10 December 1985', poster in support of SWAPO/South West African People's Organization, London, 1985.

6

4

The global presence: signs and symbols of a worldwide movement

The prime motives of the international women's movement – communicating, networking and organizing – can also be seen in the clip-art books produced by the International Women's Tribune Centre (IWTC). The IWTC was founded in New York City in 1976, following the 1975 International Women's Year conference held in Mexico City, to act as a communications support service for women's activities worldwide.

As a way of encouraging women's groups to produce their own publications and communicate with one another, IWTC has created books of logos and illustrations to be 'clipped out' and used in a variety of ways. They do, however, emphasize the need to adapt the illustrations to specific situations, ethnic backgrounds and cultures, by altering hairstyles, dress and other features. To this end, many of the illustrations exist in both outline and solid (filled-in) versions. In addition, outlined protest placards remain blank, awaiting a slogan, and crowds can be expanded, contracted or changed in style. Intended to help women everywhere to create visual aids to action, this picture language can be found dotted here and there throughout the many documents and publications of the global movement.

Covers and inside pages from three clip-art books of feminist logos and illustrations, originally published in 1984 and 1988 by the International Women's Tribune Centre and intended for use by publications and women's groups around the world. *Artists credits: Rural Women in Action: Anne S Walker; Woman: The Password is Action: Anne S Walker and Grace Jung. Source credits from Feminist Logos: Cover: from Kvinder for Fred (Women for Peace),* Denmark. Second page (top): symbol of the Women's Ecology Movement; used in Women of Europe, Belgium, no 15, May/June/July 1980, p59. Second page (bottom): graphic used in Kvinner, Norway, no 3/4, 1980, p9. Third page: symbol for the UN Decade for Women. Designed by Valerie Pettis. Copyright/Fund for the Decade for Women, Inc.

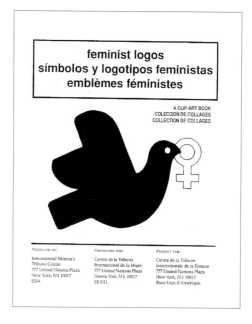

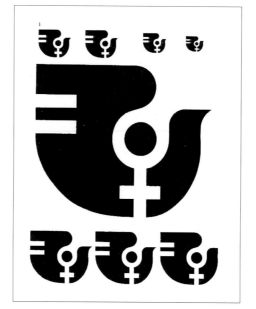

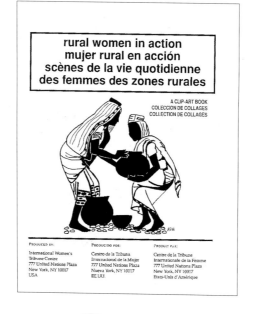

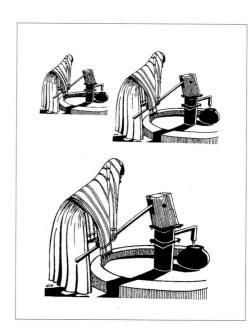

Produced by:

International Women's
Tribune Centre
777 United Nations Plaza
New York, NY 10017
USA

Preparado por:

Centro de la Tribuna
Internacional de la Mujer
777 United Nations Plaza
Nueva York, NY 10017
EE.UU.

Produit par:

Centre de la Tribune
Internationale de la Femme
777 United Nations Plaza
New York, NY 10017
Etats-Unis d'Amérique

PRIERE D'INDIQUER COMME SOURCE: SIRVASE CITAR COMO FUENTE: PLEASE CREDIT TO:

Centre de la Tribune
Internationale de la Femme (CTIF)

Centro de la Tribuna
Internacional de la Mujer (CTIM)

International Women's
Tribune Centre (IWTC)

PRIERE D'INDIQUER COMME SOURCE: SIRVASE CITAR COMO FUENTE: PLEASE CREDIT TO:

Centre de la Tribune
Internationale de la Femme (CTIF)

Centro de la Tribuna
Internacional de la Mujer (CTIM)

International Women's
Tribune Centre (IWTC)

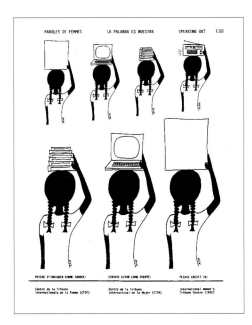

PRIERE D'INDIQUER COMME SOURCE: SIRVASE CITAR COMO FUENTE: PLEASE CREDIT TO:

Centre de la Tribune
Internationale de la Femme (CTIF)

Centro de la Tribuna
Internacional de la Mujer (CTIM)

International Women's
Tribune Centre (IWTC)

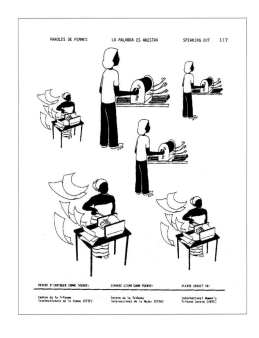

PRIERE D'INDIQUER COMME SOURCE: SIRVASE CITAR COMO FUENTE: PLEASE CREDIT TO:

Centre de la Tribune
Internationale de la Femme (CTIF)

Centro de la Tribuna
Internacional de la Mujer (CTIM)

International Women's
Tribune Centre (IWTC)

PRIERE D'INDIQUER COMME SOURCE: SIRVASE CITAR COMO FUENTE: PLEASE CREDIT TO:

Centre de la Tribune
Internationale de la Femme (CTIF)

Centro de la Tribuna
Internacional de la Mujer (CTIM)

International Women's
Tribune Centre (IWTC)

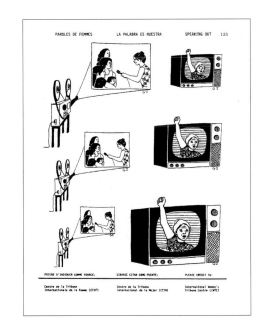

PRIERE D'INDIQUER COMME SOURCE: SIRVASE CITAR COMO FUENTE: PLEASE CREDIT TO:

Centre de la Tribune
Internationale de la Femme (CTIF)

Centro de la Tribuna
Internacional de la Mujer (CTIM)

International Women's
Tribune Centre (IWTC)

Violence against women: protest campaigns and solitary statements

Violence against women remains endemic in all countries and cultures. It cuts across barriers of race and class, and appears in many different forms: in the private sphere in the forms of rape, murder or beatings; in the institutionalized sphere in which violence is sanctioned through religious or state laws; in injurious practices that exist through tradition or custom; and in many other areas. Its recognition, and the definition of its many manifestations, became one of the central concerns of the Women's Liberation Movement of the 1970s and has consequently continued to be a major issue of the international women's movement.[7] This focus has inevitably brought to many countries a variety of activities and protests which have extensively used graphic formats for information-carrying and awareness-raising – and even, in one case shown here, for expressive, healing purposes.

Crisis hotlines and women's centres relating to rape or other forms of abuse often rely on ephemeral graphics, such as cards, stickers and press advertisements, that are floated through the environment, with the aim of providing easy access or of coaxing out a hesitant cry for help. US artist Peggy Digg's milk cartons (page 204), have a more distinct strategic mission: to deliver that hotline number into the domestic domain of the home – where most violence takes place – and within the reach of an audience that often remains invisible.

Posters, announcements and other paraphernalia still operate as awareness-raising and networking devices, whether exchanged across continents or pasted up on home ground. Examples are shown here that have emanated from women's rights organizations as far afield as Women's Action Forum in Pakistan, or CIPAF in the Dominican Republic (Centro de Investigación Para la Acción Femenina, the Centre of Investigation for Women's Action). Some of the examples attempt to raise awareness of issues by citing certain actions or demonstrations; others build solidarity by commemorating events such as the International Day of Protest Against Violence Against Women (25 November). They may also remind of tragedy: the White Ribbon campaign was organized by the Canadian men's movement in direct response to the Montreal massacre of 1989, when a male student screaming 'I hate feminists' shot dead fourteen women at an engineering school. With the aim of opposing male violence and altering male attitudes, the White Ribbon campaign quickly exceeded national boundaries – this poster's home (page 204) was a wall in a British university.

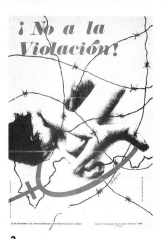

¡No a la Violación!

25 de noviembre - día internacional de la no violencia contra la mujer   Centro de Investigación Para la Acción Femenina -CIPAF-

SI A LA VIDA NO A LA VIOLENCIA

1　Advertisement for a Women's Centre, protesting against the misuse of sex determination tests which may prompt the abortion of female foetuses, India, 1987.

2　Trans: 'Donate Now in Order to Change Things'. Poster (in Hebrew) designed by Yossi Lemel for WIZO, a major women's organization in Israel, 1990s. The paragraph in large quotations says: 'A month after the wedding he started with beatings, and then suddenly I was left with nothing, no dignity, no security ... only fear, dreadful fear that he would kill me...'

3　Trans: 'No to Violence!', a CIPAF poster celebrating 25 November, the International Day of No Violence Against Women (photo-image signed K R Graficas), Dominican Republic, 1990.

4　Trans: 'Yes to Life, No to Violence', a poster celebrating 25 November, published by CIPAF (Centre of Investigation for Women's Action), Dominican Republic, 1989.

5　Trans, moving downwards: 'Are we protecting women both inside and outside the house?', 'Regal Choank (Intersection), Lahore, 12 February 1983', 'The Women's Movement of Punjab'. Poster showing a demonstration – staged to campaign for the protection of women – being suppressed by the police. Pakistan, 1980s.

5

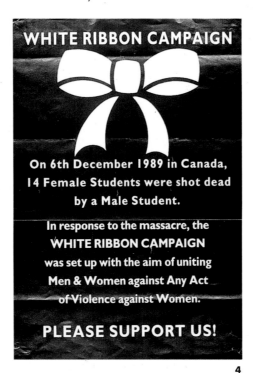

While many of these projects disturb with the intensity or meaning of their statement, some of the larger campaigns overwhelm the viewer with an added dimension – their revelation of the sheer scale of the problem being addressed. The USA-based Clothesline Project, for example, stuns with the weight of the list of statistics that inspired it. For example: 'it is estimated that 51,000 women were murdered in the United States by their husbands or lovers during the sixteen years of the Vietnam War, where 58,000 Americans [men] had died'.[8] The Clothesline Project aims to show both the extent and the impact of violence against women. It encourages women – survivors, or family and friends – to design or create a t-shirt as an expression of the abuse they have experienced; the t-shirt is then hung on a clothesline with others. This simple, evocative idea started as thirty-one shirts displayed on a clothesline in Massachusetts in 1990 and rapidly grew into a national network that saw its means of expression become massive in scale: by 1995, there were 250 lines with 35,000 shirts. The Project held a national display in Washington DC in 1995; it now incorporates another eight participating countries. Within this vast demonstration exists a counterpoint that is equally overwhelming: the expression of individual pain, which is at times courageous and moving, and at others very difficult for the viewer to confront, but which overall, in its extraordinary variety, carries a message that is eloquent and powerful. The Clothesline Project is not solely about mourning for its victims; it is about having the courage and strength to survive, reclaim a life and bring about change – the end to violence against women.

WHITE RIBBON CAMPAIGN

On 6th December 1989 in Canada, 14 Female Students were shot dead by a Male Student.

In response to the massacre, the WHITE RIBBON CAMPAIGN was set up with the aim of uniting Men & Women against Any Act of Violence against Women.

PLEASE SUPPORT US!

1, 2 'Domestic Violence Milkcarton Project' by Peggy Diggs, USA 1991–2. Working with the knowledge that supermarkets were the only public places commonly visited by abused women, the artist Peggy Diggs developed a design for half-gallon milk containers which, once purchased, would carry a domestic violence hotline number into the home – and within the reach of those who needed it. Figure 2 shows four designs developed by the artist; figure 1 shows the prototype that was selected and distributed by Tuscan Dairy.
3 Logo for the Rape Law Reform Evaluation Project designed by Lin Tobias, Australia, 1995.
4 Poster for the White Ribbon campaign, a movement by Canadian men to stop male violence against women, as a result of the Montreal Massacre of 1989. (See text, page 202.)

5 Examples from The Clothesline Project, the US national network dedicated to ending violence against women and giving survivors of such violence a voice through the medium of hand-painted shirts. (Total as of 1 February 1995: 35,150 shirts.) The different shirt colours represent a code: red, orange, pink: raped or sexually assaulted; blue, green: survived incest or child sexual abuse; yellow, beige: battering or assault; purple, lavender: lesbian bashing; white: violent death.

MY SISTER IN THE CLOSET
SITS WITH A FENCE AROUND
HER HOUSE, HER HEART
HER SILENCE IS HER PAIN
SOCIETY'S TO BLAME.

THE WITNESS

I Saw My Daddy Hit My Mommy
AGAIN, AND NOW SHE HAS UGLY
Bruses ON HeR PRETTY SKIN.
I Tried to Stop him But He's
My Dad. Why did he Hit My
Mommy Was She Being BAD?
Author:
My 5 year old Son
MARCUS Jr.

CONVICTED
FOR STEALING
1999, TWO CAMERAS,
AND A JACKET
ESCAPED...
RUNNING NAKED
IN THE SNOW
1,000 YARDS
THROUGH
PARKING LOTS, PAST
APTS, KNOWING
BUT NOT
FOR RAPE
ANY MOMENT
THE RAPIST
WOULD SHOOT
ME DEAD
HELD AT GUN POINT FOR 4 HOURS, BRUTALIZED, VIOLATED, RAPED, FOREVER CHANGED...

NOW YOU ARE AT PEACE

STOP DOMESTIC ABUSE!!

If my Daddy really loved me why did he touch me?

The ONLY TIME I GOT NEW GLASSES WAS WHEN YOU PUNCHED ME IN THE FACE, JOHN.

EVERY CHILD DESERVES A SAFE HUG

You vill not gag me anymore

Evelyn

No More Secrets!

PLEASE MOMMY HELP Me! DADDY'S Hurting Me!!!

MY NAME IS GIGI H S NAME MIGUEL

I was left torn, in tatters...
But I have begun to reclaim myself;
weaving hanging threads
into whole cloth.

And after Dark!

may there be no Sadness

VIOLENCE PEACE
WE DIDN'T CHOOSE:
to be beaten
to be violated
to be killed

blame the woman, blame the drink, blame the weather.
DOMESTIC VIOLENCE – THERE IS NO EXCUSE

In another expansive project on violence, scale served to create an absorbing visual presence on the city streets. The Zero Tolerance project, based in Edinburgh, Scotland, in November 1992 bombarded the city with messages relating to male violence against women, in a massive awareness-raising exercise with a revolutionary agenda. It wanted to redefine such violence, particularly domestic violence, in the broadest terms so as to show its widespread nature, to subvert stereotypes about who creates that violence, and to place such issues into the public domain – all in an attempt to undermine society's long-standing tolerance of violence against women. The project was also revolutionary in that it didn't demand women change their behaviour, and insisted on a feminist stance that empowered women and challenged men.

The project was initiated and launched by the Women's Committee of Edinburgh District Council, who formed a small creative team for its development and implementation. With graphic elements, including a strong logo, designed by Franki Raffles, the team formulated a highly identifiable visual campaign which, like so many sleek advertising campaigns, would by its very presence overtake and dominate the urban environment, and penetrate the public's psyche. The initiative was so successful it spread to other cities in the UK and gradually made its presence felt throughout the entire country.

Z ZERO TOLERANCE
of violence against women
A·L·A
ASSOCIATION OF
LONDON AUTHORITIES

NO
MAN
HAS THE RIGHT.

Z ZERO TOLERANCE
of violence against women

2

1   The many visual applications of the Zero Tolerance project, protesting against male violence against women. Based in Edinburgh, Scotland, November 1992.
2   Variations of the Zero Tolerance logo (black on white, and white on black) designed by Franki Raffles.
3   Poster from the London campaign that followed.

1

3

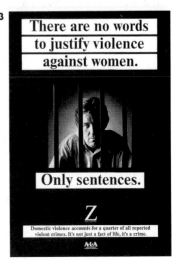

Latin American women against political repression: solidarity graphics

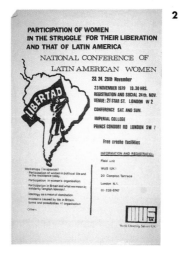

Feminism is by no means a Western invention; active and highly organized women's movements have existed in developing countries around the world since the nineteenth century, not to mention the 'indigenous feminism' that existed in many cultures long before then. Latin American women's groups, for example, have a particularly strong history this century of campaigning for women's rights in the home and the workplace. They have challenged the heavily male-orientated culture (where violence against women is a central issue) and the suffocating influence of the Church, as well as taking a stand against military dictatorships and their ongoing systems of political repression.

On the latter subject, Chile provides a strong case in point. Throughout the 1970s and 1980s, solidarity graphics permeated worldwide showing women in the forefront of the Chilean movement against the monstrous Pinochet regime, which seized power in a military coup in 1973 and conducted a reign of terror marked by torture and 'disappearances' that lasted until the late 1980s. In Britain and elsewhere, posters and other graphic products were produced by solidarity campaigns and human rights organizations – as well as by support groups set up by Chilean women forced into exile – in order to raise the world's awareness of the situation and to raise funds to help those still under threat in Chile itself.

Women in Chile and in exile abroad therefore mobilized to oppose the dictatorship, and devised many different forms of resistance. Within the country, they were the first to demonstrate openly against Pinochet. They organized into committees of the Relatives of the Disappeared Prisoners and Political Prisoners, and staged hunger strikes and public demonstrations confronting the secret services and police during the late 1970s. They sent delegates abroad to encourage international solidarity. On International Women's Day (8 March), they would hold massive marches against the dictatorship. They staged protests from home. At a chosen point in the late evenings, working-class women would step outside their houses and hit empty saucepans for twenty minutes or so, creating an organized chorus of noise intended to let the regime know that women were on the offensive. Groups of women also collectively sewed together fabric collages called 'arpilleras' that illustrated daily life and political and economic situations. The arpilleras were a particularly important medium of popular expression and denunciation of the regime during the dictatorship's worst years of censorship (1973–c 83), when only government-controlled printing and media were allowed. They were also a cottage industry and a vital means of subsistence, since they were smuggled out of the country and sold, with the revenue being used to help feed people in the poorer areas. Support groups of women in exile, such as the London-based group known as Avanza, also helped to spread the story of the people's resistance. The group members produced posters and other solidarity graphics, raised funds to sustain relatives of those killed or disappeared, and worked to maintain an international focus on the injustices taking place in their homeland.

1   *Illustration accompanying an article about the power of language, and encouraging women based in the domestic sphere to learn to articulate their demands in the public sphere.*
From Mujer/Fempress, issue no 82, Chile, July 1988.
2   *Poster for the National Conference of Latin American Women held in London by the World University Service (UK) in 1979.*
3   *Translation: 'Documentation about Women', a journal from Nicaragua, issue 7/8, April–September 1989, and focusing on Women of the Third Age (Older Women).*
4, 5 *Publications from El Salvador (1985) and Chile (1982).*

6 Poster depicting women (including an editor of a feminist magazine) who were disappeared, tortured or imprisoned in Central and South America in the 1970s/80s. Contact numbers listed include Carila Resource Centre, Amnesty International, and Chile Committee for Human Rights. Britain, early 1980s.

LILIANA MERCEDES LETONA "CLELIA 26yrs old commander of the FMLN in El Salvador she was arrested in Jan 1981 & is in Soyapango women's prison

THE UNITED STATES DOMINATES THE SOUTH AMERICAN CONTINENT BY CONTROLLING ITS GOVERNMENTS ECONOMIES AND RESOURCES RESISTING THIS POLITICAL AND MILITARY INTERVENTION. MANY THOUSANDS OF PEOPLE ARE MURDERED, TORTURED AND IMPRISONED

ALAIDES FOPPA DE SOLORZANO 60yrs old. kidnapped 19 December 1980 in Guatamala city, she is a professor at the Autonoma university of Mexico and is the editor of the feminist magazine Fem DISAPPEARED

MARIA ETTY MARIN 21yrs old a factory worker. she was arrested May 10 1979 & taken to Batallon Pichincha where she was severely tortured & raped, she now has to walk with a crutch & is being held in La Picota prison Bogota Colombia.

Being young and beautiful doesn't interest me for I don't want to be just one more for them to kill.

They've been killing me since my mothers womb in my infancy with malnutrition in my adolescence with subjection and if I don't fight, my destiny will be to serve those who always win.

But now they are going to lose

by Evelyn

NALVIA ROSA MENA ALVARADO born in Chile 26 august 1955. she was pregnant when she was detained with her husband in 1976 DISAPPEARED

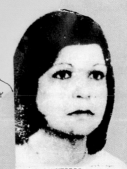

MARIA JOSEFA ESTEVEZ DE RODRIGUEZ 28 yrs old she was detained on 20 oct 1976 with her husband and two children. she was sentenced to 20 years in prison in Buenos Aires and was severely tortured.

ELENA QUINTEROS. was born on 9th September 1945 she was a teacher and leader of the teachers union. Elena v detained on 24th june 1976 Montevideo Uruguay DISAPPEARED

THOUSANDS OF WOMEN & CHILDREN ARE INVOLVED IN THIS STRUGGLE

contact
Carila Resource Centre 01 352 9270
Amnesty International 01 836 7788
Chile Committee for Human Rights 01 837 7561

1

4

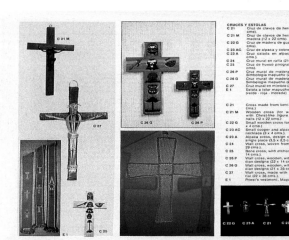

2

3

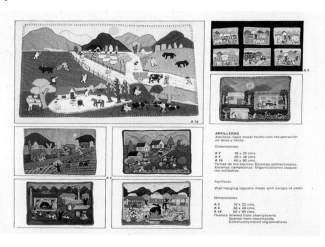

1 Photograph of women sewing 'arpilleras' (fabric collages or patchworks) in Chile, mid-1980s. Photo by Julio Etchart.

2, 3 Examples of arpilleras, carrying an overtly political protest message, Chile, mid-1980s.

4 Catalogue of items sold by the Vicaria of Solidarity Workshops Program Team which included jewellery or objects (made by people in prison out of whatever materials were to hand, including stale bread or meat bones from soup), and arpilleras. Chile mid-1980s.

5 'Don't Lose Hope Avenue', poster by Constanza Aguirre, Britain, 1985.
Under the signpost the text explains:
'After a decade of military rule under the Pinochet regime, thousands of shanty town dwellers from the neighbourhood of La Granja in Santiago, carried out the largest land occupation in Chilean history. In their long struggle for the right to a home, they named the newly created streets with both optimism and irony, such as Avenida no pierdan la esperanza (Don't Lose Hope Avenue), Pasaje ilusion de un hogar (Home Sweet Home Illusion Passage).'

6 'Chilean Women', poster by Juan Skelton, published by the Chilean women's group Avanza and printed by See Red poster collective in London, Britain, 1983.

7 Sticker (and badge) for the London-based Chilean women's group Avanza, drawing by Constanza Aguirre, Britain, 1985–6.

8 Poster by Greenwich Mural Workshop in support of Chilean Women in Exile. It declares International Women's Day as a day of National Protest against Pinochet's regime, and depicts various demonstrations including banging on saucepans, a form of protest through noise.

9 'Chile Solidarity', poster by Jane Ray for the Chile Solidarity Campaign, Britain, 1985. The woman's dress depicts demonstrations for Freedom, women sewing arpilleras, someone being beaten in a prison cell, and a more hopeful image of a peaceful village of homes.

DON'T LOSE HOPE AVENUE

AVENIDA NO PIERDAN LA ESPERANZA

After a decade of military rule under the Pinochet regime, thousands of shanty town dwellers from the neighbourhood of La Granja in Santiago, carried out the largest land occupation in Chilean history.
In their long struggle for the right to a home, they named the newly created streets with both optimism and irony, such as 'Avenida no pierdan la esperanza' (Don't lose hope Avenue) 'Pasaje ilusion de un hogar' (Home Sweet Home Illusion Passage).

5

WOMEN in CHILE

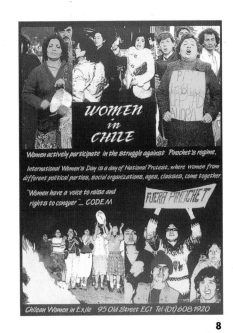

Women actively participate in the struggle against Pinochet's regime.

International Women's Day is a day of National Protest, where women from different political parties, social organizations, ages, classes, come together.

"Women have a voice to raise and rights to conquer" _ CODEM

FUERA PINOCHET

Chilean Women in Exile   95 Old Street EC1 Tel (01) 608 1920

8

9

CHILE SOLIDARITY

FREEDOM

CHILE SOLIDARITY CAMPAIGN 129 Seven Sisters Road London N7 7QG
01. 272 4298

CHILEAN WOMEN

6

7

Women against apartheid: solidarity graphics

The international anti-apartheid movement generated massive support for its cause, and inspired intense activity and concern from the international women's movement. By a vast variety of ways and means, the anti-apartheid movement encouraged resistance to the Republic of South Africa's system of apartheid, a separatist policy that imposed white minority power over the black majority, employing racial segregation, economic exploitation and the denial of basic rights to blacks, as well as Indians and people of mixed race. It also challenged the military and terrorist activities used by the aggressive South African regime in their attempts to destabilize neighbouring countries such as Namibia.

A long history of popular resistance within South Africa itself, despite harassment, detentions, torture, massacres and other atrocities, culminated in a decade of intense mass resistance in the 1980s. This brought solidarity and support from the international community in actions such as campaigning for Nelson Mandela's release from prison; support for economic sanctions; and 'divestment', the withdrawal of public funds from companies investing in South Africa. Consciousness-raising projects and solidarity posters further acknowledged the role that women were playing in the struggle and in sustaining their communities while under attack; these helped to tighten the ties of solidarity between women of different countries and cultures, and broadened their knowledge of one another.

1

2

3

1 'Boycott Products of Apartheid', poster for the Anti-Apartheid Movement, designer unknown, Britain, mid-1980s.

2 Poster designed by Jane Ray for the Women's Committee of the Anti-Apartheid Movement, Britain, mid-1980s.

3 Solidarity poster, designer unknown, Britain, mid-1980s.

4 Trans: 'Women Against Apartheid. Support the struggle of the women of the liberation movements ANC and SWAPO'. Poster by Wild Plakken for the Dutch anti-apartheid movement, Holland, 1984.

5 Poster celebrating South African Women's Day – 9 August, designed by Wild Plakken (Frank Beekers, Lies Ros, Rob Schröder) for the Dutch anti-apartheid movement, Holland, 1988.

4

'You have struck a rock': women fight apartheid in South Africa

Within South Africa itself, women played a vital part in the mass struggle against the South African government and its system of apartheid. As early as 1955/6 they organized nationwide protests against the pass laws. The most famous occurred on 9 August 1956 when 20,000 women marched on the government offices in Pretoria; this date is now known as South African Women's Day. Throughout the following decades, they mobilized, protested and suffered harsh punishment and harassment (such as detention and torture), while at the same time attempting to build a 'culture of resistance' to sustain their families and communities through crisis. This also included taking on the responsibility of looking after the families of those banished or in jail.

The 1980s brought a decade of intense mass resistance from the popular democratic movement and a surge of resistance graphics in the form of posters, stickers and t-shirts, used to announce meetings, protest against injustices, promote support for organizations, and memorialize events. Photographic documentation also filtered out through alternative media channels, including books and magazines, often produced by humanitarian organizations, solidarity campaigns or women's groups. All provided visual documentation of the people's expression of outrage and defiance. They also supplied the world with yet another insight into the courage and spirit of the women who fought and sacrificed – as well as the leadership shown by the women's organizations, mobilized by their members' determination to see a new future in South Africa for their families.

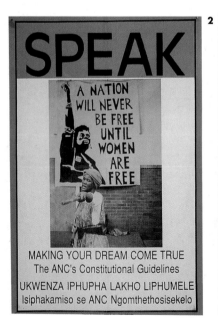

1 'Now You Have Touched the Women You Have Struck a Rock', the rallying cry emanating from the 9 August 1956 women's march on Pretoria. Screenprinted poster celebrating South African Women's Day (9 August), produced by Medu Art Ensemble, Botswana, 1981.
2 Posters advertising the feminist magazine Speak, South Africa, 1990. Speak started out in 1982 as a women's group with a newsletter, printed in both English and Zulu versions. By 1992 it had grown into an independent magazine, run by a collective, and with a national distribution of 15,000.
3 Poster originally produced by TOPS (The Other Press Service) for DPSC – Detainees' Parents Support Committee, which was then banned in February 1988. The poster was consequently issued by FEDTRAW (Federation of Transvaal Women), South Africa, c1988.
4 A demonstration on the steps of Johannesburg city hall by members of the Black Sash, a women's organization founded in 1955 and devoted to the protection of human rights and parliamentary democracy. Their name refers to the black sashes draped over their right shoulders to symbolically mourn the 'killing' of the constitution by Nationalists. South Africa, 1991. Photo by Gill de Vlieg.
5 Solidarity banner created at the last meeting of the DPSC (before banning) and carrying the names of prisoners and detainees, South Africa, c1988. Photo by Eric Miller.

3

4

5

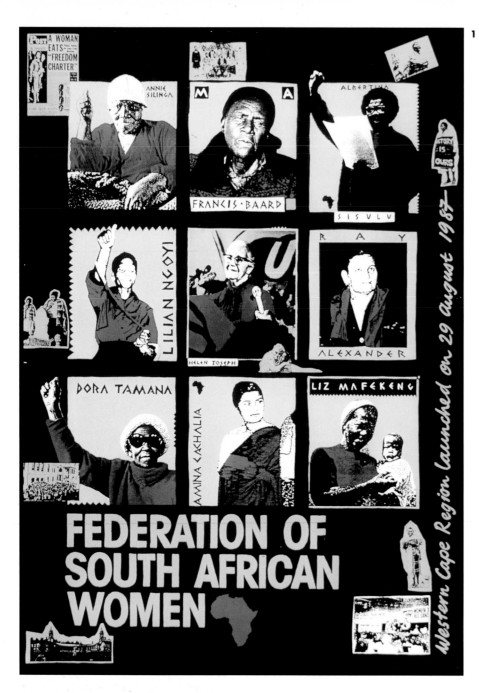

FEDERATION OF SOUTH AFRICAN WOMEN

Western Cape Region launched on 29 August 1987

This spread shows an interesting contrast in the reproduction quality of the 'graphic voice' of South Africa's democratic movement over two decades. The 'unofficial' or alternative voice of the 1980s exudes power and determination through the use of crude, spontaneous graphic layout and reproduction. The 'official' voice of the post-election 1990s employs the familiar professionalism of art-directed photography and styled typography, and is quietly confident and forward-looking.

1 Poster celebrating the launch of the Western Cape Region of FEDSAW: the Federation of South African Women, and depicting heroines of the struggle against apartheid. (Note the small cutting of Albertina Sisulu, upper right.) Produced by FEDSAW, Western Cape, 1987.

2 Photo of Albertina Sisulu, joint-president of the United Democratic Front and one of 16 UDF leaders charged with treason in 1985.

3 T-shirt for ANC Women's League, before the 1994 elections. (ANC: African National Congress)

4 T-shirt for the United Women's Congress, which through its activities and programmes emphasized the triple oppression of women – as women, workers and as black women – while promoting women's rights and national liberation. March, 1986.

5 Scarf made by the Woodstock Branch of the United Women's Congress for South African Women's Day (9 August) in 1986 – the day that annually commemorates the march to Pretoria in 1956 to protest against the pass laws.

6 Front and back of the Election t-shirt, for the first democratic election in South Africa in April 1994. The logos represent political parties (left to right): the African National Congress, the South African Communist Party, and COSATU (Trade Union Federation) – all offering policies sensitive to women.

7 T-shirt declaring 'Farewell Mama Dorothy Zihlangu', women's leader and activist, September 1991. Funerals were important gatherings used to mobilize and politicize women.

8 'Waiting for Democracy', a booklet published by the Community Law Centre in Durban, which used a cartoon-style format to teach the fundamentals of democracy, elections and voting to rural South Africans, many of whom suffered from poor communication networks and high levels of illiteracy. Both text and illustrations were tested in the communities, revealing great differences in urban and rural experience and perceptions. Two languages, Zulu and English, were presented simultaneously. Written by Jeya Wilson et al; illustrated by Tracy Brownlee, Colin Farris, and David Hadlow; designed by Artworks in Durban, South Africa, 1992.

9 Poster celebrating the 40th anniversary of the 1956 women's march to Pretoria to protest the pass laws, South Africa, 1996.

10 An ANC campaigning poster which also commemorates National Women's Day, South Africa, 1996.

6

VOTE FOR WOMEN'S
RIGHTS VOTE ANC
MALIBONGWE!

7

HAMBA
KAKUHLE

MAMA
ZIHLANGU

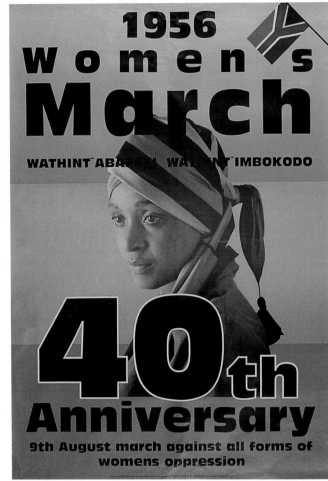

1956
W o m e n's
March

WATHINT`ABAFAZI WATHINT`IMBOKODO

40th
Anniversary

9th August march against all forms of
womens oppression

9

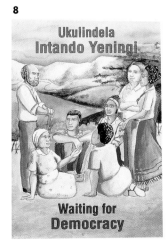

Ukulindela
Intando Yeningi

Waiting for
Democracy

8

Ukulindela Intando Yeningi

Abadlali / Characters

Waiting For Democracy

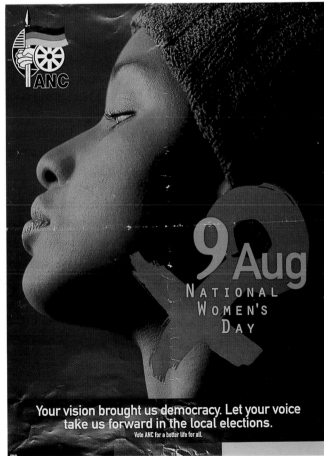

ANC

9 Aug
NATIONAL
WOMEN'S
DAY

Your vision brought us democracy. Let your voice
take us forward in the local elections.
Vote ANC for a better life for all.

10

Women and alternative media: reconstruction in the new South Africa

In addition to providing a tool for protest and a channel for communication to the outside world, alternative media also helped to combat the social and cultural destruction imposed on black communities during the apartheid years. The community project Molo Songololo addressed the impact of apartheid on children – its political repression, the unstable living conditions engendered and its disruption of education – and helped them to express their experiences through writing and drawing. In 1980 this project launched the magazine *Molo Songololo* for children, which has continued ever since to promote children's rights. ('Molo Songololo' is a Xhosa expression meaning 'hello centipede' – the centipede's legs symbolize all the children, and its segments the different communities working together.)

In the 1990s' climate of reconstruction, the pages of *Molo Songololo* reflect lively opportunities and aims. The magazine attempts to stimulate children's expression through puzzles, drawings and letterwriting; it also offers many opportunities to learn about the culture and geography of South Africa and the continent of Africa by means of colourful poster inserts or features such as 'Learn to speak Xhosa'. Furthermore, it discusses the meaning of democracy, voting procedures, and other aspects of the democratic process. The first democratic election in 1994 supplied a colourful, celebratory focus. In addition to wider activities, such as creative workshops or helping homeless children living in the street to reconstruct their lives, *Molo Songololo* keeps a firm eye on the future. It has an uncanny talent for placing children and politicians together – through panel discussions, summit conferences and other forums – in an attempt to ensure that children's rights are taken seriously by any new government.

Mediaworks (formerly known as the CAP: Community Arts Project) in Cape Town offers another example of this focus on the future, with its attempt to build creative communications projects in marginalized and rural communities, giving a voice to those not normally heard through mainstream media. Its Women's Media Watch concentrates on targeting women's lack of access to channels of communication. Media Watch members are shown here protesting against the negative and unrealistic portrayal of women in the media, and against the absence of women on an international advisory board responsible for shaping the content of one of the largest South African newspapers. Through its many activities, Mediaworks shows that 'democratizing the media' is essential to a democratic future where a diversity of voices can be heard, and it underlines the important role that alternative and community media still have to play in the new South Africa.

The beginnings of reconstruction in the new South Africa:

1   Photographs of CAP Media Watch members picketing outside Newspaper House, Cape Town, 1995. Approximately 50 women took part. Posters read 'Men Still Control the News' and zippers stuck onto mouths were used to symbolize women's lack of a voice in the media, as well as protesting their misrepresentation.

2   Two covers from Molo Songololo magazine for children, Cape Town, 1990s. The magazine originated in 1980 from an idea by Nomhle Ketelo, Nomhi Mtwecu, Caroline Long and Barbara Strachan.

3–5   Examples of posters that are inserted into Molo Songololo magazines (one per issue).

6   The Molo Songololo t-shirt, showing the well known centipede in the centre.

Women and work:
from local action to global views

The posters on this spread can only hint at some of the many work-related issues surrounding women around the world. Their intense activism in trade union movements (often struggling against the male orientation of the unions themselves), their role as supporters in strike action and industrial disputes, their demands for equal pay and for equal opportunities, and their fight against exploitation or sexual harassment in the workplace, are only a few of the many issues.

One of international feminism's most important contributions over the decades has been to persistently call for the redefinition of 'work' itself, in an attempt to encompass women's 'invisible' contribution to the labour situation – for example, work related to their family role and responsibilities, such as water-carrying, fuel-gathering and other survival activities. Graphically speaking, earlier references to women's 'invisible' or unpaid family work (and its contribution to economies) can be found in the 1970s in the work of Britain's See Red poster collective, and in other anonymous posters of the time (see Chapter Two). Changes in attitudes and definitions of work, and in information collection, brought new statistics throughout the 1980s showing women to be major contributors to the world labour force, and certainly the world's most substantial force of agricultural workers and food producers. The impact that this new vision has had on the issue of educating women can be seen in the graphic campaign shown on pages 232–5.

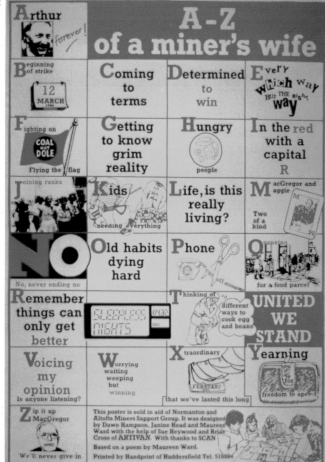

1 'KCC Women's Auxiliary', poster by Redback Graphix (designer and printer: Alison Alder) for the KCC Women's Auxiliary, Wollongong, Australia, 1984.
2 Poster created by Artivan in conjunction with members of Normanton and Altofts Miners Support Group, January 1985, during the great British Miners Strike of 1984–5.

WORKERS OF THE WORLD UNITE!

MAY DAY IS OURS!

DOWN WITH THE LABOUR BILL

COSATU LIVING WAGE CAMPAIGN

OFTEN THE BEST MAN FOR THE JOB IS ...A WOMAN!!

LEAVE IT ON THE DESK WOULD YOU, DALRYMPLE?

YOUR TEA MS. JONES

SUPPORT AN AIEU AFFIRMATIVE ACTION POLICY FOR WOMEN IN THE INSURANCE INDUSTRY

If God had intended women to think he'd have given them better jobs

© Quillan

5

3   Poster produced by COSATU celebrating May Day and promoting their Living Wage Campaign. (COSATU: Congress of South African Trade Unions). Designed by Gardens Media Group/CAP (Community Arts Project), Cape Town, South Africa, 1989.

4   Poster calling for opportunities for women in professional and/or executive positions in the insurance industry, created by Bob Clutterbuck of Red Letter Press in Melbourne, Australia, 1985.

5   Cartoon by Viv Quillin, from the book Women Draw (Women's Press, London, 1984).

6   Trans, moving downwards:
'Your shekel is worthless!
Are you worthless?
Working woman!
For every shekel that a man is paid, you are paid only 70 agorot!
Na'amat's struggle to advance women is your struggle!
Your shekel = his shekel!'
Front and back of a double-sided poster (in Hebrew) produced by Na'amat: the Movement of Working Women and Volunteers, Israel, 1990s. Na'amat is Israel's largest women's rights movement (f 1921) and works for equal rights for women in the workplace, in public and political life and in the family. It particularly focuses on economic equality for women (see also the poster on page 195).

6

100 שקל

השקל שלך שווה פחות??? האם את שווה פחות???

אשה עובדת!

על כל שקל שמשלמים לגבר - משלמים לך רק 70 אגורות!

המאבק של נעמ"ת לקידום האשה הוא גם המאבק שלך!

השקל שלך = לשקל שלו!

נעמ"ת ישראל

BANK OF ISRAEL

Women and health

The subject of women's health, in global terms, is expansive. It sits within a complex web of ever-changing factors – social, cultural, political, economic, religious – all of which differ from country to country. The role that graphic design has played in women's health issues around the world has been substantial, encompassing a variety of modes, instructional and educational as well as propagandist. Analysis of this alone would fill an entire book.

In short, it is only possible to skim the surface here, and note that examples of the relationship between graphics and health issues for women can be found throughout this book, and are slightly extended by the projects on the following four pages. The Women's Liberation Movement of the 1970s, for example, made use of the educational and awareness-raising possibilities of graphic material in the form of the classic American textbook *Our Bodies Ourselves*, and masses of leaflets and pamphlets produced by women's clinics and feminist groups. Feminist magazines and newsletters voiced new attitudes and methods (relating to childbirth, contraception, etc) around the world, while posters encouraged women to make choices, to challenge the system and to take control of their own bodies.

The 1980s and 1990s then brought graphic comments from the Pro-Life/Pro-Choice debate, with the hard-sell propaganda of the Pro-Life organizations, and the volatile illustrations and poster protests of a burgeoning Pro-Choice movement. Awareness campaigns have furthermore made HIV and AIDS a woman's issue, both in targeting women directly (in the style of Gran Fury, see Chapter Four, pages 166–7), or in the use of a broader community view, as shown here by Bronwyn Bancroft's posters. Throughout these years, graphic design has also found an angry cause in the form of violence against women (a critical health issue for women of all cultures), and cries of protest against it consequently appear throughout this book.

1 *'Care and Support are All He Needs for a New Beginning', anti-drug poster showing women and the family as support systems. (The lettering on the book reads 'drugs', on the right, and 'new life' on the left. Illustration by the artist Buhayri.) Issued by the Ministry of Health – Health Education, UAE (United Arab Emirates), c1993.*

2–4 *Three AIDS awareness posters illustrated by Aboriginal artist Bronwyn Bancroft and published by the Commonwealth Dept of Human Services and Health, and the Dept of Health, Housing, Local Govt and Community Services, Australia, 1992. Each poster carries an explanation of the imagery, as follows:*

2 *'Caring for People with AIDS':*
'This painting shows that people can safely care for family and friends with AIDS. The waves around the central image suggest the warmth of friendship and love that can greatly benefit the well-being of someone with AIDS. In the centre is an eye looking towards the future when a cure will hopefully be found.'

3 *'Education about AIDS':*
'This painting represents the need to educate people about needle exchange programs and the importance of safe sex. The small circles house the different groups that are available for counselling and education about AIDS. The flower shapes in the corner represent the spread of good information about AIDS prevention and education.'

4 *'Prevention of AIDS':*
'The two people are housed in condoms where they are safe from potentially infectious body fluids which are indicated in the outer patterning. The central image shows the continuation of normal lives without HIV infection through the use of condoms. This image also indicates the importance of protecting unborn children from AIDS.'

2

EDUCATION
ABOUT AIDS

This painting represents the need to educate people about needle exchange programs and the importance of safe sex. The small circles house the different groups that are available for counselling and education about AIDS. The flower shapes in the corner represent the spread of good information about AIDS prevention and education.
BRONWYN BANCROFT (Australian Aboriginal Artist)

© Commonwealth Department of Human Services and Health

EVERY BODY'S BUSINESS

3

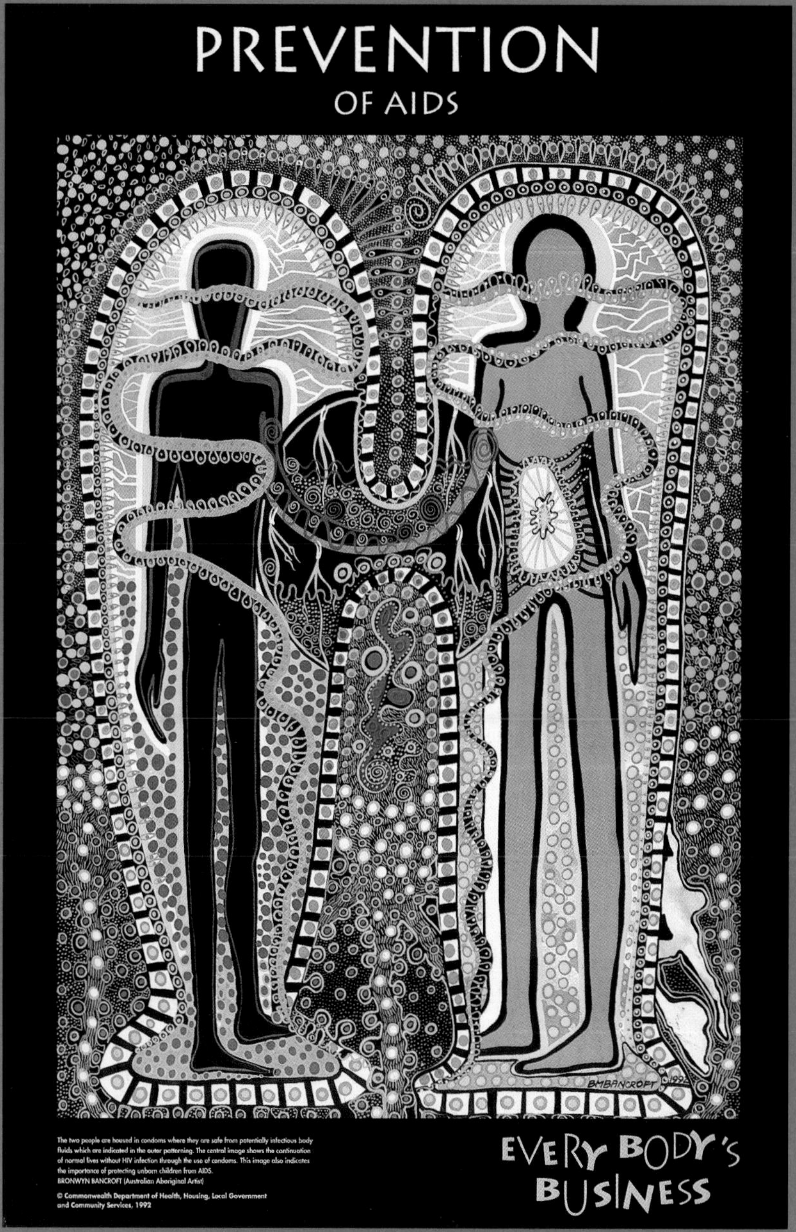

PREVENTION
OF AIDS

4

The two people are housed in condoms where they are safe from potentially infectious body fluids, which are indicated in the outer patterning. The central image shows the continuation of normal lives without HIV infection through the use of condoms. This image also indicates the importance of protecting unborn children from AIDS.
BRONWYN BANCROFT (Australian Aboriginal Artist)

© Commonwealth Department of Health, Housing, Local Government and Community Services, 1992

EVERY BODY'S
BUSINESS

1

2

3

4

STOP STERILIZATION ABUSE /ALTO AL ABUSO DE ESTERILIZACIÓN

5

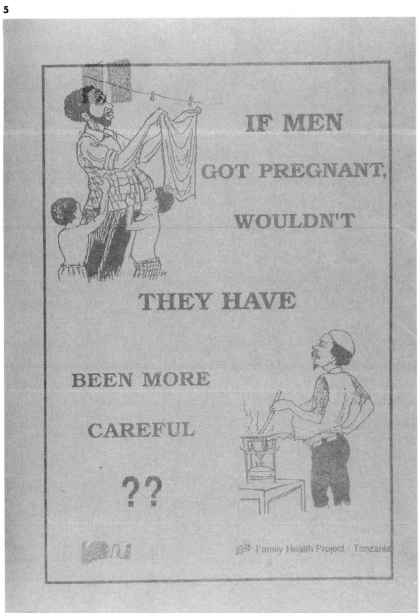

IF MEN GOT PREGNANT, WOULDN'T THEY HAVE BEEN MORE CAREFUL ??

Family Health Project - Tanzania

6

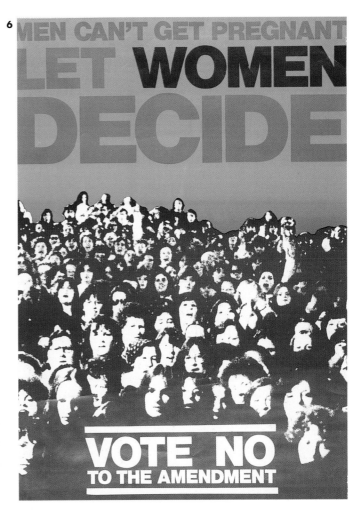

MEN CAN'T GET PREGNANT LET WOMEN DECIDE

VOTE NO
TO THE AMENDMENT

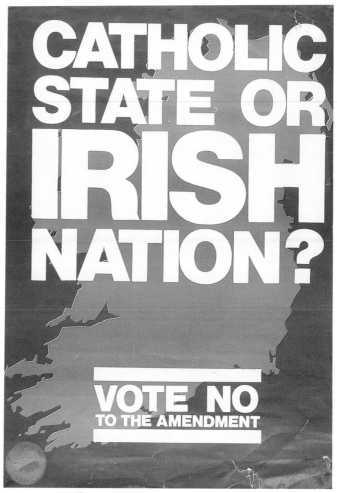

CATHOLIC STATE OR IRISH NATION?

VOTE NO
TO THE AMENDMENT

Women and nuclear disarmament: protest and peace camps

Since the early days of the suffragettes, women have organized and worked for the cause of international peace. In the early 1980s, however, this grand tradition showed itself to particularly powerful effect. NATO re-armament and the deployment of short- and medium-range missiles in Europe made the international peace movement spring into action. Women rose up in protest and maintained a high profile in the heavy stream of demonstrations that took place in the USA, Britain, Germany and other countries around the world.

1

The Women's Peace Camp at Greenham Common, which saw women camped outside the gates of a US missile base in Britain, became by far the most potent symbol of women's ability to stand up to the male military machine. Established in 1981, and at the height of its activity until 1985, the Camp's numbers grew and shrank – at times as low as a hundred, or as high as six figures. But it actually persisted in some form for over a decade – with a small contingent still existing today – and through its many activities and actions involved women from far and wide, from all age groups (from children to those in their seventies) and from all walks of life.

Greenham thrived on performance and symbolism, especially as demonstrations of solidarity and strength. Many direct actions were staged, such as 'Embrace the Base' in 1982, when over 30,000 women travelled to Greenham to link hands around the base. As the photographs by Astra Blaug on pages 228–9 show, the protesters made the camp a highly decorated environment. Visual signs of occupation were everywhere including those drawn or scribbled on the road, or woven into the hedges and bushes. Visions of spinning and webs proliferated. The perimeter fence remained a focal point throughout: it was damaged, cut through and even pulled down during demonstrations. But more often than not, it was decorated with banners, paint, paper doves, dolls, baby clothes, photographs and other mementos of humanity. Bannermaking enjoyed renewed popularity, and the Camp inspired books, songs, print portfolios and other tributes.

The Greenham women also overcame an ongoing tirade of brutal jibes from the 'popular press' (one tabloid labelled Greenham Women 'man-hating harpies' and 'woolly minds in woolly hats') as well as harassment from local vigilantes, security forces and police. Injuries such as broken arms and dislocations were common during the large-scale actions. But despite such difficulties and traumas, their spirit never failed and the Camp just wouldn't go away. The 'Greenham experience' achieved worldwide renown and remains to this day one of the great modern-day symbols of women's unity and strength.

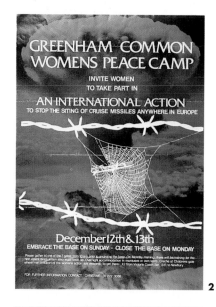

2

3

1 Poster announcement for the Women's Peace Camp at Greenham Common, Britain mid-1980s.
2 'Embrace the Base', a poster inviting women to take part in a demonstration that will join hands and encircle the base at Greenham Common, Britain, 1982.
3 Cover of The Greenham Factor, a news sheet produced to document and raise funds for the Women's Peace Camp at Greenham Common, Britain, 1983–4.
4 Badges relating to the Women's Peace Camp at Greenham Common which include popular imagery such as the spinning of webs or cutting through the perimeter fence, Britain, mid-1980s.
5 Poster produced by the Women's International League for Peace and Freedom, USA, 1979.

4

it will be a great day
when
our schools
get all the money
they need
and the air force
has to hold
a bake sale
to buy a
bomber

1 Banner celebrating the 'Women for Life on Earth' Action for Peace at Greenham Common (August 1981 to December 1983), created by Thalia and Jan Campbell and Jan Higgs, Britain, 1983. (Thalia Campbell's banners for Greenham inspired a revival of bannermaking in Britain throughout the 1980s.)

2 Badge, Britain, mid-1980s.

3 Photographs by Astra Blaug of the Women's Peace Camp at Greenham Common, from the period 1982–91. They include a banner similar to the one that led the march from Cardiff to Greenham in 1981 and became the start of the Peace Camp; the environmental art and graffiti that decorated the camp, perimeter fence and even the roads; paintings on bed sheets by Katrina Howse, hanging at Yellow Gate; and a witch with bolt-cutters painted on a tarpaulin or tent.

Women and nuclear disarmament: protest and peace camps

Another arena of intense anti-nuclear activity is the Pacific region where, since the 1960s, the French have been testing bombs at Mururoa Atoll. In the anti-nuclear climate of the 1980s, Australian postermakers and graphic workshops (including a strong contingent of female artists) created protest posters, billboards, postcards and mail-art projects in order to place a persistent focus on the growing worry of nuclear weapons and nuclear testing. Such concerns included the existence of US nuclear-related military bases in Australia, uranium mining and exporting, and testing in the Pacific Islands. Feelings intensified when, in 1985, the French Secret Service bombed the Greenpeace sea-going vessel 'Rainbow Warrior' moored in Auckland harbour (resulting in the death of the Greenpeace photographer on board) while on a mission to evacuate victims of the French nuclear testing programme.

The protests continued, shown by Australian designer Julia Church's contribution to a high-profile poster exhibition on human rights, staged in France

1

2

for the 1989 Bicentenary of the French Revolution. The poster's inclusion and display generated great controversy and concern from the French officials. Even today, in the mid-1990s, nuclear testing in the Pacific has resumed – and so have the protests – on an international scale.

3

4

1   '15 more years testing in the Pacific? NO', poster by Pam Debenham, printed at The Tin Sheds, University of Sydney, Australia, 1984.

2   'Nuclear Free Pacific', poster by Wendy Black of Red Letter Press in Melbourne, Australia, c1983. The poster incorporated French, English and Bislama Pidgin English languages, and coincided with a conference held in Vanuatu concerning the South Pacific region.

3   Fijian girl making a statement against nuclear testing at a fashion show in 1995, the year of the resumption of French nuclear testing at Mururoa Atoll in the South Pacific.

4   Poster by Australian designer Julia Church, created for the human rights exhibition of the Bicentenary of the French Revolution in 1989. It shows an island woman in a nuclear-blasted landscape with fish thrown in the air (symbolizing all of nature destroyed) – a blatant criticism of the French nuclear presence in the South Pacific.

5   'Daddy, what did YOU do...', designed by Toni Robertson and Chips Mackinolty of Earthworks Poster Collective, printed at The Tin Sheds, University of Sydney, Australia, 1977.

Empowering women worldwide: education for the future

1 Poster publicizing the United Nations Fourth World Conference on Women held in Beijing in September 1995.
2 The logo representing the NGO Forum on Women, which accompanied the Conference in Beijing, 1995.
3–6 UNFPA poster series created by Bureau design studio, USA, 1996. (UNFPA: United Nations Population Fund).

3, 4 English and Mandarin versions of the UNFPA poster 'Equal, Girl – Boy'. The English version was distributed to: Afghanistan, Bangladesh, Bhutan, Cambodia, India, Indonesia, Korea, Laos Peoples' Democratic Rep, Malaysia, Maldives, Mongolia, Myanmar, Nepal, Sri Lanka, Thailand. Mongolia also received Russian; Cambodia also received French; Vietnam received only French. The Mandarin version was distributed to China.

Over the past few decades, our views and perceptions of the status of women worldwide, their role in economies and how they live their lives have been changed by the work of development agencies, health organizations and forums, such as the UN Decade for Women (1975–85) and its world conferences in Mexico City, Copenhagen and Nairobi. The changes promise to continue through more recent efforts, including the 1994 International Conference on Population and Development (IPCD) in Cairo, and the Fourth UN World Conference on Women in Beijing, 1995. All have been involved in developing a new world view: a recognition of the vital role that women play in the development and survival of their communities, and their potential as agents of change in society.

Although it has been a long time in coming, most development agencies now acknowledge that, for women, education remains the first step towards freedom and control of their own lives and destinies. It also then leads to improvements in, and knowledge of health care, farming and marketing methods, reproductive health and other community concerns. However, gaining access to education for women often entails confronting 'invisible' barriers, such as social and family pressures insisting that 'a woman's place is in the home', everyday workload and household responsibilities, and prejudice of women's inferiority to men. In some countries, such prejudice, or favouritism towards men, can mean that the best teachers and educational facilities are reserved for male students. The partiality can reach even more basic levels, where boys are fed before, more than, or instead of girls.[9]

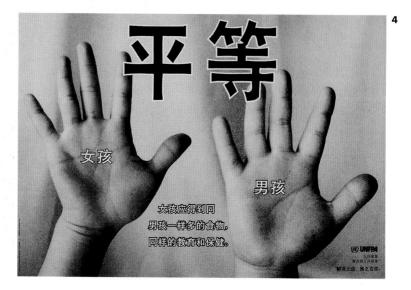

As culturally sensitive as these issues may be, an example of the way in which international agencies or forums attempt to educate and change attitudes – in this case, with the help of graphic communication – can be seen in the project shown here, following on from the 1994 Cairo Conference on Population and Development. The United Nations Population Fund (UNFPA) contracted New York design studio Bureau to create a series of posters for use by UNFPA field offices and non-governmental organizations (NGO's) throughout forty-two developing countries of the world including Algeria, Bangladesh, Iran, Morocco, Mongolia, Somalia and Vietnam, among others. The simplicity and clarity of the visual statement was therefore vital in order to avoid misinterpretation and confused meanings, particularly as the messages to be communicated were problematic in the countries in which they were to be displayed. (The posters were not intended for use in developed or 'donor' countries.)

The underlying statement of all the posters is simple and clear: empower women and the standard of living improves for everyone; women have healthier and fewer children, and more control of their own lives and the destinies of their communities, therefore everyone benefits. The messages which the posters carry, however, differ according to 'regions' (Latin

America, Arab States and Eastern Europe, Asia and the Pacific Islands) and have been tailored to the issues most pressing in that region. Bureau worked with UNFPA representatives in order to ascertain the appropriate topics. For example, the idea of 'Choice' is very important to Latin America; while in Asia, the 'gender ratio' problem is at the forefront of issues. The concept of educating women, however, remains vital across all regions; and although the notion that a girl should be educated remains politically controversial in some, it is a forward-looking concept which is being promoted with great strength, and which is certain to carry us all into the next century.

5 *Trans: 'Deprived', 'Domestic Labour Deprives Girls of Education'. UNFPA poster (in Arabic) that responded to the fact that in many Arab countries girls are drawn into unpaid domestic labour as early as age four. It was distributed to: Algeria, Djibouti, Egypt, Iraq, Jordan, Lebanon, Libya, Morocco, Somalia, Sudan, Syrian Arab Rep, Tunisia, Rep of Yemen.*

6 *(overleaf) 'Power'. This UNFPA poster (in English) was distributed to: Anguilla, Antigua and Barbuda, Bahamas, Barbados, Bermuda, Brazil, British Virgin Islands, Cayman Islands, Dominica, Grenada, Guyana, Jamaica, Montserrat, Surinam, Trinidad and Tobago. Haiti used a French version.*

Pov

ver

Education is power.

Educate a girl
and you empower
a woman, a family,
a community, a
nation, the world.

 **UNFPA**
United Nations
Population Fund

It's in your hands.

Notes

Chapter 1

1 Mackenzie, Midge, *Shoulder to Shoulder*, Vintage Books Edition, New York, 1988, p 310.
2 Reynoldson, Fiona, *Women and War*, Wayland Publishers, Hove, East Sussex: 1993, p 19.
3 Ibid, p 41.
4 Friedan, Betty, *The Feminine Mystique*, Penguin Books, London, 1992, p 14.
5 *Votes for Women* sales reached 40,000 copies per week, and an average weekly readership of 160,000. See Diane Atkinson, *The Purple, White and Green: Suffragettes in London 1906–14*, Museum of London, 1992 (exhibition catalogue), p 19.
6 Tickner, Lisa, *The Spectacle of Women: Imagery of the Suffrage Campaign 1907–14*, Chatto & Windus, London, 1987, p 13.
7 The National League for Opposing Women's Suffrage (NLOWS) founded in 1910 was an amalgamation of two earlier bodies: the National Women's Anti-Suffrage League and the Men's League for Opposing Female Suffrage, both established in 1908. Ibid, p 99.

Chapter 2

1 Broude, Norma and Garrard, Mary D, *The Power of Feminist Art: Emergence, Impact and Triumph of the American Feminist Art Movement*, Harry N Abrams Inc, New York, 1994, pp 32–8.
2 De Bretteville, Sheila Levrant, 'Some aspects of design from the perspective of a woman designer' and 'The Women's Design Program', *Icographic* no 6, International Council of Graphic Design Associations, London, 1973, pp 4–8 and pp 8–11 respectively.

Chapter 3

1 Kenna, Carol, Medcalf, Lyn and Walker, Rick (eds), *Printing is Easy...? Community Printshops 1970–1986*, Greenwich Mural Workshop, London, 1986, p 48.
2 *Shocking Pink* (It's Our Choice issue), Shocking Pink 2 Collective at the Brixton Women's Centre, c 1987, p 20.
3 Particularly vicious attacks were launched at the Greenham Women, labelled by the popular press as 'man-hating harpies' and 'burly lesbians'.

Chapter 4

1 'Louder than Words: a WAC Chronicle' by Tracy Ann Essoglou, in Nina Felshin (ed), *But is it Art? The Spirit of Art as Activism*, Bay Press, Seattle, 1995, pp 333–72.
2 'A Cyborg Manifesto: Science, Technology, and Socialist-Feminism in the Late Twentieth Century', in Donna J Haraway, *Simians, Cyborgs, and Women: the Reinvention of Nature*, Free Association Books, London, 1991, pp 149–81.
3 Crimp, Douglas and Rolson, Adam, *AIDS Demo Graphics*, Bay Press, Seattle, 1990, pp 62–4.
4 Acocella, Marisa, *Just who the hell is SHE, anyway?*, Harmony Books, Crown Publishers, New York, 1994, p 25.

Chapter 5

1 United Nations Report, 1980.
2 *Women: A World Report*, A New Internationalist Book, Methuen, London Ltd, London, 1985, p 16.
3 Sivard, Ruth Leger, 'Women ... A World Survey', World Priorities, Washington DC, 1985. (Taken from *WAC Stats: The Facts About Women*, Women's Action Coalition, New York.)
4 *Women in Action*, Issue 1987/4 (December 1987), Isis International, Rome, p 41.
5 Morgan, Robin (ed), *Sisterhood is Global: the International Women's Movement Anthology*, Penguin Books, Harmondsworth, Middlesex, 1985, pp 23-4.
6 *You Have Struck A Rock: Women and Political Repression in Southern Africa*, International Defence and Aid Fund, London, 1980, p 17.
7 Morgan, Robin (ed), *Sisterhood is Global: the International Women's Movement Anthology*, p 23.
8 Statistic compiled by the Maryland Men's Anti-rape Resource Center, and published in the Clothesline Project Press Kit, 1995.
9 Morgan, Robin (ed), *Sisterhood is Global: the International Women's Movement Anthology*, p 21.

Selected Bibliography

Acocella, Marisa, *Just Who the Hell Is SHE, Anyway?*, Harmony Books/Crown Publishers, New York, 1994

Atkinson, Diane, *The Purple, White and Green: Suffragettes in London 1906–14*, Museum of London, 1992. Exhibition catalogue

Atkinson, Ti-Grace, *Amazon Odyssey: The First Collection of Writings by the Political Pioneers of the Women's Movement*, Links Books, New York, 1974

Berger, John, *Ways of Seeing*, British Broadcasting Corporation, London and Penguin Books, Harmondsworth, 1985. First published 1972

Blum, Andrea et al (eds), *WAC Stats: The Facts About Women*, Women's Action Coalition (WAC), New York, 1992

Broude, Norma and Garrard, Mary D (eds), *The Power of Feminist Art: The American Movement of the 1970s, History and Impact*, Harry N Abrams, New York, 1994

Chadwick, Whitney, *Women, Art and Society*, World of Art Series/Thames and Hudson, London, 1994. First published 1990

Chicago, Judy, *Embroidering Our Heritage: The Dinner Party Needlework*, Anchor Press /Doubleday, Garden City, New York, 1980

Chicago, Judy, *The Dinner Party: A Symbol of Our Heritage*, Anchor Press/Doubleday, Garden City, New York, 1979

Crimp, Douglas and Rolston, Adam, *AIDS Demo Graphics*, Bay Press, Seattle, 1990

DiMassa, Diane, *Hothead Paisan: Homicidal Lesbian Terrorist*, Cleis Press, Pittsburgh and San Francisco, 1993
DiMassa, Diane, *Hothead Paisan*, Giant Ass Publishing, New Haven, Conn. Quarterly comic-zine. First published 1991

Elliott, David (ed), *Alexander Rodchenko*, Museum of Modern Art, Oxford (GB), 1979.

Faludi, Susan, *Backlash: The Undeclared War Against Women*, Vintage, London, 1992. First published (USA) 1991

Felshin, Nina (ed), *But Is It Art? The Spirit of Art as Activism*, Bay Press, Seattle, 1995

Friedan, Betty, *The Feminine Mystique*, Penguin Books, Harmondsworth, 1992. First published (USA) 1963

Goffman, Erving, *Gender Advertisements*, Macmillan Press, London, 1979. First published (USA) 1976

Goodwin, Jan, *Price of Honour: Muslim Women Lift the Veil of Silence on the Islamic World*, Warner Books/Little, Brown and Co, London, 1995. First published 1994

Greer, Germaine, *The Female Eunuch*, Paladin/Granada Publishing, London, 1971. First published 1970

Guerrilla Girls, *Confessions of the Guerrilla Girls*, Pandora/HarperCollins, London, 1995. First published (USA) 1995

Haraway, Donna J, *Simians, Cyborgs, and Women: The Reinvention of Nature*, Free Association Books, London, 1991. Essay: 'A Cyborg Manifesto: Science, Technology, and Socialist-Feminism in the Late Twentieth Century', pp,149–181

Hewlett, Jamie and Martin, Alan, *Tank Girl 2*, Penguin Books, Harmondsworth, 1995

Holzer, Jenny, *Jenny Holzer: Signs*, Institute of Contemporary Arts/Art Data, London, (revised edition) 1988

International Women's Tribune Centre, *Feminist Logos (A Clip Art Book)*, IWTC (updated edition) 1991. First published 1984

International Women's Tribune Centre, *Rural Women in Action (A Clip Art Book)*, IWTC (updated edition) 1991. First published 1984

International Women's Tribune Centre, *Woman: The Password is Action (Clip-Art for Women)*, IWTC, 1988

Jacobs, Karrie and Heller, Steven, *Angry Graphics: Protest Posters of the Reagan/Bush Era*, Peregrine Smith Books, Salt Lake City, 1992

Kruger, Barbara, *Love for Sale: The Words and Pictures of Barbara Kruger*, Harry N Abrams, New York, 1990

Mackenzie, Midge, *Shoulder to Shoulder*, Vintage Books/Random House, New York 1988. First published (USA and GB) 1975

McDonald, Ian, *Vindication! A Postcard History of the Women's Movement*, Deirdre McDonald Books/Bellew Publishing, London, 1989

Miller, Casey and Swift, Kate, *The Handbook of Non-Sexist Writing for Writers, Editors and Speakers*, The Women's Press, London, (revised British edition) 1982

Morgan, Robin (ed), *Sisterhood is Global: The International Women's Movement Anthology*, Penguin Books, Harmondsworth, 1985. First published (USA) 1984

Opie, Robert (compiler), *The Wartime Scrapbook: From Blitz to Victory 1939–1945*, New Cavendish Books, London, 1995

Orbach, Susie, *Fat is a Feminist Issue...*, Arrow/Random House, London, (new edition) 1988. First published 1978

Pankhurst, Richard, *Sylvia Pankhurst: Artist and Crusader*, Paddington Press, London, 1979

Paret, Peter et al, *Persuasive Images: Posters of War and Revolution from the Hoover Institution Archives*, Princeton University Press, Princeton, NJ, 1992.

Parker, Rozsika, *The Subversive Stitch: Embroidery and the Making of the Feminine*, The Women's Press, London, 1986. First published 1984

Chronology

Posener, Jill, *Louder Than Words*, Pandora Press/Routledge & Kegan Paul, London, 1986

Posener, Jill, *Spray It Loud*, Pandora Press/Routledge & Kegan Paul, London, 1986. First published 1982

Raphael, Amy, *Never Mind the Bollocks: Women Rewrite Rock*, Virago Press, London, 1995

Reynoldson, Fiona, *Women and War*, Wayland Publishers, Hove, East Sussex, 1993

Rowe, Marsha (ed), *'Spare Rib' Reader: 100 Issues of Women's Liberation*, Penguin Books, Harmondsworth, 1984. First published 1982

Schweitzer, Pam *et al* (eds), *What Did You Do in the War, Mum? Women Recall Their Wartime Work*, Age Exchange Theatre Company, London, (new edition) 1993. First published 1985

Seager, Joni and Olson, Ann, *Women in the World: An International Atlas*, Pan Books, London, 1986

Sharp, Saundra, *Black Women for Beginners*, Writers and Readers Publishing, New York, 1993

Sinclair, Carla, *Net Chick: A Smart-Girl Guide to the Wired World*, Henry Holt and Co, New York, 1996.

Stanton, Elizabeth Cady, *The Woman's Bible: The Original Feminist Attack on the Bible*, Polygon Books, Edinburgh, 1985 (abridged edition)

Strizenova, Tatyana, *Costume Revolution: Textiles, Clothing and Costume of the Soviet Union in the Twenties*, Trefoil Publications, London, 1989

Taylor, Debbie *et al*, *Women: A World Report* (A New Internationalist Book), Methuen, London, 1985

Tickner, Lisa, *The Spectacle of Women: Imagery of the Suffrage Campaign 1907–14*, Chatto & Windus, London, 1987

Tuttle, Lisa, *Encyclopedia of Feminism*, Longman Group, Harlow, Essex, 1986

Watkins, Susan Alice *et al*, *Feminism for Beginners*, Icon Books, Cambridge (GB), 1992

Williamson, Judith, *Decoding Advertisements: Ideology and Meaning in Advertising*, Marion Boyars, London, 1994. First published 1978

Wolf, Naomi, *The Beauty Myth*, Chatto & Windus, London, 1990

Wye, Deborah, *Committed to Print: Social and Political Themes in Recent American Printed Art*, The Museum of Modern Art, New York, 1988. Exhibition catalogue

This chronology provides a framework for viewing the graphic projects shown in this book, and is therefore not exhaustive.

1900–1919

1903–14
'Votes for Women', the women's suffrage campaign conducted by the militant suffragettes of Britain, ie members of the Women's Social and Political Union (f 1903), and the Women's Freedom League (f 1907). Also key to this period of activity: the National Union of Women's Suffrage Societies (NUWSS). The first and largest suffrage organization (f 1897), its members are law-abiding constitutionalists. See detailed chart on pages 22–23.

1914
Outbreak of First World War (1914–18).

1917
The Bolshevik Revolution takes place in Russia. After the Revolution, the avant-garde art movement, Constructivism (1913–mid 1920s), brings art and design into the service of the new Soviet future.

1918
British women over 30 given the vote.

1920s

1920
American women given the vote.

1922
Russian Constructivist Exhibition held in Berlin. Constructivist art and artists exhibited as a major movement outside of Russia for the first time.

1924
Lenin dies. Stalin begins his rise to power and by 1929 has introduced collectivization.

1928
The voting age for British women reduced from 30 to 21.

1929
Wall Street Crash marks the start of the Great Depression in the USA.

1930s

1933
Hitler becomes German Chancellor.

1939
Outbreak of Second World War (1939–45).

1940s

1946
New York psychiatrist Benjamin Spock's best-selling book *Baby and Child Care* teaches American housewives how to raise a generation of children.

1950s

The golden decade of US magazines, the main medium of advertising at that time. (Madison Avenue, New York City, becomes the advertising centre of the world.) Not only were there mass circulation, 'general editorial' magazines (such as *Life* and *Look*), but also ad-carrying magazines aimed at major groups within the population (men and women, urban and rural) and specialist audiences.

1956
20,000 women march to the government buildings in Pretoria to protest the 'pass laws' on 9 August – now known annually in South Africa as 'Women's Day'.

1960s

1960
John F Kennedy elected US President; assassinated in 1963; Vice President Lyndon B Johnson becomes President.

First commercially available contraceptive pill introduced in the USA.

1961
Contraceptive pill available in Britain.

1963
Publication of Betty Friedan's *The Feminine Mystique*.

1966
Betty Friedan founds the National Organization for Women (NOW) in Washington, DC, and becomes its first President.

1968
Feminist protest at the Miss America Contest in Atlantic City, New Jersey – the media myth of bra-burning is born.

First American National Women's Liberation Conference held in Chicago.

Abortion is legalized in Britain.

1970s

1970
In Britain, the First Conference on Women's Liberation is held in Oxford.

Judy Chicago forms the first Feminist Art Program at Fresno State University.

Publication of Germaine Greer's *The Female Eunuch*.

1971
Judy Chicago and Miriam Schapiro initiate the Feminist Art Program and Sheila Levrant de Bretteville initiates the Women's Design Program at the California Institute of the Arts (CalArts).

The book *Our Bodies, Ourselves* is published by the Boston Women's Health Book Collective, leading to the Women's Health Movement.

1972
Ms. magazine is founded in the USA.

Spare Rib magazine is founded in Britain.

1973
The Woman's Building opens (founders: Sheila Levrant de Bretteville, Judy Chicago, Arlene Raven).

Judy Chicago's large scale collaborative project *The Dinner Party* begins (–79).

US Supreme Court rules abortion is legal in *Roe vs Wade*.

1975
UN declares 1975 the International Year of the Woman (a conference is held in Mexico City).
1975–85 is designated the UN Decade for Women.

1977
'Reclaim the Night' marches begin in West Germany and Britain, protesting against violence against women.

1978
The first bombing of an abortion clinic occurs in the USA.

'Take Back the Night' rally held in San Francisco.

1979
Margaret Thatcher elected Prime Minister in Britain.

Feminist Petra Kelly founds 'Die Grünen' (The Green Party) in West Germany.

1980s

1980
Ronald Reagan elected US President.

UN Conference on Women held in Copenhagen.

1981
Founding of the Women's Peace Camp at Greenham Common, Britain.

1985
UN Conference on Women held in Nairobi (to end UN Decade of Women).

The Guerrilla Girls, an anonymous feminist art activist group, start their street poster campaigns in protest against discrimination in the New York art establishment.

1988
George Bush elected US President.

1989
March on Washington for abortion rights.

Defiance campaign in South Africa.

'The Montreal Massacre', Montreal University, Canada: 14 women are shot dead by a male student who screams they are 'a bunch of fucking feminists'; he also shoots himself to death.

1990s

1990
Publication of Naomi Wolf's *The Beauty Myth*.

1991
Publication of Susan Faludi's *Backlash*.

The Riot Grrrl movement appears.

1992
Women's Action Coalition (WAC) is formed in New York (–94).

Second major abortion rights march on Washington.

The Lesbian Avengers founded in New York.

1995
UN Conference on Women held in Beijing.

Much of the graphic work in this book has for decades been resting in non-funded archives under the care and protection of volunteers, or in the personal collections of friends and associates – usually with no proper conservation or storage facilities. It is reproduced here in its present true form with folds, cracks, stains and other markings, as this is considered to be an essential part of its character.

(Illustration acknowledgements are listed by page number followed by figure number.)

The Advertising Archives: p32, 2. Anchor Press/Doubleday, 1979: p98, 3; Anchor Press/Doubleday, 1980: p98, 2. Art Unlimited, Amsterdam: p18, 3. Artangel (courtesy Barbara Kruger): p141, 5. Artivan and Greenwich Mural Workshop: p220, 2. Attic Press: p134, 4. *Aurum Press*, 1978: p124, 1. *Bad Attitude* magazine: p115, 5; p125, 6; p175, 4. Bronwyn Bancroft: pp222/3, 2–4. Courtesy Jayne H Baum Gallery, New York, © 1992 Robbie Conal: p146, 1. Donna Binder: p164, 3. Astra Blaug: p10, 3; p14, 2; p116, 2, 4; p118, 1–3; p130, 2–4; p132, 3–6; p133, 9–13; p196, 2; p199, 4; p226, 4; pp228/9, 1, 2. Mary Boone Gallery, New York: p152, 1. Boston Women's Health Book Collective: p108, 1, 2. Marion Boyars Publishers: p84, 2. Sarah Brown: p179, 4. Bureau: pp 232/3, 3–5; pp234/5. Estelle Carol: p91, 2. Catholic Institute of International Relations, London: p13, 3. Center for the Study of Political Graphics, USA: p13, 5; p31, 3; p91, 4; p198, 3. Georgina Ashworth, Change: p12, 2. Chatto & Windus, 1987: p138, 2. Chicago Women's Graphics Collective: p86, 3; p90, 1; p91, 3. Julia Church: p114, 1; p120, 4; p125, 3; p230, 4. Class Action: p17, 6; p155, 4; pp172/3, 2, 3; p174, 1. David Collins, Saatchi & Someone: p123, 6. Courtesy *Home & Garden*, © 1943 (renewed 1971) by the Condé Nast Publications, Inc: p30, 1. CORBIS-BETTMANN: p61, 3–6; p70, 1; p75, 4. CORBIS-BETTMANN/UPI: p80, 2; p89, 6. Rosie Cross: p157, 5; p185, 2, 3. Mary Ellen Croteau, SisterSerpents: p19, 2; p16, 4; p154, 1–3; p160/61, 1–3; p178, 3. Sheila Levrant de Bretteville: p79, 5; p86, 2; p88, 1; p91, 5; p92, 1, 2; p93, 3–6; p136, 1–4. Design Documentation, UK: p20, 3; p21, 4; p24, 1; p25, 3, 4; p26, 1, 2; p27, 4; p34, 1, 3; p35, 5(top left); p41, 4, 5; p42, 5; p43, 7; p44, 2; p45, 5; p49, 3; pp56/7; p58, 1–3; p59, 4; p64, 2–5; p65, 7, 8; p73, 2. Peggy Diggs: p204, 1, 2. Mary Beth Edelson: p94, 1; p165, 4.

Noemi Escudero: p211, 5, 7. Julio Etchart, Reportage Pictures: p210, 1. Mary Evans Picture Library: p18, 1; p44, 1; p45, 4; p51, 3. Feminist Archive, Bristol: p9, 4, 5; p11, 4; p69, 2–5; p83, 4; p87, 4; p89, 2, 3; p100, 3; p101, 6; p102, 1; p105, 2, 4, 5; p110, 3; p113, 5–7; p116, 3; p118, 4; p125, 4, 5; pp128/9, 2–11; p132, 1, 2; p226, 1, 2. Feminist Library, London: p2; p11, 6; p16, 2; p33, 3; p79, 4 ; p82, 2; p83, 3; p84, 2; p86, 1; p98, 1; p102, 3; p109, 4–6; p110, 1; p111, 5; p115, 4; p119, 6; p120, 2, 3; p121, 5–8; p133, 8, 9; p134, 2; p188, 2; p190, 1; p191, 5, 6; p194, 2; p196, 1; p199, 6; p202, 3, 4; p209, 6; p211, 9; p212, 1–3; p225, 6. Gertrude Fester: p216, 3–5; p217, 6, 7, 9, 10. Forward: p191, 1, 2. Free Association Books, 1991: p156, 2. Giant Ass Publishing: p220, 4–6. Courtesy Barbara Gladstone Gallery, New York: p139, 1–4. Gran Fury (courtesy Marlene McCarty): p166, 1; p167, 2–4. Ilona Granet (courtesy PPOW, New York): p142, 1. Greenwich Mural Workshop: p211, 8; p224, 1. Diane Gromala: p156, 3; pp186/7. Guerrilla Girls: p 114, 3; p122, 1; p141, 6–8; p152, 2. Jude Harris: p81, 3(top and centre right); p105, 6. Jamie Hewlett: p180, 1–3. Henry Holt and Co, 1996: p156, 4. Hoover Institution Archives, Stanford University: p63, 6; p68, 1; p75, 3. Icograda: p93, 7. Imperial War Museum, London: p28, 2; p29, 3, 4; p31, 2; p62, 1, 2; p63, 3–5; p64, 1; p65, 6; p70, 2; p72, 1; p73, 4, 5; p74, 1, 2. Laurence Jaugey-Paget: p175, 3. Jillposters: p116, 1, p118, 5. Bethany Johns: p 159, 3; p164, 1, 2. Melanie Keen, Liz McQuiston and Feminist Library, London: pp106/7. Barbara Kruger: p122, 2; p144, 1. Ladybird Books, 1975: p84, 1. Leeds Postcards: p162, 4. Yossi Lemel: p14, 3; Yossi Lemel/WIZO, Israel: p202, 2. Links Books, 1974: p78, 2. Lynx: p176, 1. Macmillan Press, 1979: p84, 5. Marlene McCarty (Bureau): p153, 4–6; p158, 1, 2; p162, 1–3. Andy McEntee: p210, 2–4. Liz McQuiston: p183, 2. Mediaworks Collective Images Library: p218, 1. Erik Miller, i-Afrika: p215, 5. Molo Songololo: p195, 4; p219, 2–6. Mothers Against Drunk Driving (MADD): p131, 6, 7. Carrie Moyer: p151, 5; p168, 1, 2. Carrie Moyer and Sue Schaffner: p151, 4; p169, 3; p170, 1, 2; p171, 3. *Ms.* magazine: p11, 5; p15, 4; p165, 5. Museum of London: p25, 2; p27, 3; p28, 1; p34, 2; p35, 4, 5(bottom), 6; p36, 1, 2; p37, 3–6; p38, 3, 4; p39, 5; p40, 1–3; p41, 4; p42, 1–4, 6; p44, 3; p46, 1, 2; p46/7, 3;

p49, 4; p50, 2; p51, 5; p52, 1–3; p53, 4; p55, 2, 4; p59, 5. Na'amat (all rights reserved): p195, 6; p221, 6. National Black Women's Health Project, USA: p133, 8. National Gallery of Australia: pp96/7, 1–4; p130, 1, 5; p221, 4; p230, 1, 2; p231, 5. The National Museum of Labour History, Britain: p38, 1, 2; p112, 3. Collection of The Newark Museum. Purchase 1981 Harry E Sautter Bequest Fund: p194, 1. NOW (National Organization of Women, USA): p146, 2. The Robert Opie Collection: p18, 2. Paladin, 1971: p78, 3. Pan Books, 1986: p190, 4. Penguin Books, 1968: p78, 1; Penguin Books, 1975: p33, 4; Penguin Books, 1985: p84, 4; p190, 3. PETA: pp176/7, 3–6. Jill Posener: p10, 1; p124, 2. Brenda Prince/Format: p131, 8. Red Planet: p119, 7; p178, 1, 2. Redback Graphix: p220, 1; p224, 2. Rex Features Limited: p16, 3; p99, 5, 6; p116, 5. Linda Rosier: p151, 3. Saatchi & Saatchi: p110, 2. Courtesy Galerie St Etienne, New York, © 1991 Sue Coe: p14, 1; © 1983 Sue Coe: p143, 4; © 1992 Sue Coe: p147, 4. Karen Savage: p16, 1; p150, 1; p163, 5. Schlesinger Library, Radcliffe College: p8, 1; p60, 1, 2. Sheba: p134, 3. Monica Sjöö: p79, 6; p103, 4. South African History Archives: p214, 1; p215, 3; p216, 1; p221, 3. Spellbound Cards, Dublin: p17, 5. Staatliche Museen zu Berlin – Preußischer Kulturbesitz Kunstbibliothek: p69, 6. Linda Sterling (Linder): p117, 6; pp126/7, 1–5. Christine Tamblyn: p182, 1. TAMWA: p189, 5; p225, 5. Lin Tobias: p192, 1; p204, 3. United Nations Office and Information Centre, London: p232, 1, 2. Villard Books/Random House, 1992: p123, 4. Virago Press: p134, 1. Gill de Vlieg: p215, 4. VNS Matrix: p157, 6; p184, 1. *Vogue* magazine, UK: p230, 3. Deborah Wellsby, The Worcester County Clothesline Project, Massachusetts: p192, 2; p205, 5. Wild Plakken: p139, 3–6; p190, 2; p213, 4, 5. Women's Action Forum, Lahore: p12, 1; p193, 3; p195, 3; p196, 4; p203, 5. Women's Art Library, London: p81, 3(centre left and bottom right); p100, 2; p102, 2; p109, 3; p112, 1, 2, 4; p211, 6; p225, 4. Women's International League For Peace and Freedom, 1213 Race Street, Philadelphia, PA 19107-1691: p227, 5. Suzanne Perkins, The Women's Press: p135, 6. The Women's Press, 1981: p123, 3. Workshop for Women Jo-Jo: p8, 2; p137, 5–16. WUS (World University Services, UK): p13, 4; p80, 1; p196, 3; p198, 1, 2; p208, 2–5; p214, 2. Zero Tolerance Campaign/Trust and Franki Raffles: pp206/7, 1, 2.

Special thanks are given to the following for help in the production of this book: Siân Cook, Louise Ford, Ruhi Hanid, Marelle Hill, Danielle Oum, Teal Triggs, Catherine Willmore.